THINK, PIG!

Think, Pig!

BECKETT AT THE LIMIT OF THE HUMAN

JEAN-MICHEL RABATÉ

FORDHAM UNIVERSITY PRESS
New York 2016

Visit us online at www.fordhampress.com.

Library of Congress Cataloging-in-Publication Data
Names: Rabaté, Jean-Michel, 1949– author.
Title: Think, pig! : Beckett at the limit of the human / Jean-Michel Rabaté.
Description: First edition. | New York : Fordham University Press, 2016. |
Includes bibliographical references and index.
Identifiers: LCCN 2015042060 (print) | LCCN 2016000364 (ebook) |
ISBN 9780823270859 (hardback) | ISBN 9780823270866 (paper) |
ISBN 9780823270873 (ePub)
Subjects: LCSH: Beckett, Samuel, 1906–1989—Criticism and interpretation. |
Literature—Philosophy. | Theater—Philosophy. | BISAC: LITERARY
CRITICISM / General. | PHILOSOPHY / Aesthetics. | PERFORMING
ARTS / Theater / History & Criticism.
Classification: LCC PR6003.E282 Z7886 2016 (print) |
LCC PR6003.E282 (ebook) | DDC 848/.91409—dc23
LC record available at http://lccn.loc.gov/2015042060

Printed and bound in Great Britain by
Marston Book Services Limited, Oxfordshire
18 17 16   5 4 3 2 1

First edition

CONTENTS

Introduction   1

1.   How to Think Like a Pig   11

2.   The Worth and Girth of an Italian Hoagie   23

3.   The Posthuman, or the Humility of the Earth   37

4.   Burned Toasts and Boiled Lobsters   49

5.   "Porca Madonna!": Moving Descartes toward
     Geulincx and Proust   59

6.   From an Aesthetics of Nonrelation to an Ethics
     of Negation   76

7.   Beckett's Kantian Critiques   92

8.   Dialectics of Enlittlement   108

9.   Bathetic Jokes, Animal Slapstick, and Ethical Laughter   124

10. Strength to Deny: Beckett between Adorno and Badiou   134

11. Lessons in Pigsty Latin: The Duty to Speak   158

12. An Irish Paris Peasant   171

13. The Morality of Form—A French Story   182

Coda: Minima Beckettiana   200

Acknowledgments   205
Notes   207
Index   235

Think, Pig!

Introduction

Although Samuel Beckett was the only writer I was eager to meet when I was a student in Paris, I never dared approach him, so great was the awe he inspired. In the late sixties, the École Normale Supérieure had not yet memorialized his passage in the institution. No hall had been named after him yet. The students were not even sure in which room he had spent two crucial years on the premises. When I edited a collection of essays about his early work with the École Normale Supérieure press, the board felt that it was its duty to pay Beckett an homage that had been long overdue. I mailed a copy of the book to Beckett, who immediately wrote back to thank me. He inserted in his kind note, as a little joke, an "a" to the title that, out of modesty, he had abbreviated: *Beckett avant Beckett* had become "BABa."[1] This book could only be a "B. A., BA," as the French say, meaning a basic primer. Ironically self-deflating and deflating us, Beckett showed to our group of contributors that we should not take ourselves too seriously when discussing his work. He was also warning us about the danger of "explaining," that is, of reducing his work to formulas.

Despite the promptings of an Irish friend who saw Beckett regularly for late-night chats accompanied by a lot of whiskey, I never found the courage to arrange a meeting. Not only was Beckett a world-renowned writer, but he was also a man who had to be faced fully. I did not feel strong enough to meet him. I had heard of the long and painful silences that marked first meetings with well-meaning admirers. Even though I had spent more time writing a dissertation on James Joyce, I never imagined that I would have enjoyed meeting Joyce in person, had this been possible. The reverse was true with Beckett, yet the more I longed to meet him, the less this seemed conceivable.

This ineluctable distance has been reduced by the many books recently published about the most diverse aspects of his work; yet, at the time of writing, I kept wondering how to address Beckett in print only, as he was both a towering presence and a humble person. If Beckett has remained our contemporary even though he is, admittedly, the "last modernist," his work points to the future.[2] His literary eminence—following a paradigm in which one could place Eliot, Joyce, and Woolf—suggests that modernism is the classicism of the twenty-first century, our classicism. Beckett exerts an influence that goes beyond our present, for his works keep a power to move that has remained intact. However, if his words "do things," as John Langshaw Austin would say, more often than not, paradoxically, they do things by foregrounding the impossibility of doing anything. "Nothing to do": thus begins *Waiting for Godot*. While we may still be caught up in this pervasive nothingness, Beckett challenges us to turn it into something.[3] His sense of the *impossible*, a term to which I will return, made him an exception that turned into the norm. A notable and remarkable exception, Beckett has remained a rigorous and demanding artist who keeps inspiring many, as the living artists who claim him as a source of inspiration attest.[4] A relentless experimenter, Beckett reinvented himself several times by some sort of creative *bricolage*, burying a character into a mound of earth in *Happy Days*, making a blabbering mouth the main character of *Not I*, thus expanding the definition of a theatrical stage, and discovering new media such as the radio, film, video, and television. Not bothered if he disappointed audiences with his disconcertingly original approaches, he progressed by questioning his ability to go on further. And his solutions pushed the limits of each medium, each perfect in spite of mounting impossibilities. What is more is that each time, these solutions would overcome the dread of silence, sterility, and impotence.

Beyond the exemplary nature of his artistic career, anyone who has read a biography of Beckett can verify that he was that oddity: a driven artist who happened to be a good man. This is why he has been a "hero" to diverse philosophers, including Simon Critchley, Theodor W. Adorno, and

Alain Badiou.[5] Beckett's behavior throughout his life was admirable; even though he never wrote anything that can be called autobiographical, his life is undeniably present in his works, and it insists through singular and haunting images. However, a recent controversy about his personality has made opponents of James Knowlson, his prime biographer, and Stephen John Dilks, who tackled the professional side of Beckett's career. Dilks published a book stating that Beckett succeeded in his literary career by pretending not to care about literature; he pointed out that Beckett was picky in his choice of publishers, editors, and translators, and keenly aware of the impact of his photographic image.[6] Dilks's contrarian approach has the merit of resisting the temptation of an all too pious hagiography, and besides, it is true that Beckett cared for his reputation, that he managed his career skillfully and checked on the sums of money he received for his work. On the other hand, his immense generosity has been attested by all. Moreover, he objected to the label of "hero," and refused, for instance, to play any official role in commemorations of the French Resistance. He was both a humble man and a domineering author who would never relinquish control over his texts. Harold Pinter appreciated this duality when he evoked Beckett in 1954:

> I don't want philosophies, tracts, dogmas, creeds, ways outs, truths, answers, *nothing from the bargain basement.* He is the most courageous, remorseless writer going and the more he grinds my nose in the shit the more I am grateful to him. He's not fucking me about, he's not leading me up any garden, . . . he's not selling me anything I don't want to buy, he doesn't give a bollock whether I buy or not, *he hasn't got his hand over his heart.* Well, I'll buy his goods, hook, line and sinker, because he leaves no stone unturned and no maggot lonely. He brings forth a body of beauty.[7]

Pinter's earthy and pithy encomium captures what philosophers have admired in Beckett: the paradox of someone who provides all the more a model of ethical behavior as he refuses to be a model. He will never tell you what to do or what to think. Beckett's exemplarity lies in that he even avoids being taken as an example. This attitude allows him to rephrase contemporary ethics by posing simple albeit basic questions. Beckett keeps asking: "What's the point of art as form and of art for life?" With an urgency admired by thinkers as diverse as Adorno, Badiou, Critchley, but also Stanley Cavell, Jacques Derrida, or Gilles Deleuze, Beckett's strenuous efforts as a writer help us reject pseudo-values and reach a site—a linguistic and ethical position—in which one can truly think, love, live, or write. What he offers is tantamount to a radical imperative to continue living, because, for him, such an affirmative gesture implicitly underpins all our actions. While Beckett avoids telling us what to do or believe in, his extraordinary verbal energy dislodges us from any complacency about style, form, and values.

In 1945, when introducing MacGreevy's essay on Jack Yeats, Beckett harnessed the apparent paradox that philosophy can be used against philosophy: "There is at least this to be said for mind, that it can dispel mind. And at least this for art-criticism, that it can lift from the eyes, before *rigor vitae* sets in, some of the weight of congenital prejudice."[8] Instead of *rigor mortis*, we glimpse a life already dead, stiff, and stultified. Hence good art and good writing have the power to kill a death that we mistake for life. Mobilizing Proust's critique of deadening "habit" and Wittgensteinian language games, Beckett's alert writing forces us to become responsible for the forms of art by which we surround ourselves.

The situation has not changed drastically seventy years later, now that so many philosophical discourses have been used and abused about Beckett. All the possible theoretical approaches have been applied to his works without capturing what makes the texts tick. At best, spirited readings by Adorno and Badiou explain to what extent Beckett's works anticipated their theories. Other philosophers, like Martha Nussbaum, a distinguished ethicist, examine Beckett's text critically before concluding peremptorily that they convey no value. I will approach the vexed issue of the worth of Beckett's texts by combining close readings and the discussion of broader philosophical contexts. However, I will not multiply theoretical detours and psycho-biographical analyses, and promise to say as little as possible about the absurd or the precariousness of human existence. This is not a self-help book and I would hardly suggest that reading Beckett can change your life overnight, or that he will tell you how to become a better person. If this happens, it won't be by design, but as the consequence of rethinking fundamental values, above all by questioning the humanism that we take for granted. Beckett took as models poets like Walther von der Vogelweide, philosophers like Arnold Geulincx, or mystics like Blaise Pascal, none of whom gave straightforward answers to the riddles of life. Beckett liked the fresh lyrics of the *minnesinger* Walther von der Vogelweide, especially when he depicts himself physically in the posture taken by Dante's Belacqua (we will meet him again soon) and quite often by James Joyce:

I sat upon a stone,
Crossed one leg with the other leg,
Propped my elbow in,

The other hand, my chin
And one cheek was hiding.
Anxiously I pondered
How on this earth one ought to live.
There was no answer I could give.[9]

To combine honor, leisure, creativity, and a quest for salvation is no easy task. Blaise Pascal—a Catholic mystic who hoped to convert French Libertines, the group of thinkers whom he frequented in his youth—asserted: "Se moquer de la philosophie, c'est vraiment philosopher [To deride philosophy is to be a true philosopher]."[10] This could be Beckett's motto, next to that of Giordano Bruno: "In tristitia hilaris, in hilaritate tristis [Laughing in sadness, sad in hilarity]." Although Beckett kept laughing with the atomist Democritus, in order to deride philosophy philosophically and keep a balance, he would also cry with Heraclitus, the sad pantheist.[11] Even his intellectual hero René Descartes, as we will see, seemed conflicted about the power and limits of thought, and may have derided the main orthodoxies of his times in secret. Thus Beckett needed to make a detour, which was his way in and out of philosophy, thanks to his discovery of another philosopher, almost forgotten today, Arnold Geulincx. Geulincx's stroke of genius was to invert the *cogito* ("I think") of his master Descartes so as to introduce an even more productive *nescio* ("I don't know"). This inversion gave him a formidable lever with which he undermined a rationalism that he turned inside out. He gave birth to an ethics of humility via a new philosophy of the unconscious some two centuries before Schopenhauer, Nietzsche, and Freud. Such arcane references remind us that we must read Beckett as closely as possible even when selecting issues that have kept a relevance for today's readers.

Talking about readers, a reproach leveled at literary theory is that it prevents students from reading fiction, which begs the question: Should we return to a simple, unmitigated, and unmediated enjoyment of literary texts? The injunction to do so is not as simple as it sounds; most of our interests have gone elsewhere, toward documentary history, the visual arts, sexuality, cultural economics, politics, media, all of which are considered as closer to life. Literature is left for the passive consumption of romantic clichés. Beckett's works address this situation not only because one of his characters, Murphy, is a "strict non-reader," but also because his writings function as a black hole attracting and swallowing theories. Moreover, they also swallow the traditional novel. Beckett appeals most to the "non-readers," those who do not immerse themselves in romances or historical novels and prefer writing that is crisp, startling, poetic, and enigmatic—those who read fiction in the *New Yorker* and avoid the fat blockbusters recommended as summer reading. Beckett loathed Balzac's recreation of a social world, and expressed misgivings about the grand form deployed with mastery by Proust and Joyce. He remained faithful to their examples but chose a different path, which allowed him to evolve and explore.

Beckett's progression through various domains of the arts was marked by a hesitation between poetry and prose, between the stage and the page. He did not eschew essay writing, and all his life stuck to a grueling schedule of self-translation. Translation from French to English and from English to French was a huge concern, which is why translation studies have a whole field to explore there. Subtle variations in tone and meaning from one version to the other explain the difficulty of unifying Beckettian themes under one concept. If the epithet "Beckettian" calls up "bleak minimalism" or "funny despair," it has not acquired the universal ring of "Kafkaesque," for Beckett has varied his genres and media too often to become an icon of popular culture.

In a 2006 interview, J. M. Coetzee, who had written a dissertation on *Watt*, meditated on the recent changes in literary studies after literary theory stopped being applied systematically to interpretations of Beckett. Erik Grayson asked: "Do you feel that Beckett's was a 'dated' achievement, relevant only during the time it appeared or is he important even today? What relevance, if any, would the writings of Beckett have for the contemporary reader? Why would we read him today? Do we need to read him at all?" Coetzee responded cautiously: "Beckett is a great prose writer, very acute, very restless, very self-aware. Whether he is 'relevant' or not I don't know. I don't see that 'relevance,' narrowly conceived, is of much importance when we come face to face with a writer of the size of Beckett."[12] Coetzee's prudence gives us a timely warning; even though Beckett stands above "his" century, he cannot be said to have influenced many writers, Coetzee excepted. Coetzee catches the fundamental spirit of this work in another essay: "Starting out as an uneasy Joycean and an even more uneasy Proustian, Beckett eventually settled on philosophical comedy as the medium for his uniquely anguished, arrogant, self-doubting, scrupulous temperament."[13] It is because of the self-awareness of Beckett's works that my investigation will have to be both theoretical and in the field of literary history.

This does not mean that one should engage with an exploration of references, foreign quotes, or influences. At any rate, the study of influences has not been very productive; if indeed one may observe a proximity between Beckett and Kafka, Pinter, or Coetzee, these are not direct influences but spontaneous affiliations allied with a similar reluctance to play the role of the committed intellectual, and an assertion of strong ethical and political beliefs. The complete works of Beckett, which fit snugly in four volumes, occupy a much vaster cultural space. This space has expanded from the novel and poetry so as to include the theater—a medium in which Beckett achieved notoriety—and various other media, along with unclassifiable prose fragments, inventive art criticism, and dazzling letters. There are innumerable drafts and discarded fragments in various archives, plus texts published against Beckett's wishes, such as the French translation of *Proust* or the play *Eleutheria*, which was published in French because unauthorized English translations were circulating. Even when Beckett translated his texts himself, his accomplishments as a translator vary from inspired renditions to drained reductions, as evinced by his first French novel *Mercier et Camier*, which he cut by one third and toned down in the English version. It nevertheless offers gems in English. Here is one rare pastoral evocation, when Mercier and Camier consider a goat frolicking in a meadow. The scene smacks of parody despite the subdued and relaxed mood:

> The field lay spread before them. In it nothing grew, that is nothing of use to man. . . . Beyond the hedge were other fields, similar in aspect, bounded by no less similar hedges. How did one get from one field to the other? Through the hedges perhaps. Capriciously a goat, braced on its hind legs, its forefeet on a stump, was muzzling the brambles in search of tender thorns. Now and then it turned with petulance away, took a few angry steps, stood still, then perhaps a little spring, straight up in the air, before returning to the hedge. Would it continue thus all day round the field? Or weary first?
> Some day someone would realize. Then the builders would come. Or a priest, with his sprinkler, and another acre would be God's. When prosperity returned.[14]

The author puns on the "capricious" capers of "capri," Roman or Irish goats. But Ireland is not Capri, and insular caprices soon yield to the steady march of progress. He is also playing on the overtones of the verb "to hedge," suggesting to avoid giving a promise, or to protect oneself in the future. Even if religion and capitalism are bound to encroach on this forlorn area, perhaps in order to modernize it, perhaps to sell its soul, no doubt goats will go on grazing, capering as capriciously as before, whereas we will not be able to hedge our bets. The haunting overtones of the short vignette are confirmed by a later recall. Close to the end, Mercier and Camier meet Watt, who, disgusted with life, has a fit and screams several times, "Fuck life!"[15] In between these outbursts, Mercier and Camier manage to exchange a few words:

> You know what often comes back to me? Said Camier.
> It's raining, said Mercier.
> The goat, said Camier.
> Mercier was looking perplexedly at Watt.[16]

Cunningly, the author was testing the memory of inattentive readers. One learns, while progressing with the two old men whose interactions offer a blueprint for the endless non sequiturs in *Godot* that it does not matter if we get lost, since that is the point of the narrative, even if the plot is recapitulated via "summaries of preceding chapters," parodying the genre of the nineteenth-century novel after it has been destabilized by Flaubert in *Bouvard and Pécuchet*, a novel that provides a model for Beckett's absurdist travelogue.

Flaubert and Proust rejected a streamlined nineteenth-century realism in the name of dialogism, encyclopedism, and verbal experimentation, hoping that, in the end, literary language would be able to express everything, from the highest to the lowest. Beckett followed them in a spirit of parody. In *Mercier and Camier*, the contents of the two main characters' pockets reveal a lot about their daily habits, but more fundamentally aim at expressing life as such ("Punched tickets of all sorts, spent matches, scraps of newspaper bearing in their margins the obliterated traces of irrevocable rendezvous, the classic last tenth of pointless pencil, crumples of soiled bumf, a few porous condoms, dust. Life in short"[17]). Besides, these rare moments of descriptive frenzy enhance the limits of human communication, as shown by the exchange that follows immediately after:

> I was thinking of saying something, said Mercier, but on second thoughts I'll keep it to myself.
> Selfish pig, said Mercier.[18]

In order to think through these questions, we will need to move beyond the human and try to think otherwise—like an animal, perhaps like a goat or a pig. A first detour will take us through *Waiting for Godot*, when we meet Lucky, whose performance suggests that we need to think like a pig. This task was taken seriously by two French writers, Georges Bataille and Raymond Cousse. From this vantage point, we will revisit the Dantean foundation of Beckett's ethics. Such foundation was laid early, as we perceive when we see Beckett glossing the work of his literary mentor, James Joyce. Beckett's astute commentary on *Finnegans Wake* leads to critical theses about salvation and redemption—in a word: they can wait—and to the creation of an ethics of nonvalue, which soon redoubles as an aesthetics of nonrelation. With this double postulation in mind, we will see how Beckett grapples with Kantian ethics in order to usher in a philosophy of the "low."

To make sense of this literal "bathos," I will evoke Adorno's and Lacan's parallel pairing of Kant and Sade, and deduce from the idea of transgression a veritable ethics of the base, of the low, of humility. Humility leads to laughter, the hushed and dimmed laughter of the low. Hilarity bring us closer to the core of an irrational life endowed with unbreakable resilience. When he exhausts the trope that the end is never at hand, Beckett becomes an antimessianic prophet of doom and generates a peculiar form of dark humor. Adorno believed that Beckett and Kafka shared a similar outlook. I will suggest that Beckett's witty sallies, memorable puns, and pensive jokes are a far cry from K.'s smothered gasps and repressed giggles.

Less a formalist or a minimalist than a moralist of form, Beckett reiterated that we have to give expression to life as it is, which means life as it will be when it goes on without us; even if this entails that whatever we perceive is "ill seen" and "ill said," we shall continue to grope for the exact word until the tender thorns emerge from the brambles. Literature will not be spared by the malicious and capricious "hedging" of expressivity, for any pretention to the mastery of genres and styles will be denied, violently at first, and then in a process of reduction that undermines it by derision and parody. This evolution inscribes Beckett in a literary context dominated by a "writing degree zero" best exemplified by Camus and Blanchot. Such blank writing raises itself to the level of the stark ethics required by post-Holocaust times.

Beckett, reluctant to give pronouncements about positive values, ended up taking a minimalist position like Voltaire who asserted: "Il faut cultiver son jardin [We have to cultivate our garden]."[19] Beckett voices the old motto tongue in cheek, joking about the old "pseudo-couple" of nature and culture. If one can extract any wisdom about gardening from his work, it will be a cynical version of pastoralism.[20] If "man"—a loaded concept to be questioned relentlessly—or say Molloy, tends a garden full of teeming pests, one should not forget that he is an animal, too, without other redeeming qualities than his fear of death, his love of beauty, and his ability to laugh and make others laugh.

This book develops these themes by following a rough chronological outline, beginning with the readings of Dante, Joyce, and Proust (chapters 2 and 3), passing though philosophical conversations with Descartes,

Geulincx, Kant, Sade, and Freud (chapters 4 to 7), and finishing with the later texts and plays like *Endgame* and *Catastrophe* (chapters 10 to 13). This remains a loose chronology, however, since my argument is mostly theoretical and takes as its central focus Beckett's productive years from 1945 to 1955, from the essays on the van Velde brothers and the stories and plays written in French to the writing of *Fin de Partie* in 1955. This was a turning point, the moment when Beckett became a "French" writer perhaps because he was hoping to write "without style," a decision that was linked with his original mediation on art and aesthetics (as discussed in chapters 6, 7, and 8) and on the issue of laughter and comedy (chapter 9).

I will explore the concepts that underpin these central texts, situating them in dialogues with Maurice Blanchot, Georges Bataille, Emmanuel Levinas, Roland Barthes, and finally with Alain Badiou and Theodor W. Adorno. The latter two thinkers, taken together, would behave like the man in Descartes's third dream, when he tells him ominously: *Est et Non*, which means: Yes and No.[21]

CHAPTER I

How to Think Like a Pig

The furious commandment "Think, pig!" comes both as a surprise and a relief for the audience in *Waiting for Godot*. It is the order barked by Pozzo to Lucky, who is obliged to "perform" the act of thinking for Vladimir and Estragon. *Waiting for Godot* breaks the tedium it has created by repetitive and sterile exchanges between Didi and Gogo with the entrance of a second couple, Pozzo and Lucky. Lucky, also called a "hog," grants another voice to dispossession, disenfranchisement, and slavish acquiescence. In French, the order is made more powerful with its redoubled plosive consonant: "Pense, porc!"[1] We would never have known that Lucky was able to think had Pozzo not made him perform. Before, we are told, Lucky could dance or sing; now he can only think—this being the last level of human performance, a weak remainder of Cartesian certainty. In fact, *thinking* means releasing a torrent of words, unleashing a hilarious delirium moving in concentric circles from God's creation to an epileptic stutter verging on aphasia. Its inception is marked by a recurrent "quaquaquaqua," identical in the French and English versions: "Given the existence as uttered forth in the public works of Puncher and Wattmann of a personal God quaquaquaqua with white beard quaquaquaqua outside time."[2] Even if this tirade imitates a psychotic delirium, which was often the case in performances supervised by Beckett himself, we may take the injunction seriously; we may try to think like a pig so as to engage with a mode of excess that goes beyond Lucky, whose botched performance joins the bestial and the divine in a self-canceling obliteration of human rationality.

Thinking like a pig, we would approximate what Georges Bataille used to call "sovereignty"—a pure paroxysm, an awareness of excess in a moment of total overcoming, a limit experience when the act of thinking turns into bodily production whether by laughter or excretion, when the conflation of glory and abjection opens up a space beyond madness and rationality. Bataille, one of the first to hail Molloy as a masterpiece, had really imagined what it might mean to think like a pig. In "The Practice of Joy before Death" (1939), first published in Acéphale,[3] Bataille associates the intense joy of being alive to predatory fantasies of Sadian violence. He participates in the violent struggle for mastery over other animals, but his drift is not toward the annihilation of others. His own self will vanish, as his meditation concludes ecstatically with a paean to destruction: "Before the terrestrial world whose summer and winter order the agony of all living things, before the universe composed of innumerable turnings stars, limitlessly losing and consuming themselves, I can only perceive a succession of cruel splendors whose very movement requires that I die: this death is only the *exploding* consumption of all that was, the joy of existence of all that comes into the world; even my own life demands that everything that exists, everywhere, ceaselessly give itself to be annihilated."[4] This essay begins lyrically: "All this I am, and I want to be: at the same time, dove, serpent and pig,"[5] a Nietzschean quote from the three metamorphoses of man into animals in *Thus Spoke Zarathustra*.

Ten years before, Bataille had searched for a similarly agonized extremity of affect in Salvador Dalí's painting *The Lugubrious Game*. In his view, Dalí had depicted subjects seized by inhuman forces, transformed into animal forms transcending beauty and ugliness. The contemplation of the painting was so overwhelming that it triggered in him laughter, a hilarity powerful enough to destroy conventional morality: "My only desire here—even if by pushing this bestial hilarity to its furthest point I must nauseate Dalí—is to squeal like a pig before his canvases."[6] Ironically, this intemperate and intempestive tribute led Dalí, who should have been a fellow practitioner of transgression, to feel nauseated. After this, he broke off completely with Bataille.

The thought of Bataille, so complex and paradoxical, was not unknown to Beckett, who had collaborated with Georges Duthuit when the latter relaunched *Transition* magazine in 1948, a Paris-based English-speaking avant-garde review that had both Georges Bataille and Jean-Paul Sartre as editorial advisers. Bataille, who in 1946 had founded his own review, *Critique*, published an essay in the first issue, named *Transition 48*, no. 1, in which he presented his original notion of the "Ultimate Instant."[7] This essay provides perfect definitions of key concepts like excess, sovereignty, and expenditure. Here is how Bataille sketches his notion of the sovereign:

> Poetic frenzy, religious emotion, like laughter and sensuality, have in themselves a value detachable from the meaning we assign to them, a *sovereign* value which is "in the service of nothing and nobody." . . .
> Thus it comes about that, in a variety of ways, men are led to expend certain quantities of energy which cannot be placed "in the service of anything or anybody" and which have no real meaning other than instantaneous, and are *sovereignly* wasted. Men sing, dance, get drunk, gamble and work themselves up in endless ways in order to rid themselves, without reason, of their surplus energy.[8]

Bataille gives an example of what he means by the "ultimate instant" by quoting a long letter by Caterina da Siena who relates a mystical experience. At the last minute, Caterina had managed to convert an atheist condemned to have his head chopped off; she made his terror vanish by suggesting their impending mystical marriage in heaven; after the execution that she attended, upon receiving the severed head of the young man from which blood was still spurting, she experienced an orgasmic spasm allied with a shattering religious and erotic ecstasy.

In *Transition 48*, no. 4, Maurice Nadeau discussed Bataille's groundbreaking mixture of poems, philosophical meditations and novelistic fragments, *The Hatred of Poetry*, which contained the tantalizing prose texts called "Story of Rats." Nadeau saw Bataille engaged in a heroic struggle similar to that of Pascal, Sade, Rimbaud, and Nietzsche.[9] This assessment full of high praise quoted an immortal line from "Story of Rats" that must have delighted Beckett (this will become clearer later): "Nakedness is but death, and the tenderest kisses have an after-taste of rat."[10]

All this explains why Bataille was one of the first critics to perceive and state clearly the radical novelty of *Molloy*. In May 1951, his review was published in *Critique* under the title of "The Silence of Molloy." Bataille highlights the themes of silence and of animal life in *Molloy*. Since Bataille and Beckett were both living in Paris at the time, the review was followed by a meeting, and there was an exchange of texts and letters.[11] Bataille found in Beckett an artist close to him: both were relatively lonely even

though they had belonged to avant-gardist groups before World War II—
Beckett wrote for the experimental literary journal *transition* (1927–1930),
Bataille was associated with the Surrealist dissidents of *Documents* (1929–
1930). Both had barely escaped from the horrors of the war. They were
groping in the dark, trying to produce an experimental prose that questioned the values to which their contemporaries were eager to return.
Against a regressive desire for humanist balance, they wished to think
through the limits of humanity. As Molloy says: "What I liked in anthropology was its inexhaustible faculty of negation."[12] Bataille and Beckett
questioned the foundation of humanism, including the existentialist variety, or subverted them by deploying a double strategy of debasement and
excess that freely mixed literature and philosophy. Literature was to criticize philosophy's goal to arrive at total human experience; philosophy was
to question an ancient confidence in art's representational ability.

Exceptionally, since the tone of reviews in *Critique* was neutral, Bataille's
essay turned personal.[13] A footnote described a novel that he had begun
and abandoned, which contained a scene identical to the meeting with a
tramp in *Molloy*. Molloy meets an old tramp in the woods and kills him
savagely, without any reason. Bataille saw that this was done "in the hope
of reaching out to the animality of his victim."[14] The review ended with a
meditation on lies, which links literature and ethics. "Molloy or rather the
author *writes*: he writes and what he writes is that the intention to write
gets lost in him . . . It doesn't matter if he confesses: *I have always behaved
like a pig*."[15] Here, Bataille quotes *Molloy* directly:

> And if I have always behaved like a pig, the fault lies not with me but
> with my superiors, who corrected me only on one point of detail
> instead of showing me the essence of the system, after the manner of
> the great English schools, and the guiding principles of good manners,
> and how to proceed, without going wrong, from the former to the lat-
> ter, and how to trace back to its ultimate source a given comportment.
> For that would have allowed me, before parading in public certain
> habits such as the finger in the nose, the scratching of the balls, digital
> emunction and the peripatetic piss, to refer them to the first rules of a
> reasoned theory.[16]

Scatological jokes and the exhibition of dirty habits all work to under-
mine the self-domination of a rational self in a clean body. These jokes are
taken seriously by Bataille:

> There is no human prohibition that has not collapsed into an indiffer-
> ence that would like to be final but is not final; how can one not be

indifferent to an indifference that goes half-way and remains imperfect? If the author is not faithful to his decision to *behave like a pig*, confesses that he is lying, ending his book with: "*Then I went back into the house and wrote, It is midnight. The rain is beating on the windows. It was not midnight. It was not raining*"—it is because he is not Molloy. Molloy *in truth* would confess *nothing*, for he would write *nothing*.[17]

As Bataille asserts, we fear the possibility of becoming Molloy, this "impotent moron," but there will be no escape from the same dead-end if we identify with Moran. Moran's fruitless quest for Molloy parodies the same theories, whether theological or philosophical, when it repeats and duplicates Molloy's abortive itinerary. What stands out is the conflation of "horror and rapture" linked by an effort at pure survival; such affects are captured by a literature like that of Beckett that takes higher risks by introducing us to the generic universality of defenseless life.

Surprisingly, Beckett happened to have given precise form to an old literary project abandoned by Bataille; what is more, he had achieved this with a savage wit and a verbal energy that Bataille lacked. Bataille grasped immediately that Beckett's main theme was the inhumanity of man. This exploration of human limits would launch a new antiliterature and produce a writing constantly destroying or negating itself. The personal vignette of his meeting with a tramp served to explain how it feels to be exposed to radical destitution. In the state of destitute homelessness experienced by a tramp lying in a ditch, the boundary between humanity and animality collapses. Such an utter destitution called up for Bataille "the silence of animals," which opens up to the "unnamable": "This thing we name through sheer impotence *vagabond* or *wretch*, which is actually *unnamable* (but then we find ourselves entangled in another word, *unnamable*), is no less mute than death."[18]

The silence of what remains "unnamable" (the word may have suggested the title of the last installment in Beckett's trilogy) haunts *Molloy* in a double sense: it is a silence about humanity and a silence about literature: "*literature* may have already taken the same meaning as this silence, but it still shrinks from the last step that would be embodied by pure silence. Likewise, this Molloy who incarnates it, is not exactly dead. He evinces the deep apathy of death, its indifference facing any possibility, but such apathy finds in death itself a limit."[19] Bataille's friendship with Maurice Blanchot, who at the time was working on Sade's concept of apathy, the passion for stillness paradoxically produced by sexual and morbid excess, was important for Beckett, whose letters evince a steady and strong admiration for Blanchot as a critic.

The meeting with Bataille was to leave durable traces (at his death, Beckett's library contained a copy of *Madame Edwarda*, with copious underlinings of the preface[20]); soon after, Beckett added to a draft of *Texts for nothing* a reference to Bataille's preface to Marquis de Sade's *Justine*.[21] In that preface, Bataille quoted Maurice Blanchot. The latter's book, published in 1949, was the groundbreaking *Lautréamont and Sade*.[22] Immediately after, Beckett read Blanchot's book, which begins with a meditation on "Sade's Reason." Blanchot confronts Sade's extraordinary contradictions in a magisterial analysis:

> At every moment [Sade's] theoretical ideas set free the irrational forces with which they are bound up. These forces both excite and upset the thought by an impetus of a kind that causes the thought first to resist and then to yield, to try again for mastery, to gain an ascendancy, but only by liberating other dark forces by which, once again the ideas are carried away, side-tracked and perverted. The result is that all that is said is clear but seems at the mercy of something that has not been said. Then, a little further on, what was concealed emerges, is recaptured by logic but, in its turn, obeys the movement of a still further hidden force.[23]

Having grasped the rationale of this perverted logic, Blanchot formalizes the paradox of Sade's transgressive doctrine:

> [H]e draws up a kind of Declaration of the Rights of Eroticism, with for a fundamental principle this idea, applying equally to men and women: give yourself to anyone who desires you, and take anyone you desire. "What harm do I do, what offence do I commit, if I say to a beautiful creature I meet: 'Lend me the part of your body that can give me an instant's satisfaction, and enjoy, if so pleases you, the part of mine you prefer.'" To Sade such a proposition is irrefutable. . . . But what does he conclude from that? Not that it is wrong to do violence against anyone and use them for pleasure against their will, but that no one, so as to refuse him, can plead as excuse an exclusive attachment or "belonging to anyone."[24]

One could not find a better summary of the twisted logic of *Watt*. This excerpt could also sum up Beckett's entire program in the trilogy, *Molloy*, *Malone Dies*, and *The Unnamable*.

Bataille expresses similar concerns in his review of *Molloy*:

> Literature necessarily gnaws at existence and the world, reduces to *nothing* (but this *nothing* is horror) our ventures that make us move

bravely from one result to another, from one success to another. This does not exhaust the possibilities granted to literature. But these two domains—horror and rapture—are closer to each other than we thought. Would the felicities of poetry be accessible to someone who turns away from horror, and would authentic despair be any different from Molloy's *golden moment* in the hands of the police?[25]

The "golden moment" evokes a strange feeling of bliss that overwhelms Molloy when the policeman drags him to the police station. He stops, hearing a distant music, which triggers in him a sense of ecstatic dispossession, a feeling of peace and freedom:

> I gave myself up to that golden moment, as if I had been someone else. . . . Was there one among them to put himself in my place, to feel how removed I was then from him I seemed to be, and in that remove what strain, as of hawsers about to snap? . . . Yes, I was straining towards those spurious deeps, their lying promise of gravity and peace, from all my old poisons I struggled towards them, safely bound. Under the blue sky, under the watchful gaze.[26]

The intuition of an excessive depth and heightened tension then triggers a reversal, the sense that all men can exchange places and share identical experiences. Such a radical freedom achieved for an instant—"Forgetful of my mother, set free from the act, merged in this alien hour, saying, Respite, respite"[27]—generates an experience of subjective dispossession coupled with a paradoxical bliss. The bliss encountered here becomes a dominant theme in the following works: the power of minimization brought about by a sense of subjective alienation, better perceptible in the French text: "Y en avait-il un seul pour se mettre à ma place, pour sentir combien j'étais peu, à cette heure, celui dont j'avais l'air, et dans ce peu quelle puissance il y avait, d'amarres tendues à péter."[28] By coincidence, Beckett's passage anticipates the title chosen by Bataille when he completed the abandoned novel mentioned earlier, *Le Bleu du Ciel* (*Blue at Noon*).

The providential meeting of Bataille and Beckett in May 1951 brought to light a convergence in their positions: both were launching a critique of humanism in the name of the "impossible," a concept that underpins Bataille's novels and Beckett's essays on painting. Both founded their writing practices on an experience of dispossession and unknowing. In 1928, Bataille's first novel, *Story of the Eye*, published under a pseudonym, gave a parodic dimension to his post-Sadian ethos. Its strange mixture of horror and laughter, of zany poetry and inhuman transgression, makes it a masterpiece of late Gothic pornography.

After the war, Bataille's trajectory went in a different direction when he elaborated a philosophical system in which waste, excess, and sovereignty were reconfigured as "heterology," and led to a new economic science of the "accursed share." The conceptual differences became more visible because Bataille brought a different library to bear on similar issues: Mauss, Hegel, and Nietzsche were his main sources of inspiration. Beckett preferred to quote Spinoza, Geulincx, and Democritus. Thomas Trezise has analyzed the historical links between Bataille and Beckett, which include a common fascination for Sade.[29] Beckett and Bataille shared a determined animus against postwar humanism; both critiqued the "human" and the "anthropomorphic machine" presupposed by such a term, often using the obscene body or "low" animals like rats or pigs to set a humorous limit to higher aspirations.

This postwar antihumanism is perceptible in "La peinture des van Velde ou le Monde et le Pantalon,"[30] a fifteen-page text from early 1945 written directly in French, in which animals like pigs and sheep keep reappearing. Unlike Breton, but like Duchamp, Beckett exonerates Dalí from the reproach of being a bad painter. Above all, his main theme is a satire of the bourgeois audience wishing to reduce art to a source of satisfaction:

> For it is not question here of the grotesque and despicable animal whose specter haunts artists' studios, like the tapirs one is likely to find in the dorms of the *Normaliens*, but of the inoffensive barmy one who rushes, as other people go the movies, into galleries and even into churches, seized by the hope—listen carefully now—of enjoying himself [*de jouir*]. He doesn't want to be taught, the pig, or become better. He only thinks of his pleasure.
> He is the one who justifies the existence of painting as a public thing.
> I dedicate to him these remarks, all made to make him even dizzier.
> He only wants to enjoy. The impossible is made to prevent him from enjoying.[31]

"Tapirs" is *Normalien* slang for high-school students who were privately taught by the students at the École Normale Supérieure (a dictionary entry described these exotic animals as having "a tasteless but nourishing flesh"). It meant by extension the instructors themselves. The reference cannot detract us from the ambiguity of those "pigs." Is Beckett simply attacking the hedonism of bourgeois philistines, or is he their accomplice?[32] Has he just moved from the simple dichotomy, I like it or I don't like it, to reach an encounter with the "impossible," a term that keeps echoes of Rimbaud's main concept?[33] In the next two pages, Beckett argues that a hedonistic approach is not to be rejected straightaway because it might offer a better comprehension of the painter's efforts than moralistic assertions.

Screaming like a pig is a better mode of expression than bleating with the sheep: "A similar bleating would salute, 150 years ago, free verse and diatonic scales."[34] The pig emblematizes the "amateur" while those who try to teach him are banal ideologues. Sheep-like critics never tell the truth to those "pigs": "They never tell him this: 'There is no painting. There are only paintings. These, not being sausages, are neither good nor bad.'"[35] Beckett hopes to transform the life of an "amateur" of art, an illusion he will lose soon after, as we will see in his dialogues on art. Here, the supreme illumination comes from the experience of the absence of the thing; this thing is motionless in the void and is apprehended in the "darkness that can fill the mind with light."[36] The essay praises the paintings of the brothers van Velde in terms similar to the contents of Murphy's mind. In the third zone, Murphy finds the darkest space in which he reaches freedom. There, he can perceive the pure generation of forms condensed as a "matrix of surds." The same ideas and terms recur in the French essay:

> Here everything moves, swims, flees, returns, gets undone, redone. Everything ceases, ceaselessly [*Tout cesse, sans cesse*]. This looks like the insurrection of molecules, the inside of a stone one millionth of a second before it disintegrates.
> This is literature.[37]

In the network of metaphors deployed here, an exploding stone releases centrifugal molecules and contrasts starkly with those sausages made up of minced pork meat. Here is the last metamorphosis of the spirit. This process of "sausagification" has another name, that of "the human," for Beckett adds: "To conclude, let's talk of something else, let's talk about the 'human.'" He goes on:

> Here is a word, no doubt a concept too, that has to be reserved for times of huge slaughters. One needs the pestilence, Lisbon and a major religious butchery [*boucherie*] for people to think of loving one another, of leaving the neighboring gardener in peace, of being radically simple.
> This is a word that is being bandied around today with an unrivalled fury. Just like dum-dum bullets.
> They fall on art communities with a peculiar abundance. It's a pity. For art should not to need cataclysms to be able to be practiced.
> The damage is already considerable.
> With "this is not human", one has said it all. Throw it to the garbage can.
> Tomorrow one will require that *charcuterie* be human.[38]

Playing on the double meaning of *charcuterie*, Beckett moves from "cooked pork meats" to the "massive slaughters" caused by wars. Facing wholesale destruction, like the Lisbon earthquake of 1755 that made eighteenth-century philosophers rethink their ideas about God, chance, and progress, artists like the brothers van Velde hold out and stick to their chosen solitude stoically, which will not yield recognition: "This painting's least particle contains more true humanity than all a procession toward their happiness of sacred sheep."[39]

In the end, we can disregard the opposition between sheep and pigs— they all end up slaughtered anyway. The relentless slaughter that we call "progress" is the triumphant march of humanity. Beckett was skeptical about such a "progress," which is just another name for legalized barbarism. His bête noire was the grandiose and inflated self-delusion of anthropomorphism. As he states, anthropomorphism is always an "anthropopseudomorphism," if we quote *Mercier et Camier* in the original version: "C'était la vraie campagne déjà, haies vives (vives!), boue, purin, mares, rochers, bouses, taudis, et de loin en loin, un être indubitablement humain, un véritable anthropopseudomorphe."[40] Surprisingly, Beckett avoids translating it: "It was the true countryside at last, quickset hedgerows, mud, liquid manure, rocks, wallows, cow shit, hovels, and here and there a form unmistakably human scratching at his plot."[41] He failed to render terms referring to linked issues: life (Beckett puns on the French phrase of *haie vive* in order to query what is "alive" in a hedge) and *anthropopseudomorphe*, which might be translated as anthropopseudomorphic. A lie (*pseudos*) is wedged in the middle of the main symptom of humanism: the projection of the human everywhere.

In *Molloy*, Moran rephrases the debate after his second meeting with Gaber—in a passage to which I will return in chapter 7. Gaber praises life as being "a thing of beauty" and "a joy for ever." Startled by the echo from Keats's "Endymion" that affirms the bounty of life, Moran wonders: "Do you think he meant human life? . . . Perhaps he didn't mean human life."[42] This worry turns into a wholesale interrogation that recurs throughout Beckett's works. The interrogation about a human or nonhuman life surfaced in a recent debate opposing Giorgio Agamben and Jacques Derrida about the concept of life, and the conversation throws light on what is at stake in the notion of "anthropopseudomorphism."

What matters most is the possibility of thinking life in general; in Greek, life is called either *zoe* or *bios*. Thus *bios* would be life as experienced by the "human animal." In 1995, Giorgio Agamben launched the concept of bare life (*vida nuda*), a concept exemplified by the death camps, in which one sees how a totalitarian control over men, women, and children reduces them to their "bare life." To define humanity as *zoe* and not *bios*, Agamben argues that even if "*zoon politikon*" means a "political animal," *zoe* should be reserved for the simple fact of living common to plants, animals, and men, whereas *bios* refers to human beings living alone or in groups.[43]

Agamben attacks forcibly the "anthropological machine" of humanism as an "apparatus" that suspends man between a celestial and a terrestrial nature.[44] In 1997, Derrida questioned the legitimacy of the distinction between *zoe* and *bios*, and he deployed another logic aiming at subverting the frontier between animality and humanity when presenting himself as an "autobiographical animal."[45] Whereas Agamben had given the subtitle of "Man and Animal" to *The Open*, Derrida published *The Animal That Therefore I Am*. Their long and bitter confrontation over the issue of "negative anthropology," as the Spectator puts it in *Eleutheria*, has generated tensions, unresolved queries, and philosophical dead-ends.[46] While Beckett's effort at "thinking like an animal" should be inscribed in this theoretical framework, it cannot be divorced from a theological framework that I will sketch when discussing a first identification of the young Beckett, his early and lasting fascination for Joyce.

The reference to pigs was literalized when the self-taught French writer Raymond Cousse was befriended by Beckett. Beckett, who had been addressed by Cousse who had written to him for help, assisted him with great generosity in his literary efforts. Cousse's main novel, called *Death Sty: A Pig's Tale*,[47] is a funny and dark text about a pig that is getting prepared for a slaughter that will produce—and that is the source of his pride—the best hams in the world. Here we have a talking pig full of self-importance, eager to reach a last metamorphosis through his own butchering and dismembering.

Cousse gives a painstakingly detailed account of the many levels of preparation of the slaughter, from the stunning by a blow or a shot in the brain to the exsanguination, the plunging of the carcass in boiling water, the scalding of the bristles, the evisceration, the beheading and the halving of the body. This will be followed by the carving, the cutting, and the deboning. The series of operations is known and eagerly expected by the pig, whose compliant narrative turns into a hilarious indictment of slaughterhouse practices, a little as if the human clones of Kazuo Ishiguro's moving novel *Never Let Me Go* knew exactly what is to happen to their organs once they are harvested one by one until a final transition kills the willing donors. Undeterred by the agony to come, Cousse's stoic pig imagines his posterity under the form of sausages, pâtés, and hams regally disseminated throughout the world.

The novel was adapted successfully as a one-man show. For a while, Cousse, a burly man, played the part of the enthusiastic pig and turned each time into a sarcastic "law-abiding hog." Walking on all fours during the entire show, he would deliver a breath-catching monologue in which echoes of *The Unnamable* could be discerned. In his friendly letters, Beckett advised Cousse to be as spare as possible in his style, and wrote with typical concision: "*Enlever toute fioriture*." (Get rid of all the frills).[48] Cousse followed this sound advice. Here is an excerpt from the last pages of *Death Sty*:

> With a debonair whistle, the butcher orders the chain into action.
> The next in line will harvest my boudin. Relieved of that burden, I
> brace myself for my purifying plunge into the vat of boiling water.
> Then comes the rotary machine which removes the bristles and also
> makes the nude parts a tiny more supple. The duration of this inter-
> lude depends upon how ill-humored the butcher is. If the Master is
> having a good day, the whole thing can provide an opportunity for
> dancing a jig on the rotary machine for hours on end.[49]

Alas, in the end, Cousse was unable to write another great text. Para-lyzed by the fame reaped by his all too human pig, he fell back in drunken delinquency and suicidal melancholia. Cousse had begun as a suburban petty thief, who would steal whole hams in supermarkets by stuffing them in his coat; he had been a talking pig, and now he wanted to be Beckett. A literalist to the end, he turned into a suicidal doppelgänger of his literary hero. Cousse committed suicide on December 22, 1991, on the second anniversary of Beckett's death. This cautionary vignette testifies to the impact of Beckett's work on younger French writers; it suggests as well that the neatest of literary identifications can be dangerous.

CHAPTER 2

The Worth and Girth of an Italian Hoagie

Beckett had barely turned twenty-three when he launched his career as a literary critic with "Dante . . . Bruno. Vico . . Joyce," his dense and thought-provoking essay devoted to Joyce's *Work in Progress,* the not yet named *Finnegans Wake.* The witty and fast-paced essay begins with an enigmatic caveat: "The danger is in the neatness of identifications."[1] The sentence strikes and baffles at once; it warns its readers while questioning the clarity and neatness of its own enunciation. As for identifications, we have quite a few here: four proper names—Dante, Bruno, Vico, and Joyce—separated by six periods, one per century, span a history of European thought from premodern times to modernism, from the early Italian Renaissance to a twentieth century marked by Joyce's incomparable brilliance. Beckett cautions readers who might be taken in by the formulaic density and the abrupt pontifications of the essay they are reading: they risk being blinded by an all too brilliant (the etymology of "neat") father figure. Wary of flashy formulas, Beckett nevertheless produces the most stylish essay of *Our Exagmination Round His Factification for Incamination of Work in Progress.* Having understood *Finnegans Wake* more than ten years before its publication in

1939 (his essay was begun in 1928 and published in 1929), he whispers to himself: "Beware of turning into too neat a Joycean clone."

The Dynamism of the Intermediate

Perhaps because he is recoiling against the neatness he evoked, Beckett flaunts his school-boyish humor while flirting with bad taste: "The conception of Philosophy and Philology as a pair of nigger minstrels out of the Teatro dei Piccoli is soothing, like the contemplation of a carefully folded ham-sandwich. Giambattista Vico himself could not resist the attractiveness of such coincidence of gesture" (*D*, 6). When the essay on Joyce was published,[2] Beckett had not yet translated Nancy Cunard's *Negro: An Anthology*. A few years later, he would render in English the sarcastic humor of Georges Sadoul with "Sambo without tears" and adapt René Crevel's obscene rants in "The Negress in the Brothel." I will return to these texts, which are much more shocking than the glib remark on "nigger minstrels"; moreover, they are political throughout. Never mind that the reputed Teatro dei Piccoli never exhibited minstrel shows or black-face comedians, even if its repertoire included *Ali Baba* as it toured the cities of Europe,[3] what Beckett hints at was formulated with more gusto in "The Negress in the Brothel" when Crevel condemns the double standards of the bourgeoisie: "when for one reason or another he [the generic Frenchman] is obliged to remain at home he demands to be entertained and debauched by the exotic curiosity that lifts him clear of the national fact into an illusion of renewal. Hence the popularity of Martinique jazz, Cuban melodies, Harlem bands and the entire tam-tam of the Colonial Exhibition."[4]

Yes, Beckett is hamming it up, and chooses words that evince poor judgment; however, the contemplation of a carefully folded ham sandwich generates a series of dialectical images that are threaded imaginatively throughout the essay. They reappear forcibly in an assault on contemporary audiences' inability to accept Joyce's new language: "And if you don't understand it, Ladies and Gentlemen, it is because you are too decadent to receive it. You are not satisfied unless form is so strictly divorced from content that you can comprehend the one almost without the other. This rapid skimming and absorption of the scant cream of sense is made possible by what I may call a continuous process of copious intellectual salivation" (*D*, 26). The attack on bad readers takes Rebecca West to task for her nasty comments on Joyce that she had published in an essay from 1928, "The Strange Necessity." West had presented Joyce as a sentimental narcissist, "a great man" perhaps, but "entirely without taste."[5] West explained that she was purchasing hats in Paris when she discovered a new book by Joyce in which she found her key. It was *Pomes Penyeach*, allegedly a sequence of mediocre poems that would betray Joyce's stylistic limitations and his absence of taste. In his sarcastic rejoinder, Beckett literalizes the concept of taste upheld as an obsolete value by West. Taste condenses British smugness and sanctimoniousness. In a facetious evocation, West turns into a Pavlovian dog, and needs a stimulus in order to salivate; stylistic propriety is truly "old hat" next to Joyce's wild new language:

> When Miss Rebecca West clears her desk for a sorrowful deprecation of the Narcisstic element in Mr. Joyce by the purchase of 3 hats, one feels that she might very well wear her bib at all intellectual banquets, or alternatively, assert a more noteworthy control over her salivary glands than is possible for Monsieur Pavlov's unfortunate dogs. The title of this book is a good example of a form carrying a strict inner determination. It should be a proof against the usual volley of cerebral sniggers: and it may suggest to some a dozen incredulous Joshuas prowling around the Queen's Hall, springing their tuning-forks lightly against finger-nails that have not yet been refined out of existence. (*D*, 26–27)

The "nigger minstrels" have now morphed into the "sniggers" of uncomprehending intellectuals. What book is alluded to so cryptically? Lawrence Rainey suggests *Finnegans Wake*, assuming that Joyce would have disclosed the title to Beckett.[6] More likely, Beckett refers to *Our Exagmination* whose very title conveys the thrill of linguistic experimentation typical of *Work in Progress*. Beckett, the latest contributor, was the only one who could allude explicitly to the weird-sounding title. More than idiosyncratic words like "exagmination," he stresses the first word, "Our." If one must have read *Finnegans Wake* to recognize Latinate words ending in *-tion* as signaling the presence of the evangelists or apostles, no one can miss Beckett's insistence on a possessive plural stressing communal ownership. "Joshuas" puns on Eugene and Maria Jolas, the ringleaders of the group. In *A Portrait of the Artist as a Young Man*, the artist was described as a god paring fingernails, and "refined out of existence." Like modern Joshuas, the twelve "disciples" go around the citadel of the Queen's English, but rather than blowing their trumpets to destroy it, they sound semantic tuning forks in order to assess its linguistic and musical purity. The analogy with Jericho suggests that these avant-gardist "exagminers" want to make literature collapse. One question remains: who is hiding inside the walls, the Queen of England, or any author who believes in his divinity as an artist?

Beckett's praise of the zany title leads to a discussion of Vico's etymologies. From Vico to Joyce, Beckett maps the recurrent dream of a total equation of thought with language. This sketches a formalist utopia in which Joyce seemed to be "stuck." Beckett's essay thus hesitates between queries facing the unity of form and content and the debunking of traditional literary values upheld by Rebecca West. As soon as language and thought, form and content, and meaning and gesture are equated, Beckett retreats; he is all too aware of the idealist danger that such a postulated or sought-after unity can create. At the same time, he does his best to comply with his assignment, his mouthful turning into a handful: "And now here am I, with my handful of abstractions, among which notably: a mountain, the coincidence of contraries, the inevitability of a cyclic evolution, a system of Poetics, and the prospect of self-extension in the world of Mr. Joyce's *Work in Progress*" (*D*, 19). In fact, Beckett's essay had been masterminded by Joyce, who even tried to get it translated into Italian at some point. It is remarkable that Joyce should have asked Beckett to write this essay just one month after they met. The sudden offer of a task to a newcomer anticipates Joyce's proposition to James Stephens a few years later, when he suggested that Stephens should finish *Finnegans Wake* in his place. Beckett acknowledges that much when describing the process—Joyce controlled everything:

> It was at his suggestion that I wrote "Dante . . . Bruno. Vico . . Joyce"—
> because of my Italian. I spent a lot of time reading Bruno and Vico in
> the magnificent library, the Bibliothèque of the École Normale. We
> must have had some talk about the "Eternal Return," that sort of thing.
> He liked the essay. But his only comment was there wasn't enough
> about Bruno; he found Bruno rather neglected. They were new figures
> to me at the time. I hadn't read them.[7]

Joyce was right, of course. In an essay that flaunts four names, Bruno functions as a mere bridge toward Vico's linguistic theories.

A bold generalization ("[Vico's] exposition of the ineluctable circular progression of Society was completely new, although the germ of it was contained in Giordano Bruno's treatment of identified contraries" [*D*, 20]) segues into a breezy survey: "To this six-termed social progression corresponds a six-termed progression of human motives: necessity, utility, convenience, pleasure, luxury, abuse of luxury: and their incarnate manifestations: Polyphemus, Achilles, Caesar and Alexander, Tiberius, Caligula and Nero. At this point Vico applies Bruno—though he takes good care not to say so—and proceeds from rather arbitrary data to philosophical abstraction" (21). Then

Beckett sums up Bruno's concept of the identity of contraries in the domains of heat, speed, and geometry: an infinite circle is identical to a straight line, as Nicolas de Cues had argued one century earlier. However, the application to Vico is surprising: "The maximum of corruption and the minimum of generation are identical: in principle, corruption is generation. And all things are ultimately identified with God, the universal monad, Monad of monads. From these considerations Vico evolved a Science and a Philosophy of History" (21). If the forces of corruption bring about generation, the point hardly proves that Vico's historicism derived in any way from Bruno's dialectical ontology. Because history avoids the contraries of fate and chance, Vico would opt, in Beckett's reading, for a divine Providence that remains inscrutable. Did Vico "identify" contraries such as chance and fate by subsuming them under the heading of Providence? This is doubtful, especially if we can all admit, as Beckett does, that Vico calls Providence "divine" with his tongue in his cheek (22).

Moreover, Beckett's presentation of Vico's tenets is predicated upon a philosophical rejection of Benedetto Croce's idealism: "Giambattista Vico was a practical roundheaded Neapolitan. It pleases Croce to consider him a mystic, essentially speculative, '*disdegnoso dell' empirismo.*' It is a surprising interpretation, seeing that more than three-fifths of his *Scienza Nuova* is concerned with empirical investigation" (*D*, 19). Croce saw in Vico's Providence a superior agency, and he equated it with Hegel's cunning Reason, a Reason leading to the realization of absolute knowledge. Beckett rejects this Hegelian language, but since all the Italian passages from Vico that he quotes come from Croce's *La Filosofia di Giambattista Vico* (1911), his reading cannot but have been inspired by Croce who presents Vico as a precursor of Hegel. Croce repeatedly established parallels between the two thinkers: Vico would announce Hegel's philosophy of history while compensating for the failings of Hegel's aesthetics. In matters of aesthetics, Croce contended, Hegel was "dead."[8] Hegel's aesthetics should be replaced or complemented with the "living" insights about language, metaphor, and the body that abound in Vico's *Scienza Nuova*.

While the philosophical derivation linking Bruno and Vico is far from convincing, the postulated identity between the principle of the coincidence of contraries and the historical evolution of poetic language via tropes and metaphors has more serious credentials, at least because this conceit underpinned Joyce's creation of a new language. Having gained this point, Beckett returns to Bruno via biographical issues, quoting Joyce's pamphlet "The Day of the Rabblement," noting that Joyce's cryptic allusion to Bruno of Nola as "the Nolan" had been misunderstood as alluding to "Nolan," an unknown Irish writer. Here, too, Beckett jumps from his Vico-Bruno continuum to Dante's works without any justification.

Why is this youthful, conceited, and immature essay quoted so often? The answer is simple: it contains the best analysis of Joyce's use of Vico's linguistics in *Finnegans Wake*. Beckett is acutely aware of the novelty of his mentor's enterprise. Croce, for one, never took Vico's linguistic investigations seriously because he distrusted his fanciful popular etymologies. Beckett explains best what Vico brought to Joyce when he takes the example of the Latin word *lex*. He shows that *lex* evolved from a "crop of acorns" to the act of gathering them, then to the law, to public assemblies, and finally to reading: "Legere = To gather together letters into a word, to read" (D, 25). Such etymologies were indispensable to Joyce who would weave them endlessly in his text.

Here, the specific derivation of "legs" could point further to Martin Heidegger's meditation on Heraclitus's concept of *logos* in an essay translated into French by Jacques Lacan.[9] For Heidegger, too, *logos* was identical with the act of reading, especially his own act of reading which entailed attempting to translate the untranslatable etymologies contained in Greek concepts. If the German verbs *legen* (to lay) and *lesen* (to read) do sound like cognates of *legein* in Greek, it is not just a coincidental homophony; their intimate proximity sends us back to a pre-Socratic philosophy striving to think a *logos*. Such *logos* condenses the essence of poetic and philosophical language as a "Laying that gathers."[10]

Jolas and his friends were similarly and actively engaged in the construction of a new logos, but this *logos* was used to launch a new mythos. The *transition* group explored the so-called "language of the night," a universal language of images disclosing a collective unconscious. For Jolas, the new mythos would bridge the gap between the high modernism of Ezra Pound and T. S. Eliot and his preferred German romanticism. If he had to define in what it consisted, he would answer that Joyce's verbal creation gave substance to this mythos. Hence *transition* privileged expression over communication. The syntax of a dream world will create its own reality, while tapping images from a universal history, and also piling up many cultures and languages. Missing from the previous essays on Joyce's "Work in Progress" was a careful analysis of Vico's philosophy of history, etymology, and linguistic derivations. Only this philosophy of language—which had found one earlier model in Giacomo Leopardi's *Zibaldone*,[11] and had been sketched here and there by Croce, but always too vaguely—would provide a basis for the parallel exploration of historical and semantic universals. This is what Beckett provided with perfect pitch.

Our Exagmination offers a polyphonic accompaniment to Joyce's "Work in Progress" by disclosing its law, the gathering *lex* presupposing the creation of a new reader, or rather of a new collective body of readers, first embodied by the group of "apostles," who will be the twelve first true readers of *Finnegans Wake* when it is published. Even though their styles and tones are different from each other, they have a common task: they have to root for the fallen "acorns" embedded in the humus of the text. In thrall to a Circean text, they will gather them and eat them. However, in his disquisition on *lex*, Beckett refrained from mentioning one meaning Vico regularly associates with *lex* and law in *The New Science*: Vico showed that the main term deriving from *lex* was *religio*, that is, a collective act of gathering, not religion as we know it. Symptomatically, Beckett never mentions the religious fervor with which the twelve disciples envisaged their mission, all sooner or later turning into apostles. One of the twelve, John Rodker, had presented Joyce's achievement as leading to a "complete symbiosis of reader and writer."[12] This symbiotic exchange would be recycled ironically in *Finnegans Wake*. Joyce himself would make fun of the title of the collection: "His producers are they not his consumers? Your exagmination round his factification for incamination of a warping process."[13]

For his part, Beckett had performed his own act of *religio* when he postulated that three literary and philosophical masters anticipated the fourth: Bruno's identification of contraries, Vico's poetic wisdom, and Dante's divine comedy converge on Joyce's new babelic universe whose "word" in constant revolution is underpinned by a logic of regeneration. A bold step is taken when Beckett calls this process "purgatorial": "This inner elemental vitality and corruption of expression imparts a furious restlessness to the form, which is admirably suited to the purgatorial aspect of the work. There is an endless verbal germination, maturation, putrefaction, the cyclic dynamism of the intermediate" (*D*, 29). Hence, by an unforeseen twist, Joyce appears almost as a Hegelian, for his new language imitates the plastic dynamism of the continuum between nature and spirit, Hegel's starting point in the preface to the *Phenomenology of Spirit*. Hegel's restlessness of the negative and Joyce's linguistic organicity merge so as to combine the flux of history and the generation of semantic forms. Such a combination rests upon an excess of content, since the new coinings invented by Joyce keep multiplying their meanings thanks to the endless resources of the natural languages proliferating on the surface of the earth. The phrase of "dynamism of the intermediate" chimes in with a Hegelian vision; it defines style as more than a medium, it is more precisely an active mediation that is caught in a restless movement. Apparently Croce had convinced Beckett, in spite of himself, of the ultimate truth of Hegelian dialectics, but with one main difference: Joyce's Hegelianized Viconian philosophy of history will never be equated with the position of an absolute or of Absolute Knowledge.

Ascending or Descending Purgatories

Beckett sensed a discrepancy between Vico's cyclical history, Dante's steady progress upward in his entire Commedia from *Inferno* to *Paradiso* and Joyce's own verbal purgatory. The difference would lie in the geometries that they deployed, hence in the symbolic geographies that they created. Beckett systematizes the distinction between types of purgatories:

> A last word about the Purgatories. Dante's is conical and consequently implies culmination. Mr. Joyce's is spherical and excludes culmination. . . . In the one, absolute progression and a guaranteed consummation: in the other, flux—progression or retrogression, and an apparent consummation. In the one movement is unidirectional, and a step forward represents a net advance: in the other movement is non-directional—or multi-directional, and a step forward is by definition, a step back. (*D*, 33)

Joyce's idea that there is no progression reappears in a parody, the terse exchange between Clov and Hamm in *Endgame:*

CLOV: Do you believe in the life to come?
HAMM: Mine was always like that.[14]

In 1929, considerations of a spherical purgatory devoid of any progression led to a last identification, Beckett's fascination for Dante's Belacqua, a real person and a character in the epic, a minor character representing an important narratological problem in Dante's *Divina Commedia*. Belacqua, the hero of Beckett's first novel, *Dream of Fair to Middling Women*, reappeared in later texts. In the first lines of "Dante and the Lobster," the first story of *More Pricks Than Kicks*, Belacqua appears "stuck," or "bogged," to sound more Irish: "It was morning and Belacqua was stuck in the first of the canti in the moon. He was so bogged that he could move neither backward nor forward."[15] This is, somehow, the Belacqua introduced in *Purgatorio*. Dante was walking on with Virgil when they heard a voice saying: "Perhaps you will / have need to sit before you reach that point!"[16] It came from a boulder under which a group of men had gathered, lounging listlessly in the shade. One of them, even more exhausted than the rest (he is "listless" and "languid"), spoke out: "Climb, then, if you're so vigorous!" (Canto 4:114). Just before, when Dante had expressed fears of being too weak to follow his guide, Virgil reassured him. No sooner had Dante regained strength than his eagerness to ascend the mountain of purgatory was derided by Belacqua, a new speaker identified by his slowness:

> The slowness of his movements, his brief words
> had stirred my lips a little toward a smile;
> then I began: "From this time on, Belacqua,
> I need not grieve for you; but tell me, why
> do you sit here? Do you expect a guide?
> Or have you fallen into your old ways?"
> And he: "brother, what's the use of climbing?"
>
> (Canto 4:121–127)

Belacqua's idiomatic expression, *O frate, andar in sù che porta?* ("Bro', why keep moving up?"), triggers Dante's "wan smile," a half-smile often evoked by Beckett; it is called "Dante's first quarter-smile" in *Company*.[17] "The Lost ones" shows Belacqua "in the attitude which wrung from Dante one of his rare wan smiles."[18] Indeed, the smile must have frozen on Dante's lips, for Belacqua's question is brutal despite its tone of easy camaraderie. Belacqua, because he had waited until the last minute to repent for his sins, had when he died to linger in ante-purgatory as many years as he had spent on earth. Belacqua's background is provided in *Dream of Fair to Middling Women* (in March 1932, the section was published in *transition* as "Sedendo et Quiescendo"):

BELACQUA

we had to call him and no indolent virgin is his sister (indolent virgin!) and he does not much care whether he plays the tinkle-tinkle of a fourhander or not but he won't facing the keyboard observe the rule of the road (a megalomaniac you see with his head in his thighs as a general rule) so we ask you to humour now what naturally looks merely like so much intestinal incohesion, remember he belongs to the coster-monger times of a pale and ardent generation, pray that he will let a few good sighs out of him ere it be too late and speedy promotion from the Godbirds.[19]

This passage could have been lifted from Joyce's mocking presentation of Shem the Penman in *Finnegans Wake*. It sounds so much like a pastiche of Joyce's "Wakese" that we realize how true was Beckett's repeated complaint in the 1930s that he could not get out from Joyce's influence: he had caught the Joycean "stink."[20] In order to struggle free and achieve independence, he would need another identification, this time with Belacqua. Indeed, all his fictional alter egos like Murphy or Molloy do experience a "Belacqua bliss" at some point;[21] this bliss defines the ability to live in one's mind by pure contemplation, the momentary peace of suspended action. Because there is this bliss, the rest seems to matter less. Hence the subsequent question, whether aggressive or derisive: "What's the point of this frenzied activity all around?"

The original Belacqua is not to be found among the Sullen of *Inferno*, Canto 7, to whom I will return in chapter 11. He does not belong to the Slothful described in *Purgatorio*, Canto 18, those sinners whose tongues never stop blabbering. In fact, Belacqua does not fit neatly in the symbolic geography of the purgatory. He sits in an ante-purgatory, a transitional space between the *Inferno* and the *Purgatorio*, a limbo for adults who have never been properly born. From the start, Belacqua is an exhausted ironist, an indolent questioner, a medieval Bartleby who seems, on top of all this, to enjoy himself. In spite of his "head in his thighs," he is called a "megalomaniac." This skeptical critic is "stuck," whether by his own lack of will or by divine decree, but then from this stymied position of blockage, he can voice the most devastating antiheroic objection to the grand pattern of the quest. Belacqua's question problematizes the teleology of Dante's progression, hence the entire notion of "progression" still implied by Joyce's very "work in progress." Belacqua's passive subversion is a global refusal to go on that undermines from within a narrative structure up to then taken for granted, which anticipates Beckett's deep worries facing Joyce's and Proust's epic schemes.

The Belacqua fantasy is deployed in the context of what French historian Jacques Le Goff has called the "invention of Purgatory" in the middle ages. Le Goff provides an archeology of the "third place" rejected by Luther and most Protestants. The concept imposed itself slowly from the tenth to the twelfth century before finding its apotheosis with Dante.[22] The early fathers of the Church had only Hell and Paradise to work with, until Origen and Saint Augustine stabilized eschatological hope by defining "purgatory punishments" for the sinning souls. In the twelfth century, the "purgatory" fire morphed into the Purgatory, now a place and not just a process of purification. Beckett's effort is to understand how this essentialist metamorphosis, which keeps exerting effects on modern imaginations, can be undone by language.

A turning point for the young Irish writer was the intuition that Joyce's new language enacted a process but did not entail a progress—thus process alone would displace the Purgatory as a stable theological site. With Joyce, *purgatory* would become an adjective again. His language would destroy, through its restless punning and bold deployment of linguistic monstrosities, the ancient social perversion produced in the name of the Purgatory. In *Dubliners*, especially in "Grace," the penultimate story, Joyce had taken up Dante's fight. Both used the weapons provided by literature to attack "simony," the act of selling grace and redemption.

Simony had been linked with the creation of an intermediary site halfway between Hell and Heaven in the Middle Ages, when sinners paid handsome sums to reduce the length of their postmortem stays. There would be no need to bribe anyone if one was sure of being damned. The Church profited hugely from the sale of indulgences in a swindle denounced by Dante. The spatial organization of moral judgment had become dogma when the reality of the Purgatory was promulgated by the Council of Lyons of 1274 and confirmed by the Council of Florence of 1439. In between, it was left to Dante to map out an intermediary world of dead souls by granting poetic prestige to the tripartite zones in which the souls move, squirm, and suffer, with one exception: the exhausted Belacqua and his friends.

The theological crisis was paralleled by a crisis in language. Taking stock of this, Dante composed his poem not in Latin but in a synthetic idiom made up of words culled from most Italian dialects. Dante's creative use of the vernacular for his *Commedia* triggered hostile reactions, exactly as Joyce's invention of a new English would six centuries later: "We may also compare, if we think it worth while, the storm of ecclesiastical abuse raised by Mr. Joyce's work, and the treatment that the Divine Comedy must certainly have received from the same source" (*D*, 32). Moreover, Dante's monarchism contested the Church's wish to wield a temporal power embodied in a papal state. Two centuries later, Luther would attack the notion of an intermediate zone, arguing that Purgatory had no foundation in the Scriptures.

Beckett's Protestant origin did not predispose him to foreground Purgatory. At times, he would return to the binary opposition of Hell and Heaven, as in *From an Abandoned Work* (1957): "Ah my father and mother, to think they are probably in paradise, they were so good. Let me go to hell, that's all I ask, and go on cursing them there, and them look down and hear me, that might take some of the shine off their bliss."[23] Let us take their bliss for granted and not be cynical like Villiers de l'Isle-Adam who quoted in *Nouveaux Contes Cruels* the anecdote of Abbé Tussert, an inveterate gambler. As he was losing at cards and needed money, he sold the hidden secret of the Church: there is no Purgatory.

Beckett's central concept of purgatory shares with Joyce's own a loss of all absolutes: "In what sense, then, is Mr. Joyce's work purgatorial? In the absolute absence of the absolute" (D, 33). The rejection of an absolute belief underpinned Joyce's skepticism facing philosophical theories used in *Finnegans Wake*: "This social and historical classification is clearly adapted by Mr. Joyce as a structural convenience—or inconvenience. His position is in no way a philosophical one" (D, 22). For instance, Joyce denied that he strictly believed in the theories of Vico or Bruno.[24] Uncomfortable with this skepticism, Beckett would have preferred a solid philosophical position. This led to his own skepticism facing Joyce's linguistic utopia. He had not yet learned, as the Unnamable will, that the only way one can be an "ephectic," or a skeptic, is by remaining "unaware" of the fact.[25] This could only come to him after the Belacqua fantasy of nondoing was relayed by Geulincx's phenomenology of nonknowledge.

For Joyce, culmination was excluded because the verbal machine had to drone on in a process that regenerated itself endlessly. Hence the circular text, virtually infinite, of *Finnegans Wake*. Can one imagine an endless purgation? In 1937 Beckett was more skeptical when he wrote to his friend Axel Kaun in German that his "program" had nothing to do with that of Joyce, then about to publish the completed *Finnegans Wake*. For Beckett, Joyce was still thinking in terms of the "apotheosis of the word." He adds wistfully: "Unless perhaps Ascension to Heaven and Descent to Hell are one and the same. How nice it would be to believe that in fact it were so."[26] The mystical or paradoxical idea that the way up and the way down are one and the same, at this point, seemed even more exhausting to Beckett who preferred to find relief in a comforting Nothing. However, the bi-directional apotheosis might lead to a solution if only it is rephrased by Marquis de Sade. For Sade, as we will see in chapter 8, any Ascension to Heaven will have to turn into a Descent to Hell.

All this brings us back to Belacqua's rebuttal, his "Why go on?" questioning both the eschatological teleology of Redemption and the measured theology of Damnation. Such a radical questioning forces us to meditate on the values presupposed by the simple fact of "going on." Here, however, we can guess that Belaqua's exhaustion will not prevent him from indulging his idleness and, why not, will be softened by the consumption of ante-purgatorial delicacies (the historical Belacqua was rumored to have a sweet tooth). Before I return to the ethics implied by his ironical questioning, a word about material comforts.

Beckett's central image of a "carefully folded ham-sandwich" containing all of Italian culture, plus Joyce's last work, plus universal history, has to be identified more decisively. It seems to fit the idea of what is called an "Italian hoagie" in Philadelphia. Hoagies were invented in South Philadelphia, the Italian section of the city, during World War I. To this part of the city, innumerable "roundheaded Napolitans" and Southern Italians had come in the first decades of the twentieth century, most of them to work in the shipyards. The hoagie is a ham sandwich still highly popular in Philadelphia. Hoagies are found in a geographical arc going from Pittsburgh to Southern New Jersey; in New York or Boston, the hoagie is called a sub or a hero. The hoagie consists of a bread roll packed to burst with several types of ham and salami, cheese slices, lettuce, tomatoes, onions, sweet peppers, oregano, salt, pepper, and olive oil. The sandwich has to be thick and hold a lot. Its official width is that of a strong clenched fist—so much for Vico and his metaphors based on the human body!

The hoagie provides an equivalent for Beckett's essay: being young, greedy, and not easily frightened, he crams as much as he can into it and yokes his four masters in less than twenty pages. This is how culture would appear to an omnivorous young Beckett: a nearly exploding ham sandwich. Culture spelled out a surfeit of knowledge that was at the antipode of the diminutive Proustian madeleine that Beckett's monograph on Proust briefly discusses, presenting it as a first "fetish," that is as the first of the many "visitations" that will bring the narrator to a full and final epiphany.[27] However, we know from manuscripts for *À la recherche du temps perdu* that Proust's madeleine experience was triggered when he dipped a "toast" into tea: the real life model for the vaunted madeleine was simply a banal biscotto.

Beckett knew that it was Proust's massive work that could, much better than Joyce's magnum opus in fact, be compared with a "carefully folded ham-sandwich." Indeed, Proust had written the beginning and the ending of *À la recherche du temps perdu* first, and then kept on adding new narratives, theories, character developments, all he could find to season the whole, making the "middle" acquire an enormous length. How to prevent the sandwich from bursting open? It was an inbuilt principle of form or metaphoricity that would serve this purpose. For Proust as for Vico, metaphors always send us back to the human body. The text has to turn into a body, a shapely body if possible, which entailed that it would be limited in space and time; finally, its ultimate resource would rely on an identification of thought with poetic language. Neither Proust nor Joyce could resist the idea of a total identification of thought with language, no more than Belacqua Shuah could resist the vision of smelly Gorgonzola cheese spread on a charred toast.

To move beyond dangerous identifications with Joyce and Proust, Becket would have to find his own route, thus identify differently—skipping Vico, Bruno, and Dante, he would become Belacqua in order to avoid becoming Joyce. No doubt, Belacqua the indolent sensualist would have enjoyed the typical South Philly hoagie, relished its multiple layers, rich strata of Genoa salami, prosciutto, mortadella, cappicola, and provolone cheese. Its almost obscene girth might evoke the image of a pregnant animal. When one opens one's mouth, the enormous size of the object and the muscular effort required to swallow the "carefully folded ham-sandwich" inevitably produces the kind of bliss Belacqua was craving for: in a second, the mind goes blank. Then the world is reduced to no-know, to nonknowledge. It is pure Bataillean unknowing condensed in an excess of edible matter, a posthuman reduction of spirit to base materialism.

However, unlike Kafka, Beckett's materialist minimalism eschews anorexia. For him—as for Belacqua who prepares his toasts with so much care— there are creature comforts, and they can even bring a form of minimal happiness, the happiness ensuing after the glut, after the devouring of all that matter. This is confirmed by the narrator of *Ill Seen Ill Said* at the very end of this spare and condensed late text: "Not another crumb of carrion left. Lick chops and basta. No. One moment more. One last. Grace to breathe that void. Know happiness."[28]

CHAPTER 3

The Posthuman, or the Humility
of the Earth

Before entering the convoluted and post-Babelian world of Joyce's invented idiom, in which a first description of H. C. Earwicker, the main male character of *Finnegans Wake*, introduces him as a composite "creature in youman form,"[1] when did Samuel Beckett hear the word *posthuman* for the first time? It was most likely in Paris, when discussing *Ulysses* with its author. As I mentioned, Beckett came to the École Normale Supérieure on November 1, 1928, and by the end of the month ended up as a regular visitor on intimate terms with the whole Joyce family. The speedy convergence of minds between the two Irish men had an electrifying effect on both. Joyce found a younger alter ego in the eager scholar from Trinity College, who, like him, knew Dante by heart. Also, he imagined that Beckett would make a perfect son-in-law. Sadly, soon after, Joyce concluded that Beckett had played with Lucia's infatuation before jilting her, which had led to her mental disturbance—he then excluded the young disciple from the tightly knit circle. Joyce was wrong, but this is another story.

Beckett knew Joyce's works before he came to Paris. In July 1927, he gave a copy of the just-published *Pomes Penyeach* to a golf partner;[2] he read *Dubliners* and the two novels during the 1927–1928 academic year, which

he spent first in Dublin, then in Belfast. When his friend MacGreevy introduced the young scholar to Joyce's group, Beckett was ready to be con-
verted to the Joyce cult. Fall 1928 was a crucial moment for Joyce—his
collective workshop was humming feverishly at a time when each issue of
transition carried fragments from the new text. The recently launched
review had become "la maison de Joyce," as Marcel Brion said.[3] Beckett
was marked all his life by this moment of artistic collaboration and intellectual complicity.

The fact is that Beckett chose Joyce as a mentor and literary role model.
It was Beckett's first encounter with a supreme artist (and he would meet
many others); here was a writer for whom work was sacred. Joyce believed
that everyone coming within his proximity shared a duty to help him complete his magnum opus, the *Work in Progress* soon to be named *Finnegans
Wake*. Readers of *Finnegans Wake* know that the polyglot epic is partly a
commentary on *Ulysses*, above all because it was built on a principle that
Joyce had discovered when meditating about his "day" novel. It was when
he thought about the problems posed by his immortal heroine, Molly
Bloom, that he decided to move from the human to the posthuman. The
narratological logic that connects *Ulysses* and *Finnegans Wake* rests on a
simple idea that Joyce elaborated when reaching the end of *Ulysses*: he
would replace characters like Leopold Bloom, Stephen Dedalus and Molly
Bloom, each endowed with individual traits and psychology, with a set of
sigla, idiosyncratic narrative functions invented to represent generic roles
or narratological functions like "Father," "Mother," "Daughter," "Sons,"
"Drinkers in the pub," and so on.[4] The device would allow him to univer-
salize their actions and it would also render these actors capable of reen-
acting all the stories of the world at once.

Joyce intuited this principle when he presented Molly Bloom as posthuman early in 1922. This was in a letter sent to his friend and patron Miss
Weaver, along with a draft of the last episode. Joyce explained to her that
Molly was not only a Homeric "Penelope," which by then was obvious to
anyone who knew the links between the novel and the *Odyssey*, but also
embodied Gaia-Tellus, the goddess of the Earth. Miss Weaver commented
that she felt that Molly was prehuman, by which she meant coarse, crude,
low, or unrefined. Joyce corrected her with a diplomatic rebuke: "Your
description of it also coincides with my intention—if the epithet 'posthuman' were added. I have rejected the usual interpretation of her as a human
apparition—that aspect being better represented by Calypso, Nausikaa
and Circe, to say nothing of the pseudo Homeric figures. In conception
and technique I tried to depict the Earth which is prehuman and presum-

ably posthuman."[5] Molly Bloom should not simply be understood as a "real" or "realistic" human being, a person whom we could meet in the street, but as a verbal construct relying on chains of associations that were fundamentally allegorical in nature.

The complexity of Molly's psychology is the cumulative effect of an accretive process piling up numerous contradictory remarks. Joyce's idea was to make her appear as generic and universal as possible. In the end, she represents the inhuman and posthuman figure of the revolving Earth. If Molly Bloom is to become the Earth, such a construction pushes her character beyond any human psychology.[6] This method—a different mythical method from what T. S. Eliot had observed about systematic parallels between *Ulysses* and the *Odyssey*—would provide an original paradigm from which the young Beckett learned much. A similar wish to move beyond naturalism and psychology will account for Beckett's subsequent development.

Beckett discovered slowly, after several explorations and a few aborted ventures, that the issue would be to overcome the mixture of basic psychology and naturalism underpinned by age-old humanism that he called "anthropomorphism." Beckett wanted to craft a different writing capable of reaching a hard core whose model was the inorganic essence of the Earth. He became conscious of this evolution in his thinking in the late 1930s. By a strange coincidence, he developed the idea in a letter in which he mentions another Molly—Molly Roe, a cousin visiting the family in 1937 at the occasion of the marriage of Beckett's brother Frank. The stress of the family gathering proved overwhelming for Beckett who wrote to his aunt Cissie Sinclair: "At least I am escaped from Cooldrinagh, the Liebespaar & Molly."[7] The same letter discusses paintings by Jack Yeats, the brother of the poet and an artist admired by Beckett. Beckett loved the way in which Jack Yeats suggested "the inorganism of the organic." Here is how he develops the idea: "all his people are mineral in the end, without possibility of being added to or taken from, pure inorganic juxtapositions."[8] Nevertheless, Beckett concludes that this special quality, shared by Jack Yeats with Watteau, derived from the fact that Yeats seemed to him "rather inhuman."[9] Was this pure praise, or did the remark betray a certain disappointment?

Another letter written at the same time throws light on Beckett's complicated sense of the *human*, along with his growing cynicism facing the term. Watching the presents offered to the soon-to-be-married pair pile up led him to make snide remarks about gongs and tea-trolleys. In his growing "social cynicism," he observed that the law of marriage seemed to

be that "the human personal element" has to be smothered by the ownership of superfluous things.[10] Such feelings, not original in themselves, testify to a rejection of the bourgeois ethos upheld by his family. Moreover,
one can perceive in the very juxtaposition of the two letters that Beckett
evinced a deep ambivalence facing the human.

What Beckett praised in Jack Yeats's portraits in 1937 ("A kind of petri-
fied insight into one's ultimate hard irreducible inorganic singleness"[11])
does sound like D. H. Lawrence commenting on *Women in Love*, were it
not for the rejection of vitalism. In fact, these terms develop a thought that
Beckett had expressed three years earlier, when observing Paul Cézanne's
self-portraits next to celebrated paintings of the Montagne Sainte Victoire.
Beckett was in London at the time, writing to McGreevy: "What a relief
the Mont Ste. Victoire after all the anthropomorphized landscape," Beckett exclaims, after which he lists Dutch painters to dismiss them, along
with Claude Lorrain and even Watteau who is said to be "paranthropo-
morphised."[12]

The critique of anthropomorphism is a recurrent theme sounded with
great regularity in the letters from that period: "Cézanne seems to have
been the first to see landscape & state it as material of a strictly peculiar
order, incommensurable with all human expressions whatsoever."[13] Cézanne
has the merit to give viewers an "atomistic landscape with no velleities of
vitalism," an effort that he praises as a heroic task.[14] A week later, Beckett
explains himself more amply to McGreevy: "[W]hat I feel in Cézanne is
precisely the absence of a rapport that was all right for Rosa and Ruysdael
for whom the animizing mode was valid, but would have been false for him,
because he had the sense of his incommensurability not only with life of
such a different order as landscape but even with life of his own order, even
with the life . . . operative in himself."[15] We will have to understand the
articulation of Beckett's recurrent argument, a strong theory of art account-
ing for his desire to usher in a new poetics or a new ethics of nonrelation in
which distance, dehiscence, and incommensurability are key terms.

Ethics and aesthetics are knotted together, for the terms quoted apply
to both domains; they explain why Beckett's theater, for instance, aims at
debunking naturalism, and remain in line with his appreciation of Jack
Yeats and Ireland, both evoking "a nature almost as inhumanly inorganic as
a stage set."[16] They explain why Beckett's social ethics and politics would
be marked by a virulent rejection of Jean-Paul Sartre's notion of a committed, engaged, or public intellectual—a position always loathed or derided
in the 1950s.

The fact that his remarks on Jack Yeats and Cézanne date to the 1930s suggests that the problematics of the posthuman cannot be attributed to the trauma of the war, for these statements predate the period when Beckett had to flee Paris and find a refuge in Roussillon, where he wrote *Watt*. The struggle with an inorganic world was not a consequence of his having known what Agamben called "bare life" in his harsh daily life when hiding in the South of France. On the contrary, there is a logical progression from the first texts showing an intense absorption in the visual arts to the later texts exploring the dead ends of post-Cartesian subjectivity. I will analyze Beckett's theory of an art of nonrelation, one of the dominant issues in the dialogues with Georges Duthuit.

If I insist on Beckett's ambivalence, it is because I am wary of making what might look like a logical deduction, which would be to categorize him as a thinker, writer, and practitioner of the posthuman. Today, the term usually calls up analyses of subjectless technology, cyborgs, and mutants, or post-Deleuzian organic machines and "bodies without organs." However, given Beckett's twisted sense of paradox, no sooner do we meet formulations that anticipate Deleuze's and Guattari's idea of a "body without organs" than we meet the old couple of God and the human. This happens in *The Unnamable*, when the speaker describes his own body and discovers that it has lost all trace of sexual difference:

> Why should I have a sex, who have no longer a nose? All those things have fallen, all the things that stick out, with my eyes my hair, without leaving a trace, fallen so far so deep that I heard nothing, perhaps are still falling, my hair slowly like soot still, of the fall of my ears heard nothing. Mean words, and needless, from the mean old spirit, I invented love, music, the smell of flowering currant, to escape from me. Organs, a without, it's easy to imagine, a god, it's unavoidable, you imagine them, it's easy, the worst is dulled, you doze away, an instant. Yes, God, fomenter of calm, I never believed, not a second.[17]

God and man are locked in an articulation that frustrates the Deleuzian impulse to push the speaking and desiring subject beyond the human altogether. Just at this moment, the narrator decides to stop making any "pause," and indeed one will not find any paragraphs or textual breaks after this passage: he will continue speaking uninterrupted, no matter what. The unstoppable speaker is "a big talking ball," round as an egg, and he is adamant that he has abjured any "right to silence."[18] What to do in this context of those gods, or God? One could imagine that the speaking egg sees himself (should one say "itself"?) as a sort of god—but no, on the contrary. God has been called "fomenter of calm" (in the French original, "fauteur de calme"[19]). The calm is then rejected as a lie, as *trouble*, a term which would have been the usual complement of *fauteur de* in French. The speaking egg is resolutely atheistic. The divine equanimity of a static God is undermined by the speaker's endless restlessness—an inherently atheological negativity adheres to this restive speech. Such verbal negativity excludes anything stable because it never allows one to be a creator or even a creature. God and his creatures are fictional beings whose shape cannot be changed—they will have to be exploded one after the other. Another passage makes the point more clearly:

> Me, utter me, in the same foul breath as my creatures? Say of me that I see this, feel that, fear, hope, know and do not know? Yes, I will say it, and of me alone. Impassive, still and mute, Malone revolves, a stranger forever to my infirmities, one who is not as I can never not be. I am motionless in vain, he is the god. And the other? I have assigned him eyes that implore me, offerings for me, need of succour. He does not look at me, does not know of me, wants for nothing. I alone am man, and all the rest divine.[20]

The obfuscating syntax of the sentence "one who is not as I can never not be" is less strange in French: "En voilà un qui n'est pas comme moi je ne saurai jamais ne pas être,"[21] or literally: "Here is one who is not like me, I will never be able not to be." We guess that "being human" implies both "to be" and "not to be"—as Hamlet would say. To be human is to evade all fixed definition, whether it be that of a fictional character like Malone, presented in the same passage in French as "muet, soutenant sa mâchoire,"[22] an archaic caveman condemned to death by the very title of the previous section of the trilogy, *Malone Dies*, or that of a God representing the ultimate projection of the divine artist from Shakespeare, Balzac, and Flaubert to Proust and Joyce. Beckett's previous characters—Watt, Murphy, Malone or Molloy—all assumed the same divine stature as the godlike novelists whom he had tried to emulate until then. Joyce and Proust were the two masters and guides whom Beckett felt obliged to reject. Their self-important arrogance is replayed in Pozzo's boastful exclamation in *Waiting for Godot*, when he rebukes Didi and Gogo for not knowing his name. When Estragon explains weakly that they are strangers in this area, he replies haughtily: "You are human beings none the less. (*He puts on his glasses.*) As far as one can see. (*He takes off his glasses.*) Of the same species as myself. (*He bursts into an enormous laugh*.) Of the same species as Pozzo! Made in God's image!"[23]

Philosophically, the opposition between the "human" and the "divine" calls up the basic theses of existentialism, then the dominant philosophical discourse in France. As Sartre explained in *Being and Nothingness*, published in 1943, taking his cue from Hegel and Heidegger whom he generally distorted, Being with a capital B was on the side of pure essence, an essence often condensed by the name of God, whereas the concept of existence entailed freeing the power of negativity ascribed to human consciousness: human consciousness would keep negating both the facticity of the world and the essences of ancient gods. However, as Adorno states in the elaborate discussion of *Endgame* to which I will return, Beckett's proximity to existentialism is misleading. In fact, one can say that *The Unnamable* debunks existentialist themes by reducing them to a series of absurd equations.

It is not that the narrator shirks from a confrontation with the absurd, a theme deployed in Sartre's novel *Nausea*, which had impressed Beckett, or in Camus's *The Stranger* and his subsequent essays, as we see from this ironical aside: "That the impossible should be asked of me, good, what else could be asked of me? But the absurd! Of me whom they have reduced to reason. It is true poor Worm is not to blame for this. That's soon said. But let me complete my views, before I shit on them. For if I am Mahood, I am Worm too, plop. Of if I am not yet Worm, I shall be when I cease to be Mahood, plop. On now to serious matters. No, not yet."[24] As this passage proves (similar ones could be excerpted), the point is to show that the new sequence of Mahood, a castrated or diminished manhood, and Worm, suggesting organic life thriving in the earth after the human body has died and consciousness been annihilated, is nothing but the effect of a specific game of language. This game is not serious since it is compared with defecation: we literally hear two verbal turds fall on the page ("plop")! This game can be more serious if it confronts itself with the "Impossible" (a loaded term to which I will return), but cannot be so serious as to posit an absurd defined as the reverse of reason. All these terms are first of all forcibly uttered, said, written, defecated, or produced by an agency that keeps dissolving in language. *The Unnamable* teaches us, again and again, by changing points of view and arguments, by endlessly contradicting itself, that the speaking voice is nothing but language: even its nonlanguage (its very onomatopoeias) is language. Moreover, this language is not "his," that is that it does not belong to the Unnamable because, in many senses, it is the language of the others.

However, if language fails to capture the speaker's singularity, it also grants him an existence—understood as an ecstatic being of nonbeing—but only as long as he speaks. Given language's essence as a social and collective formation, the speaker can only speak of himself in the third person, which is why he changes his identities now and then. The third person is regularly negated by the first; the speaker goes on, negating and asserting at once, inhabiting the page as long as words pour from his mouth, pen, or any other hole including the rectum. Beckett has added to Sartre's and Camus's existentialism the missing element, a medium that for them remained invisible, and whose omission had dire consequences: the constitution of subjectivity by language, a theme that came to prominence with Maurice Blanchot in the late 1950s, then relayed by Roland Barthes a little later, before being taken as a red thread by Jacques Derrida when he revised Husserlian phenomenology in the 1960s.

That Beckett's writing seems to anticipate deconstruction did not escape Derrida, and two excellent books have explored those fascinating parallels.[25] In a sense, *The Unnamable* provides a fictional equivalent of *Voice and Phenomenon*. Whereas Sartre had read Hegel, Husserl, and Heidegger as if they were merely commenting Descartes's *cogito*, Beckett—who has read Descartes earlier, with more irony and more critical attention than Sartre (I will highlight this point in chapter 5 when discussing how "Whoroscope" rewrites the Cartesian *cogito* as "Fallor, ergo sum!," which replaces any subjective foundation with self-deception)—understood that the problematics of language could not but destroy the certainty of a self-positioned subject condensed in the famous "I think therefore I am." When an extreme experience of language is unleashed, an experience that can be called "literature" as Blanchot insisted, even if what we usually call "literature" gets undone in the process, no master remains the haunted castle of consciousness. Such a limit experience, fraught with paradoxes and contradictions, undermines from within any self-present mastery, any transcendent or transcendental subjectivity. My aim is not to add another chapter to the competent discussions comparing the philosophy of deconstruction and Beckett's works, but to use this conversation as a lever in order to argue that one cannot simply enlist Beckett in the camp of the posthuman. It would be impossible to state that Beckett sits squarely on one side of the divide between the human and the posthuman in its contemporary sense.

Joyce again functioned as a model up to a point. We know that Molly Bloom performs several roles in *Ulysses*: first, she is Calypso in the first episode of the second section, in which Bloom eats a pig kidney before starting his "exile" for the day; then she is Circe in the brothel scene in which men are turned into pigs; finally, she is Penelope who reconciles the frankly sexual and the heavenly via the annulling mediation of the spinning Earth. In *Finnegans Wake*, however, Joyce deploys a new division of the writing hand before the synthesis provided by the ideal family of his tale—this is why he lets the brothers Shem the Penman and Shaun the Postman struggle, in a fight for domination that lasts for all eternity. They are opposed as the artist is opposed to the politician, or as writing is opposed to the living word.

Once more, the Earth provides a synthesis, but this time the synthesis reconciling the opposites appears as a systemic recombination haunted by death. Here is how the very site of the text, near Dublin, is evoked: "And thanacestross mound have swollen them all. This ourth of years is not save brickdust and being humus the same rotourns."[26] The ancestral mound is the property of Thanatos, and it has swallowed all the living. Our old Earth has seen the collapse of all civilizations, to which human remains are mingled. Human and humus have become one in the eternal indifference of a revolving globe. Here is the root of the new humility one can discern in the later Joyce, a humility shared by Beckett who will find it extolled as the supreme virtue by his favorite philosopher, Arnold Geulincx. Humility does not mean moral abnegation or abasement but a reconciled sense that one will remain close to the Earth, an Earth that contains the ashes of all the dead along with the fertilizing humus for future plants.

Whereas Joyce strives to be funny despite the pervasive gloom of his later prose epic, Beckett's frequent disquisitions on his own physical disappearance display a refreshing jollity of tone, as can be seen in a typical passage of "From an Abandoned Work":

> Oh I know I too shall cease and be as when I was not yet, only all over instead of in store, that makes me happy, often now my murmur falters and dies and I weep for happiness as I go along and for love of this old earth that has carried me so long and whose uncomplainingness will soon be mine. Just under the surface I shall be, all together at first, then separate and drift, through all the earth and perhaps in the end through a cliff into the sea, something of me. A ton of worms in an acre, that is a wonderful thought, a ton of worms, I believe it.[27]

In this text, as in *The Unnamable*, Beckett's philosophical position allows him to speak and write as if speaking and writing were a single process. He is sitting on both sides of the fence at once, in the same way as we see Belacqua, come back from the dead, therefore pale, wan and ghostly but still kicking and game for adventure, at the beginning of the unpublished short story "Echo's Bones." Belacqua is presented "as he sat bent double on a fence like a casse-poitrine in delicious rêverie."[28] Like his character in that story, Beckett *is* his writing, a writing that is close to death but keeps on surviving, a writing often presented as an ear; it may also be a hand, or an eye, since each organ will anyway try to negate all the others:

> I'll have said it inside me, then in the same breath outside me, perhaps that's what I feel, an outside and an inside and me in the middle, per- haps that's what I am, the thing that divides the world in two, on the one side the outside, on the other the inside, that can be as thin as foil, I'm neither on one side nor the other, I'm in the middle, I'm the parti- tion, I've two surfaces and no thickness, perhaps that's what I feel, myself vibrating, I'm the tympanum, on the one hand the mind, on the other the world, I don't belong to either . . .[29]

What Beckett attacks, before and after the trilogy, is anthropomor- phism, in which he recognizes humanism pure and simple. To achieve his program, he decides to stay on the fence between the human and the inor- ganic. Thus he never finds a solid foundation for being beyond language, but because he discovers an undecidable at the place of the fence or the border, this creates an endless torture of thought through language. Such a torture nevertheless manages to punch "holes" in the continuum of our *doxa*, our innate and inane trust in the human as the fountain of value, as I will show in chapter 10 when tackling Beckett's ethics and politics and contrasting the positions taken by Alain Badiou and Theodor Adorno.

In *The Unnamable*, the right to remain silent and the duty to keep on speaking (or writing, or both at once) mesh up in a productive tension, a dynamic torsion of incompatibles; they are bound by a nondialectical fusion of the contraries. Such a double oxymoron (right versus duty, speech versus silence) defines the site of a struggle; at times it generates a logor- rheic verbal production, at times minimalist reductions in the multiplica- tion of pauses and silences. The clash of the opposites is an ethical clash since it examines the limits of language, while doubling as an aesthetic struggle; it is such a productive hesitation that I will attempt to analyze. However, before it can be structured along theoretical lines, this hesitation accounts for the beauty and the strange humor of the texts. They create a pervasive hilarity, a human and posthuman comedy of sorts that finds its sporadic discharge in jokes, sallies, or witticisms.

The rationale of this comic spirit has to do with the fact that the unde- cidable middle is also the site of laughter, even when this laughter appears deprived of any subjectivity. Typically, *The Unnamable* pairs freedom and necessity, a central ethical couple, and suggests that their opposition can be reconciled in laughter: "Yes, the big words must out too, all be taken as it comes. The problem of liberty too, as sure as fate, will come up for my consideration at the pre-established moment. But perhaps I have been too hasty in opposing these two fomenters of fiasco. It is not the fault of one that I cannot be the other? Accomplices therefore. That's the way to reason, warmly. Or is one to produce a tertius gaudens, meaning myself, responsible for the double failure?"[30] The "laughing third," a third party who profits by the unresolved antagonism of the warring opponents who end up losing everything, was a concept introduced by Georg Simmel in sociological analysis.

Such a *tertius gaudens* served Beckett as a way out of other dichotomies, as we can judge from a note for *Dream of Fair to Middling Women*, which quotes Jules de Gaultier's *De Kant à Nietzsche* (1900): "Instincts of Knowledge & Life engaged in their comic warfare."[31] What is perceived as comic provides incentives for the reader's insatiable curiosity: "Curiosity focused on relations between the *object* & its *representation*, between the *stimulus* & *molecular disturbance*, between *percipi* and *percipere*."[32] Beckett made abundant use of the last couple of concepts for *Film;* it also recurs in *Murphy*. However, the point is less to follow the serial reappearance of these concepts in his work, or play with such important philosophical notions, than to observe Beckett's strategy, his choice of a third point of view, that of the detached and amused observer, an interested but critical scholar.

By foregrounding the idea of a limit, I will imply an overdetermined link between Beckett and Kant's transcendental philosophy for which the question of the limits of domains like art, freedom, and our perception of the world produce knowledge and lead to truth. I will examine Beckett's Kantianism; however, we will see that Kant is always accompanied by his more sinister double, Marquis de Sade. Taken together, the impact of their questions is directed at the venerable issue of what makes the human human, or of what "Manhood" consists in. In *The Unnamable*, the narrator becomes Mahood, that is "Manhood" without the *n*, or "man" turning into "Ma," a syllable always associated with the narrator's mother in the trilogy. This will entail horrible treatments for the narrator's mother and his whole family. We had been warned, however, for "the mere fact of having a family should have put me on my guard."[33] Thus, when Mahood returns home to discover the remains of his family members killed by poisoned food, he stomps on the rotting entrails of his mother with some relish before setting off again.[34] The narrative can only start when it becomes aware of its matricidal impulse, otherwise the speaker would be like "the infant who has been told so often how he was found under a cabbage that in the end he remembers the exact spot in the garden."[35]

One needs to take a closer look at Beckett's anti-Oedipal garden, a matricidal and unhallowed place to which the speaker dreams of returning, still hoping to make one with the Earth after the paradises, which have never been totally lost, are left to rot, ferment, and decompose in the imagination. This accounts for the last metamorphosis of the narrator of *The Unnamable* when he imagines his residual existence as a less than conqueror "Worm." In the trinity of speaking agencies of which Worm is the last, Beckett parodies a pedagogical situation: "Pupil Mahood, repeat after me, Man is a higher mammal. I couldn't. Always talking about mammals, in this menagerie. Frankly, between ourselves, what the hell could it matter to pupil Mahood, that man was this rather than that?"[36] Following the theme of animals, beginning with pigs and rats and ending with worms and termites, we will perceive that the question of the humanity of man presupposes two limits: the domain of God on the one hand, and on the other, the animal realm, which extends from mammals to humbler crustaceans like lobsters. To assert that narrative agencies like Worm and Mahood are just "creatures" like the others will not bring a resolution, for, in fact, they don't know who they are ("What can you expect, they don't know who they are either, nor where they are, nor what they are doing").[37] Given such a pervasive ignorance, one can say that to be human has to be reduced to the ability to witness and register a catastrophe, in a movement that enacts, once more, the collapse of reason; thus the narrator of *The Unnamable* has a point when he observes coolly: "So they build up hypotheses that collapse on top of one another, it's human, a lobster couldn't do it."[38]

CHAPTER 4

Burned Toasts and Boiled Lobsters

What do lobsters have to contribute to issues of ethics? A lot, especially when they are boiled alive. But since they cannot speak, in Beckett's works, the question of ethics will have to be posed by a voice displaying the author's prerogative: the voice wields absolute power, for it has the power to interrupt the narrative with an intrusive negation. This may mean bringing the fiction, like the poor lobster, to an untimely end. Later, the imperiousness of this authorial voice will be diminished, questioned, demultiplied, endlessly qualified, but in Beckett's first collection of stories, a peremptory voice reminds us that we are indeed reading a "short" story and not a novel. No ampler narrative will be allowed, as the abrupt closure of "Dante and the Lobster" underlines:

> She lifted the lobster clear of the table. It had about thirty seconds to live.
> Well, thought Belacqua, it's a quick death, God help us.
> It is not.[1]

Belacqua has fetched a lobster for his dinner with his aunt. Believing the animal to be dead, he carries it along when taking an Italian lesson with

Professor Adriana Ottolenghi. He is surprised when the French teacher's cat tries to catch it, only to discover that the lobster was alive all the time. The ending of the story returns to Belacqua's bafflement about Dante's canto about the spots in the moon—an interpretation vigorously dismantled by Beatrice. The "vulgar" interpretation of these spots at the time was that they showed God's treatment of Cain, unceremoniously thrown out to the moon, but not killed on the spot as he should have been. Is this a proof of divine compassion for Cain?, Belacqua wonders.[2] Compassion extends to everyday ethical issues, as in the issue of whether McCabe, the notorious Malahide murderer, had to be executed, or in the question whether it is right to kill animals in order to eat them. McCabe had bludgeoned to death six victims for sordid reasons and he was executed by hanging at Mountjoy Jail on December 9, 1926. As to the lobster, the aunt has no qualms about boiling it alive; she even makes fun of her nephew's queasiness: she knows that Belacqua will devour the lobster once cooked and served.

Would "Dante and the Lobster" have been as effective if the aunt had opened oysters? Probably not, even if one is supposed to gulp oysters alive. It may be easier to identify with a lobster than with an oyster. What triggers the ethical shock is the hero's empathy for an animal whose struggles can be relived: "In the depths of the sea it had crept into the cruel pot. . . . It had survived the Frenchwoman's cat and his witless clutch. Now it was going alive into scalding water. It had to. Take into the air my quiet breath."[3] The moral issue is not simply whether it is wrong to boil lobsters, or worry about their pain when they are plunged alive in boiling water, or whether it is more humane to kill them before boiling them, but how to reconcile mundane or everyday life concerns within a grand scheme of things in which we move from God's possible compassion for Cain to scenes of sadistic violence in the *Inferno* where damned souls are plunged in boiling blood like the violent souls of the seventh circle of Hell.

Beckett told Ruby Cohn that he had wanted to change the ending to: "Like Hell it is," but changed his mind because he preferred three words instead of four.[4] The stylistic preference for concision was wise: the allusion would have been too obvious, it would have echoed Belacqua's position halfway between Hell and Heaven, "stuck" in glosses of the moon canti, too obviously. Even if Beckett had changed "It is not" to "Like Hell it is," this would not have affected "God help us." God's help remains beyond negations and affirmations. As Heine had quipped, God will help, that's his job. What is worrying is that human suffering seems to have a role to play in that job. Here is the ground of Beckett's ethics, which deploys itself between a religious realm, whether God exists or not, and the actuality of a phenomenology of suffering.[5]

The issue of pain in a system of divine sadism reappears in "Text 3," an early poem investigating suffering, pity, and the impenetrability of God's justice. It begins with the first word spoken to Virgil by Dante the character: "*Miserere*," a word not in Italian but in Latin ("*Miserere* di me," "Have pity on me," [*Inferno* Canto 1:65]), which announces Dante's synthetic language and Joyce's experiments. Proust is then quoted:

> Proust's cook is in the study,
> she is grieved in a general way for the abstract intestine.
> she is so engrossed that she does not hear the screams of her assistant,
> a sloven she,
> and the dying spit of a Paduan Virtue,
> for alas she has stripped her last asparagus,
> now she is smashed on delivery.
> She rises,
> her heart is full of murder and tears,
> she hunts down the pullet with oaths,
> fiercely she tears his little head off.[6]

The famous portrayal of Françoise, the old and faithful servant who was a fixture in the narrator's family, is the starting point for Beckett's meditation on the juxtaposition of goodness and sadism, this mixture of cruelty and compassion recurring in Proust's characters. Françoise has an assistant, a younger and sickly kitchen maid, moreover pregnant, whom she harasses and forces to leave. That summer in Combray, the narrator's family is surprised to find asparagus served in all their dishes; Françoise, knowing that the kitchen maid is prone to asthma attacks when peeling asparagus, orders her to prepare asparagus endlessly.[7] When the maid screams in pain after hard labor, Françoise grudgingly fetches a medical manual but never comes back to help. A little later, she is discovered engrossed in its pages, crying out in compassion: "Holy Virgin, it is possible that the good Lord would want a wretched human creature to suffer so?"[8] Here is the function of literature! Earlier, the narrator had surprised Françoise in the kitchen, as she was about to kill a chicken. To perform the bloody operation that would have been the maid's task had she not left, she had to scream at the animal, "Sale bête!," after which she chopped its head off.[9] Shocked, the narrator's immediate reaction is to complain and get her fired; he then reflects that without Françoise, he would not get his culinary delicacies. He decides to pardon her. Beckett's poem insists on Françoise's cruelty,

whereas Proust makes room for moral laxity by invoking "cowardly calculations"[10] that we all make in similar circumstances. Françoise condemns the
"pullet" to death in order to accomplish her menial tasks without remorse.
Such inverted ethical impulse is missing in Belacqua's aunt, who also calls
the lobster a "beast":

> "What are you going to do?" he cried.
> "Boil the beast" she said, "what else ?"[11]

Her equanimity never appears scandalous, because she has made a general
rule of it: "lobsters are always boiled alive. They must be."[12] There are
indeed good reasons for such an evil but common deed—otherwise, the
meat would not be tender, and so on. Here, Beckett closely follows Proust
when he meditates on affective ambivalence, on the proximity of ethical
contraries, and on the function of moral allegory.

Beckett's poem calls the sickly kitchen maid from Combray the "spit of
a Paduan Virtue." This refers to Swann, the aesthete, who had noticed her
resemblance with Giotto's Charity. Giotto's Charity is depicted as a banal-
looking woman in the Allegories of Virtues and Vices that one can see in
the chapel of Padua. The narrator, who keeps a reproduction of the "Cari-
tas" figure in his room (given to him by Swann), is surprised by the way
Giotto, who, by the way, was an exact contemporary of Dante, decided
to portray the Virtues: they are all earthy, stolid, mannish, almost vulgar
women—they do look like kitchen maids. At first, the narrator cannot
fathom why Swann, his role-model and a fastidious disciple of Ruskin,
praises a "Charity without charity" so enthusiastically. In a similar manner,
Swann loves Giotto's allegory of Justice; for the narrator, it was "a Justice
whose grayish and meanly regular face was the very same which, in Combray, characterized certain pretty, pious and unfeeling bourgeois ladies I
saw at Mass, some of whom had long since been enrolled in the reserve
militia of Injustice."[13] Proust's narrator will need more time to understand
that modern allegories are material fragments of a whole, and how symbolic meanings happen to be grafted on material bodies.

Proust's neat juxtaposition of figures of Justice and Injustice recurs in
Beckett's works. Ethics is predicated upon an awareness of this baffling
reversibility. This theme is deployed in *How It Is*, a dark novel narrating the
progression through mud of a narrator who finds Pim, another quester,
whom he tortures by carving words on his buttocks with a can opener. In
part three, we learn that the sadistic couplings described follow and obey
"our justice." In a revealing paragraph, a most violent language testifies to
a sort of metaphysical despair:

the fuck who suffers who makes to suffer who cries who to be left
in peace in the dark the mud gibbers ten seconds fifteen seconds of
sun clouds earth sea patches of blue clear nights and of a creature if
not still standing still capable of standing always the same imagination spent looking for a hole that he may be seen no more in the middle of this faery who drinks that drop of piss of being and who with
his last gasp pisses it to drink the moment it's someone each in his
turn as our justice wills and never any end it wills that too dead or
none[14]

Jonathan Boulter has interpreted this passage as exemplifying Jacques
Derrida's idea that Justice cannot be deconstructed.[15] Much as I admire
Derrida's "Force of Law" essay and the subtlety of Boulter's "posthuman"
interpretation, Derrida's definition of Justice as a transcendental concept
underpinning an experience of the impossible does not look that relevant
here.

Why is Beckett's Justice calculating, adding up numbers, and ensuring
that the same be always repeated identically? The paradox embodied by
this passage is that, once more, one cannot distinguish Justice from Injustice. Justice means here more the law of eternal return, in the parody of a
Nietzschean idea made cruder and more sinister by generating a vision of
life as a perpetual crawling through mud, muck, and shit, an aimless and
desperate progression from which even death cannot free us. Beckett
reveals how deeply he has been fascinated by Dante's excremental Hell.[16]
Hence there is no clear difference between this "piss of being" ("cette
goutte de pisse d'être"[17]) and the statement that "we have our being in
justice" ("on est dans la justice"[18]). The context is clear: "nothing to be
done in any case we have our being in justice I have never heard anything
to the contrary."[19] The echo of the opening sentence of *Waiting for Godot*
signals that "Justice" does not gesture toward an opening to the incalculable
but signals a sad necessity, a mortal and moral fate. The ethical experience
proposed by Beckett with a rare rigor—here, the voice uttering something "to the contrary," the ethical voice, is silent—takes place outside the
domain of Justice.

Throughout his work, Beckett's notion of Justice remains indebted to
Dante's concept of *contrapasso*, which formalizes a homology between the
sins committed on earth and the punishments meted out in Hell. The grid
of correspondences between crimes and punishments displays Dante's
invention in finding powerful images exemplifying his view of divine justice. Justice in *Inferno* is portrayed as a matter of precise, almost mechani-

cal, dispensation. In Canto 5, Minos, the "connoisseur of sin," moves his tail and the number of its coils indicates the level of damnation, which in turn determines the types of torture a given sinner will undergo. All sinners are assigned their proper torments in a machinery of suffering. This mechanization of pain shows that God's justice is impersonal and utterly without pity; it is meted out according to a codified, if opaque, system of allegorical equivalence. Marquis de Sade could hardly do any better. Sade had indeed scripted in advance the main narrative of *How It Is* when he wrote to Mademoiselle de Rousset: "Wretched creatures, thrown for an instant onto this little heap of mud, must it be then that one half of the herd should persecute the other half?"[20]

How It Is is told by a narrator who crawls through a mass of mud in the gloom. He discerns other sufferers and chooses one whom he attacks and calls Pim. After having tortured Pim for a while, he feels that they will have formed a "couple," and concludes that they may well have loved each other in spite of all. The time will come when roles are shifted and he is to be tortured by a new crawler. Why this mud? It comes first from Dante's *Inferno*. In case we had missed the reference, a passage distorts hilariously a famous line: "dream come of a sky an earth an under-earth where I am inconceivable aah no sound in the rectum a redhot spike that day we prayed no further."[21] The reference is to Paolo and Francesca falling in love: "that day we read no further" (*Inferno*, Canto 5:109) as they are reading a book together.

This deliberate distortion ("pray" replaces "read") echoes Beckett's remark in his hostile 1934 review of Giovanni Papini's book on Dante, *Dante Vivo*. Papini's main theme was that Dante paid dearly for his success as a writer by having failed in all his other endeavors. Papini argued that we should not reduce Dante to literature; we should see him as a man, and love him. Beckett rebukes him forcibly: "But who wants to love Dante? We want to READ Dante—for example, his imperishable reference (Paolo-Francesca episode) to the incompatibility of the two operations."[22] Beckett's *lex*, the law of logos and "reading," replaces here the Christian law of love. Such a disjuncture underpins the situation of Pim facing the sadistic narrator of *How It Is*: no doubt LOVE is capitalized, but it keeps its question mark, and above all is inscribed in letters of blood on the tormented victim's back.

Canto 7 of *Inferno* introduces the Sullen, the *Tristi*, those sad ones whose souls have been gnawed away by *acedia*. The Sullen have sunk into a slimy bog of wet mud, from which they compose a hymn explaining their punishment. Sadly, they cannot really sing it because of the mud that enters their throats: "This hymn they have to gurgle in their gullets,/because they cannot speak it in full words."[23] Then Dante renders in his evocative idiom the gurgling sounds issuing from throats attempting to sing under muddy water: "Quest' inno si gorgoglian ne la strozza."[24] The pervasive and invasive mud as a medium is a recurrent trope in *How It Is*. Mud as a substance is both nourishing (it provides liquid for the mouths of the questers) and suffocating, gagging if not entirely disgusting. This ambivalent slime represents what Beckett will at times call "bathos," the sublime despair oozing from the lowest of the low. One soon guesses that this slime is partly made up of anal refuse issuing from the narrator's mouth or anus. It is his "quaqua," the remainder of a sickening and damaged discourse hesitating between logorrhea and diarrhea.

In *How It Is*, the most developed fiction of Beckett's anal fascination, a scatological mud invades everything and becomes the substance of the world. Beckett develops Leopardi's line "e fango è il mondo."[25] Following this radical equation, all his characters are bogged down in Napoléon's fifth element, mud. Mud and slime are the substances of an excremental world that extends to verbal matter, which connects Lucky's "quaquaquaqua" with the word for derisive verbiage in German, "Quatsch quatsch quatsch."[26] If the world is mud, and if language is slime, one can barely distinguish them. *How It Is* presents this desperate crawling in the mud as the horizon of ontology and of ethics.

This trope literalizes Joyce's conceit that the writer of the Wake, Shem the Penman, is penning his text (the text we are reading) with an ink made from his own excrements, and that he scrawls the lines on his own body. A passage in Latin narrates the production of this special ink, combining feces and urine ("crap in his hand, sorry!" and "did a piss," in order to produce "faked O'Ryan's, the indelible ink").[27] Beyond the Joycean allusion, the situation of *How It Is* combines a number of elements disseminated in other Beckettian texts. We remember how Molloy communicates with his mother through knocks on the head according to a simple series of signals. These knocks evoke the cruel code elaborated for Pim: "first lesson theme song I dig my nails into his armpit right hand right pit he cries I withdraw them thump with fist on skull his face sinks in the mud his cries cease end of first lesson."[28] Another passage posits an explicit comparison between this situation and the usual Sadean punishment; Pim is imagined thinking: "not that I should cry that is evident since when I do I am punished instanter/sadism pure and simple no since I may not cry."[29]

We understand why "Text 3" had spliced Dante's allegories and Proust's allegories. Dante and Proust share a similar sadism, a point made first by

Georges Bataille who had insisted on Proust's sadism in his essays and
books, especially in *Literature and Evil*. Here, Dante and Proust teach
Beckett how to overcome an initial reflex of compassion by contemplating
"Justice," knowing fully that it is indistinguishable from Injustice. Here is
how the souls of the damned speak:

> We are proud in our pain
> our life was not blind.[30]

For the eternally damned, there is nothing to expect from death, which is
a source of despair but also of pride. This leaves aside the problem of compassion.

> Lo-Ruhama Lo-Ruhama
> pity is quick with death.[31]

Lo-Ruhama—the daughter Hosea had with Gomer, a prostitute—
symbolizes Israel in Hosea 1:6, because her name means "not pitied." This
lack of pity leads to the line that bothered Belacqua: "Qui vive la pietà
quando è ben morta" (*Inferno*, Canto 20, line 28), meaning "Here, in Hell,
pity is alive when it is fully dead." The line is spoken by Virgil who rebukes
Dante for his untoward display of pity; Dante recoils when he sees the fate
of the magicians, a group including Tiresias, whose punishment is to walk
with their heads twisted backward—it is, as Signorina Ottolenghi says, one
of "Dante's rare movements of compassion in Hell."[32] How can one translate this perfect oxymoron? In "Dante and the Lobster," Belacqua has
chewed on the magnificent pun, perhaps hesitating on the senses of "pity"
and "piety": "Why not piety and pity both, even down below?"[33]
   At any rate, Belacqua feels totally unable to translate Virgil's remark.
The Italian teacher's superb response ("Do you think, she murmured, it is
absolutely necessary to translate it?"[34]) is rigorously parallel to the question Belacqua poses facing Dante the character in his *Commedia*: why
translate, if *translatio* signifies "to displace," "to transfer," why keep on
moving further, pushing along human bodies, words, or even animals?
Belaqua has at some point to name the animal he has in a bag to the French
teacher. Since he does not know the term, he tells her that he has a fish,
which leads to a surprising comparison with Christ: "He did not know the
French for lobster. Fish would do very well. Fish had been good enough
for Jesus Christ, Son of God, savior."[35] Indeed, in the sentence from *The
Unnamable* I quoted at the end of the previous chapter—"it's human, a
lobster couldn't do it"—the French original was "langouste" and not
"homard."[36] Belacqua's exhausted indifference facing his own salvation and

that of creatures as diverse as a lobster (or even Christ) seems to betray a despair about the communicability of poetry, hence of all language. Both the Dantean Belacqua and Beckett's Belacqua appear as "bogged," "stuck," caught in a dead end of history, and therefore unable to move from a passive to an active will.

This active will was the object of Dante's "epic of judgment," his summation of political theology encased in an epic founded on an ethical framework. Its immense scope required the creation of a new language, as was the case with *Finnegans Wake*. However, Joyce's Viconian or Hegelian historicism prevented him from posing the question of ethics. Beckett shared Dante's and Joyce's antiabsolutism but not their linguistic optimism. If for Joyce, the verbal machine kept producing meaning in a process that would regenerate itself endlessly, for Beckett, the need of an ethical interruption came first. Such an interruption has to be "untimely." As the case of Belacqua has shown, one cannot bypass the ethical moment of questioning, which manifests itself by a sudden and brutal halt in progress.

In order to overcome the dead end of a Justice looking like Injustice, or of a process of purgation revolving blissfully and obliviously upon itself, Beckett needed an even more powerful lever than Belacqua's disabused exhaustion. After having probed the problems left unresolved by Cartesian dualism, he found a solution when he chanced on Arnold Geulincx's *Ethics*. For Geulincx, ethics is the result of a combination of absolute determinism (everything that happens, including my body's movements, happens because God wills it) and absolute freedom (I can always will a contrary gesture, hence be free marginally). *Molloy* condenses this paradox in one striking image: "I who had loved the image of old Geulincx, dead young, who left me free, on the black boat of Ulysses, to crawl towards the East, along the deck. That is a great measure of freedom, for him who has not the pioneering spirit."[37] Beckett told the German translator of *Molloy* that he alluded to the boat boarded by Ulysses for a last adventure, following Dante's startling evocation of a shipwreck in which the aged hero perishes in *Inferno* Canto 26.[38] Geulincx provides a more solid position for Belacqua's refusal of the epic quest than Descartes's reversibility between the domain of reason and that of dreams, for Geulincx asserts that even marginal and minimal freedom can perform a miracle.

In the mid-1930s, Geulincx's philosophy of nonknowing added a philosophical dimension to the lessons of psychoanalysis taught by Bion to Beckett. Occasionalist nonknowing led to a philosophical doctrine of humility, which was also an ethics of compassion. This is exemplified when we follow Belacqua who prepares a lunch with rotten Gorgonzola cheese spread on a burned toast. The cheese is so green that it is "alive," the toast has been reduced to the status of "burnt offering."[39] Belacqua's toast, closer to the Proustian *biscotte* than a thick hoagie, reveals everything about the past and the future because it imitates the map of the moon. Its singed allegorical surface displays all the marks of Cain's sin:

> For the tiller of the field the thing was simple, he has it from his
> mother. The spots were Cain with his truss of thorns, dispossessed,
> cursed from the earth, fugitive and vagabond. The moon was that
> countenance fallen and branded, seared with the first stigma of God's
> pity, that an outcast might not die quickly. It was a mix-up in the mind
> of the tiller, but that did not matter. It has been good enough for his
> mother, it was good enough for him.[40]

The "good-enough mother" of British psychoanalysis will offer some solace. More than Cain's countenance, the charred toast evokes the smiling face of the Virgin Mary, or perhaps Christ's bloody face, as if Belacqua was contemplating an edible shroud of Turin. Projective hallucinations may be invoked as an excuse, but the real quest is for a sublunary refuge. We trust that the mother's recipes will be passed on to the cursed son, and that they will include the fruit that Joyce had called "cainapple" in a wonderful conflation of Cain, Abel, Adam and Eve.[41] No need to make amends by a nihilistic withdrawal; the son's power of negation will establish new rules of behavior.

It may even happen that the son curses the mother. If the son invokes the mother as a "Porca Madonna," (an idiomatic expression in Italian that, as Signorina Ottolenghi would say, it is not necessary to translate), it may not be to convey that, as a substitute of the Virgin Mary, she is a pig, or a sow to be more precise. Although Beckett had slyly played on the confusion between an old "bitch" who has dropped her young and his own mother's distracting attentions in the poem "Serena II,"[42] he is not ready—as Dalí did in a notorious drawing that brought him a lot of trouble—to "spit on his mother,"[43] neither will he, like Bataille, write a scandalous novel, *My mother*, developing the sacrilegious potentialities offered by a mother-son incest. With this shocking profanity uttered by Descartes, we may not have encountered the most blasphemous statement of Beckett's poem "Whoroscope" yet. We will need to read the poem closely in order to understand how Cartesianism led to Occasionalism. Such a movement gave Beckett a chance to formulate the maxims of his own ethics, but he had first to play a little trick on one of his French intellectual heroes.

CHAPTER 5

"Porca Madonna!": Moving Descartes toward Geulincx and Proust

Beckett's poem "Whoroscope" presents a complex and conflicted portrait of Descartes, a philosopher as much "moved" as "moving" when negotiating with a newly decentered worldview:

> We're moving, he said, we're off—Porca Madonna!
> the way a ferryman would be, or a clockwork hare.
> That's not moving, that's *moving*.[1]

The philosophical itinerary followed with determination by Descartes was decided after he was struck by the experience of having three intense dreams, and then of finding a precise interpretation for them. In one of these, he saw the Latin: *Quod vitae sectabor iter?* (What road in life shall I follow?), a quote from a poem by Ausonius. As we have seen, it was followed by another Latin quote: *Est et Non* (Is and Is not). Descartes's genius consisted in linking the two propositions, both offered to him in a vivid series of oneiric visions.[2] Beckett's poem keeps this hallucinatory quality—it is crucial to understand that Beckett began his poetic career with a poem that he had dashed off in one day. The punning title of "Whoroscope" is still in

the Joycean mode. Beckett's notes partially help to reconstruct the logic of
an obscure and highly allusive poem.

Formally, "Whoroscope" is a dramatic monologue in the manner of
Browning; it presents the final thoughts of a dying Descartes, reliving his
past life while mixing up family matters and personal quarrels with theoretical issues of his doctrine. His untimely death might have been caused
less by the freezing cold of the Swedish mornings to which he was subjected because of Queen Christina's early hours than because he would
have been poisoned by courtiers jealous of his influence on the queen. The
monologue reels off recurrent obsessions and dark superstitions. Beckett's
point of departure is the philosopher's habit of eating omelets with specific
dietary requirements, a feature noted by John Pentland Mahaffy, the per-
ceptive philosophy professor at Trinity who had died in 1919. His short
book on Descartes was used by Beckett as a first guide, and he came across
this: "his taste must have been odd, since he recommends as a special delicacy an omelette made up of eggs hatched from eight to ten days; if longer
under the hen, he adds that the result is disgusting."[3] Of course Mahaffy
passes to other matters, the more serious elements of Cartesian doctrine.
Beckett stops there in order to reconsider the philosopher's theories of
time, gestation, and conception, as if Descartes's main theoretical statement was to be found in the treatise on man and the formation of the foetus, his *Tractatus de homine et de formatione foetus* dating from 1634 in which
Descartes puts forward his idea that the human body is a machine.

The Shuttle of a Ripening Egg

In a wonderfully erudite book, Edward Bizub has argued that "Whoroscope" is not a learned joke or a literary spoof but that it condenses a philosophical program; it is moreover an aesthetic and intellectual statement
containing all the seeds of the work to come.[4] If most commentators have
insisted on the links between Descartes and Beckett, Bizub goes further,
unpacking each element of the zany poem. Bizub points out Beckett's deep
ambivalence facing Descartes, and his reliance on a more capacious, both
ironical and generous, understanding of the French philosopher. In Bizub's
reading, "Whoroscope" provides the foundations for the literary work of a
whole life. Far from being a simple parody (the notes can remind one of the
famous endnotes Eliot added to *The Waste Land*, to Beckett's annoyance),
the witty and gnomic poem condenses a whole ethics and aesthetics. It
does so by portraying Descartes not as the "modernist" embodiment of a
newly unleashed Reason, but as a very irrational man.

The centrality of "Whoroscope" for an understanding of Beckett's works had been a thesis presented by Lawrence Harvey's groundbreaking *Samuel Beckett, Poet and Critic*, a book fact-checked and revised by Beckett himself. Harvey analyzed in great detail Beckett's "Cartesian beginnings," and also took the enigmatic poem as a touchstone for ulterior developments. Beckett had been working on Descartes at Trinity College two years before coming to Paris. He knew the work of Mahaffy, who pointed out his absurd superstitions and his reliance on dreams, but assumed that Descartes outgrew these apparently absurd or archaic fixations. Mahaffy also mentions the little girl with cross-eyes, the paradigm for Descartes's subsequent love objects, but above all he is eager to press forward with serious philosophical discussions.

When Beckett came the École Normale Supérieure, he was tutored in philosophy by his friend and would-be lover Jean Beaufret, a significant philosopher later in analysis with Lacan, as well as a translator and commentator of Heidegger. Beaufret gave Beckett an anthology of texts by Descartes, the *Choix de Textes*,[5] which was still in Beckett's library at his death, proving that it kept its relevance. Bizub adds to this a new reference that is compelling. He suggests that the rapid composition of "Whoroscope"—dashed off in one day, June 15, 1930—had been inspired by the recent publication of a book on Descartes, *Descartes, le philosophe au masque*, by Maxime Leroy. The book had been published in 1929, as Beckett was tackling Descartes again in Paris. Even though Beckett does not mention this book, it was inevitable that his *Normalien* friends like Beaufret (called Chas in *Dream of Middling to Fair Women* and *More Prick Than Kicks*), who was deeply immersed in Descartes then, would have discussed it. It was the time of Beckett's many trips to Latin Quarter bookstores, when he was not going the rounds of the bars in nearby rue Mouffetard, well evoked in a poem from 1932, "Sanies II":

> there was a happy land
> the American bar
> in rue Mouffetard
> there were red eggs there
> I have a dirty I say henorrhoids
> coming from the bath[6]

Beckett's puns may not be in the best taste, but they condense a juvenile humor revolving on post-Joycean and post-Freudian portmanteau words all evincing an obscene or blasphemous slant. Meanwhile, Leroy's two volumes elicited considerable attention in Paris for one reason: his book included a letter by Freud on Descartes. Leroy had written to Freud, sending him the account of the three dreams of Descartes. Obligingly, Freud replied with a two-page letter that was then translated and quoted in full by Leroy.[7] In his reply, Freud remained hesitant as to the meaning of the famous dreams, even if Descartes had managed to provide his own detailed interpretation of all of their elements. Freud pointed out, not unexpectedly, that the melon mentioned at some point was a sexual symbol. Freud concluded that the intellectual crisis represented by the outcome of the dream must have been triggered by the philosopher's unconscious conflicts.

Leroy took Freud's limited insights as a confirmation of his view that Descartes was a deeply divided person, a passionate and enthusiastic rebel who felt the need to hide under a conventional mask to avoid persecution. On his view, Descartes was a political reformer in advance of his times, who tried all the same to play it safe by hiding and disguising himself. Indeed, we know that Descartes remained all his life a perpetual exile; he made intricate plans to hide from public view wherever he happened to live, whether he was in Germany, Paris, or in the Netherlands. Moreover, he could only think well when lying in bed and being allowed to get up very late, which he did most of his life—all idiosyncrasies shared by Beckett.

Leroy, a prolific writer who began his career as a philosopher of law and political science, betrayed in his 1929 book his leanings to the left; he depicted Descartes as a proto-socialist, the scion of impoverished nobility at heart close to the people, a thwarted mystic with sympathies for the Rosicrucians, a rebellious intellectual *avant la lettre* who fled France because he was afraid of religious persecution, only to be disappointed when he realized that Amsterdam was barely more tolerant. His use of disguises, his cunning correspondence, his equivocations had all the same aim: to avoid censorship and pave the way for a slow dissemination of his ideas until the truth would impose itself. Descartes was a "masked thinker" whose motto was "*larvatus prodeo*" (I proceed masked). He strictly adhered to it, and rarely said or wrote exactly what he actually thought. Here is why, Leroy surmises, one should read Descartes symptomatically, in the gaps and contradictions of his texts, by linking his body, his private life, his erotic confessions, and even his dreams with his scientific work. If Leroy sees Descartes as a genius, a thinker who planned and achieved the destruction of the ancient world of Aristotelian delusions and confusions, he points out that the philosopher was also deeply split. He may have remained a Rosicrucian all his life, which is why he would be superstitious about his horoscope.

Leroy's wish to start his portrait from Descartes's contradictions gave Beckett the idea of structuring "Whoroscope" by marshaling contrarian "biographemes" and conceptual riddles whose cumulative force leads to a subversion of the usual equation between Descartes and classical rationalism. In that sense, like Leroy, Beckett agrees with the recent picture of Descartes provided by Kyoo Lee: Descartes would be on the side of the "blind, mad, dreamy and bad" much more than on that of an emerging positivism or scientism founded on metaphysical dualism.[8]

As we saw, the point of departure for "Whoroscope" was Descartes's description of an ideal omelet. His taste, in the words of a recent biographer, was weird indeed: "And Descartes put Clerselier on royally when he told him that there is nothing better than an omelet of eggs that have been brooded eight or ten days. Clerselier solemnly repeats Descartes's admonition that the result is detestable if the eggs have been brooded either less or more than eight or ten days. Do you know what is inside eggs that have been brooded eight or ten days? Yech."[9] This bizarre recipe provides Beckett's poem with a recurrent gag:

> What's that?
> A little green fry or a mushroomy one?
> Two lashed ova with prostichiutto?
> How long did she womb it, the feathery one?
> Three days and four nights?
> Give it to Gillot.[10]

The tone and style are typically Joycean, with a pun on prostitute and the Italian for ham, *prosciutto*. At the end of the poem, we understand that the omelet is finally ready because the hour of death has come to the sick philosopher in Sweden:

> Art thou then ripe at last,
> my wan, my svelte, my double-breasted turd?
> My! But she do smell prime!
> She has aborted to a tee!
> I shall eat her with a fish-fork,
> white and yoke and down.[11]

The conceit that an egg is only an aborted chick is a recurrent trope in Beckett's earlier poems, from "Enueg 1" to "Sanies 2,"[12] but in "Whoroscope," the main issue is Descartes's revisionist, and perhaps skeptical, views on the doctrine of transubstantiation (the same Claude Clerselier to whom he wrote about eggs also received a series of letters from Descartes about his theory of transubstantiation; moreover Clerselier edited and published Descartes's treatise on man and the genesis of foetuses already mentioned).[13] As Beckett comments in his tantalizing notes: "The shuttle of a ripening egg combs the warp of his days."[14] Descartes aims at displacing Aristotle (presented as the "master of those who know" by Dante) by letting science examine squarely the base foundation of bodily functions:

> They don't know what the master of them that do did,
> that the nose is touched by the kiss of all foul and sweet air,
> and the drums, and the throne of the faecal inlet,
> and the eyes by its zigzags.
> So we drink Him and eat Him
> and the watery Beaune and the stale cube of Hovis
> because He can jig
> as near or as far from His Jigging Self
> and as sad or lively as the chalice or the tray asks.
> How's that, Antonio?[15]

The materialism hinted at here is a key issue in Leroy's book. Leroy notes that when Descartes discussed the dogma of "real presence," that is the presence of a divine being in the consecrated host, he "compared the highest miracle of Christian faith with the phenomenon of human digestion."[16] Hence, we should not trust Descartes when he asserts tongue in cheek that he believed in transubstantiation:

> No I believe every word of it I assure you.
> Fallor, ergo sum!
> The coy old frôleur!
> He tolle'd and legg'd
> and he buttoned on his redemptorist waistcoat.
> No matter, let it pass.
> I'm a bold boy I know
> So I'm not my son
> (even if I were a concierge)
> nor Joachim my father's
> but the chip of a perfect block that's neither old nor new,
> the lonely petal of a great high bright rose.[17]

Beckett added the baffling endnote: "He proves God by exhaustion," which appears misleading if it refers to those lines only.[18] In fact, the lines echo more directly Joyce's theory of mystical paternity linking Stephen Dedalus to God. There is a *lex eterna* residing in God's will, and it passes directly from creator to creature. It is divorced from the accidents of human copulation, conception, and generation.[19] Here, in the poem, Descartes is thinking about his biological father, Joachim, to hint that Joachim had little to do with him as a son. His true father is the divine knot of light appearing at the end of Dante's *Divine Comedy* as an unfolding mystic rose. But like the tree of *Waiting for Godot* with its single leaf in the first act, the divine rose bears only *one* last and lonely petal.

The issue of human as opposed to divine generation in the vignettes gathered by Beckett points to the failure of an absolute foundation for philosophy in human consciousness, even though Descartes's work ended up, as posterity rehearses it, launching modern sciences like optics, physics, and mathematics against a worldview dominated by theology. If most of the anecdotes quoted in "Whoroscope" were already provided by Mahaffy's book on Descartes known to Beckett, it was Leroy who incited Beckett to read Descartes against the grain. Descartes is captured via his hidden side, caught in an unconscious network of fears and fascinations. His rationalism appears as the reverse of an irrational devotion to omens and dreams—crucial dreams that motivated him to become a philosopher. Descartes famously refused to divulge the hour of his birth; he was afraid that someone would guess him too well by having his horoscope drawn.

Murphy testifies to this oneiric beginning when the hero laughs so much at his own bad joke that he sinks down "on the dream of Descartes linoleum."[20] It is as if the poem's very title had planned the whole program of *Murphy*, even though it was only begun several years later. "Whoroscope" sketches not only the beginning of the plot, when Celia the golden-hearted prostitute brings Murphy his horoscope to force him to find a proper job, but also organizes the rest of the novel, when we realize that the Cartesian hero devoid of a *conarium* or pineal gland, hence split between his body and his mind, betrays an unhealthy fascination for institutionalized psychotics. Madness, displayed first in its seductive then horrifying aspects, appears as the exact reverse of arrogant rationalism.

"Whoroscope" is a foundational poem less because it shows a divided subject who cannot reconcile an affective and desiring body with pure thought than because it presents a driven and obsessive thinker progressing through mistakes and fantasies, superstitions, dreams, and delusions. Here is why "Whoroscope" replaces the Cartesian motto of *Cogito ergo sum* with its true source, Augustine's celebrated "*Si enim fallor, sum*," from Book XI, 26 of *De Civitate Dei* (*City of God*): "If indeed I am deceived, I am." Thus Beckett rewrites Descartes's dream of an absolute foundation via subjective certainty as "I am deceived, therefore I am." *Fallor* is the passive form of *fallo*, "I am mistaken, I deceive, I cheat," from which the past participle *falsus* derives. Such a universal deception allegorized by Descartes's *malin génie* can also function as a *proton pseudos*, a first mistake capable of bringing about the collapse or the abortion of the entire system. The theme of abortion, so crucial for Beckett's birth trauma, is developed masterfully in the image of hatched eggs in which one recognizes aborted chickens.

The program of "Whoroscope" is to unveil the un-thought of Descartes's thought. Its dramatic staging of feverish hallucinations at the time of an untimely demise in Sweden evokes the death of Bergotte, or the fears exposed by the narrator at the end of Proust's *Recherche:* he has done little of the huge work to come, he fears that death will prevent him from completing his masterpiece. Beckett translates Proust's famous culinary metaphors (the whole book is compared with Françoise's masterful *Boeuf en daube* in *Time Regained*) into this suspicious omelet in which we see boned and feathered chicks caught in the egg paste as in the traditional *balut*, the delicacy well-known to Philippinos, Laotians, Cambodians, and Vietnamese gourmets. These duck eggs (and for Descartes, one can include brooded hen eggs) must have been fecundated and hatched long enough for the little baby birds to appear with some down, their bones brittle enough to be crushed by human teeth. The main result is that the dish is aphrodisiac, as the legend goes, which sends us back to the "whore" evoked by the poem's title. Alas, Thanatos lurks behind Eros, for the whore hiding in the horoscope is nothing but a disguise for Death, and Death catches the philosopher unawares—the thinker of the *ego cogito* cannot foresee the madness of an unthinkable death looming in his eggy horoscope.

Jacques Derrida and Michel Foucault were once opposed in a controversy about the function of madness in Descartes's hyperbolic doubt in the first two *Meditations*.[21] Unsurprisingly, Beckett anticipates Derrida, for his poem presents a Descartes haunted by madness and the irrational. The persecutory *malin génie* provides a powerful metaphor for psychosis, it embodies an always lurking threat of unreason in Descartes's *Meditations*, as Derrida argued. Foucault stated in his *History of Madness* that the first and second *Meditations* allegorize the sanitation performed by Reason; Reason has to conjure up and then exclude madness before embarking on more serious matters (most commentators of Descartes, like Mahaffy, do this). Derrida saw on the contrary the return of an irrational ghost in the heart of Reason. If Derrida wins the contest, we understand why the influence of Descartes on Beckett leads to the later motto of the "torture of the cogito" not before generating its opposite, however, the statement of the impotence of reason. The boiled or fried body of a volatile, a nonhuman agent resisting the operation of transubstantiation, will parody the Paraclete, much as Flaubert made fun of the religious hallucinations of the dying servant Felicité at the end of his tale *A simple heart*, evoked in the line "a pale abusive parakeet in a mainstreet window."[22]

It was thanks to Joyce that Beckett had had to explore the collected works of Giambattista Vico, with whom he became conversant when preparing his essay on *Work in Progress*. Beckett could not fail to notice that Vico systematically attacked Descartes, whose antihumanist scientism he refuted vehemently in all his theoretical works. The domain that Vico made available for historical investigation was that of myth, epic simile, metaphor, finding in the names of gods and heroes, in poetry and ritual the remainders of struggles between antagonistic nations or rival social groups memorialized by their cultures. If "Whoroscope" contains the lineaments of a Viconian inheritance, it leaves room for the insertion of another post-Cartesian thinker, Arnold Geulincx. Lines 8–10 of the poem provide an allegory about freedom, as they point to the minimal freedom granted to whoever walks on the deck of a ship against its general direction—as Geulincx argued.

> We're moving he said we're off—Porca Madonna!
> The way a ferryman would be, or a clockwork hare.
> That's not moving, that's *moving*.[23]

Even though Beckett had probably not read Geulincx yet when he wrote those lines, he was on a track that would lead him to the Flemish post-Cartesian ethicist of humility. These lines quote the thirteenth section of Descartes's *Principles of Philosophy* to present what Beckett's note calls a "sophism" used to refute Galileo's theory of the movement of heavenly bodies. A man who stands in a boat cannot perceive the motion of the ship, whereas the movement is visible for those who are on the shore. This non-perception slips into the mathematics of bodies a whole anthropology of emotions, later condensed in Descartes's treatise on the passions of the soul. The insult to the Virgin leads to a meditation on automata, which makes us shift from the physics of movement to an anatomy of emotions: if we do not move, we are moved.

When physics and passions are interconnected, unmoored movement gives birth to the ethics of paradoxical freedom established by Geulincx. In between, the Italian profanity (*Porca Madonna!*) betrays Descartes's unconscious anger at the mother who died so young. He exhibits his wish to be directly begotten by God without any feminine intervention, and to that end engages in a complex negotiation with sexuality, paternity, and filiation. But while asserting that the virgin is a pig or a sow, he slips into the position of the deluded victim, the blind "boy" who, at the end, will fall prey to "the whore of the snows," the murderous Queen "Christina the Ripper."[24]

Such a movement of thought underpinned by irrationality more than rationality ushers in a new ethics; this explains why for Beckett, Descartes had to be relayed by Geulincx. The Flemish philosopher fully deployed an ethics of humility and impotence, whose emergence had been prepared by the inversion of Cartesian rationalism into an utter nonknowing. If "I err, therefore I am," such an erring then generates an ethics of nonvalue. As Descartes exclaimed, hoping that the Queen's doctor would stop drawing his blood in a superfluous blood-letting, "Spare the blood of a Frank," he was requesting a reprieve, his "second/starless inscrutable hour."[25] This hour of truth would not be granted to him but to his wayward disciple, the Flemish occasionalist Arnold Geulincx, who also happened to suffer for his beliefs: twice Geulincx lost his university tenure because he insisted upon teaching Cartesian philosophy and not orthodox scholasticism.

Ubi nihil vales, ibi nihil velis

In order to grasp the links between Beckett's nonconformist vision of Descartes and his endorsement of Geulincx's theses, it helps to retrace the progression of Beckett's reading. Both *Murphy* and *Molloy* contain the blueprint for the negative cogito discovered in the works of Geulincx, whose main concept was *nescio* (I do not know). Beckett translates Geulincx's "Ubi nihil vales, ibi nihil velis" as "Where you are worth nothing, you will want nothing," a sentence that can also be translated as: "Where you have no power, you will have no desire." This is what Anthony Uhlmann and Martin Wilson assume, but not David Tucker.[26] The anaphoric force of the double syntagm *ubi nihil/ibi nihil*, reinforced by the repetition of *v/l* linking *vales* and *velis*, condenses an untranslatable shape of thought, a thinking form so prized by Beckett.

The passage that had attracted Beckett's attention is in Geulincx's annotations to his *Ethics*, where he reiterates an argument about the observation of the self that introduces the doctrine of humility: "The axiom, *Wherein I have no power, therein I do not will*, embraces both parts of Humility: *I have no power* denotes Inspection of Oneself, *I do not will* denotes Disregard of Oneself."[27] Geulincx explains that we do not know how our muscles or nerves move our limbs. If we see the beauties of the world, all this beauty reinforces our sense that we have created nothing, not even our bodily movements. Unable to imagine how our nerves connect with our brains, how our muscles lift any limb, we don't know anything. The consequence is that whenever I move or speak, I am not making that motion—it is God who acts since only God "makes" in fact. The proof is that I move, walk, or dance better when I am distracted and do not think. Geulincx concludes that I am a "mere spectator" of a machine engineered and driven by God. The supreme Actor must be a true Creator, for only God *makes* things happen.

In an essay on Geulincx and Beckett, Thomas Dommange has delineated the conditions of a "mechanics of the ineffable" underpinning occasionalist philosophy.[28] He connects two terms that recur in Beckett's works, "puppets" and "grace." Dommange shows that the philosophy of Geulincx—founded as it is on the principle that since I know nothing of what happens, all happens because God wills it—proposes less a philosophy of impotence than a philosophy of the permanent miracle. This doctrine turns all subjects into God's puppets. By splicing Kleist's meditation on the uncanny grace of puppets in the *"Marionnettentheater"* of the world with the workings of divine grace, once the principle of causality has been abolished, we are offered the chance of the comical and touching grace of nonhuman automata animated from the outside.[29] Grace, miracle, and comedy blend together, a subtly haunting combination often achieved by Beckett's plays and texts which I will explore in chapter 9 when discussing his humor.

The counterintuitive philosophy of occasionalism launched by the post-Cartesian Malebranche, then relayed by Geulincx, led by degrees to the immaterialism of George Berkeley, another philosophical acquaintance of Murphy. In each case, human discordance concerning the apprehension of a series of percepts is repaired by the intervention of a divine will. God brings back volition and order to the serial chaos of the world. Friedrich Nietzsche mentions Geulincx in *On the Genealogy of Morality*; for Nietzsche, Geulincx presents an extreme case of self-contempt, and exemplifies the "ascetic will" displayed by priests. However, Nietzsche concedes that something can be gained in such abasement and dispossession: "With the growth of the community, a new interest is kindled for individuals as well, which often enough will lift him up of the most personal elements in his discontent, his aversion to himself (Geulincx's *despectio sui*)."[30] Ascetic priests, according to Nietzsche, generate an "excess of feeling" (*Gefühls-Ausschweifung*). Excess leads to enthusiasm and rapture, and finally plunges the soul into an abyss until the subject hankers for more and asks to be closer to God.[31]

Nietzsche, who insists so much on health, understood perfectly that when Geulincx promoted humility as the main virtue, he aimed at displacing the human in him and at regaining his own health through God. Geulincx states this in a paragraph about the "Inspection of Oneself" that references Plato:

Humility has two parts: Inspection of Oneself, and Disregard of One-self. As to the former, it is nothing other than the celebrated saying of the Ancients, KNOW THYSELF, once inscribed over the portico of the Temple of Apollo. *One can see this inscription as a greeting as it were from God to men, instead of a "Be well" to bid us be well. Be well! As if it were not fitting to say "Be well," and greet each other in this way, but that we should rather bid each other to live temperately.* Such is that divine saying of Plato in his Charmides, whose words dazzle me: "As if it were not fitting to say 'Be well', and greet each other in this way, but that we should rather bid each other to live temperately."[32]

Geulincx's *Ethics* was originally published as *Gnôthi Seautòn, sive Geulincx Ethica* in 1675 (Know Thyself, or Geulincx's Ethics). Here, paradoxically, the concept of knowing oneself generates an ethics of ignorance coupled with a decision to be well and live well. Indeed, Geulincx's axiom, *Ubi nihil vales, ibi nihil velis,* relies on the ambiguity of the verb *valeo.* In Spain, "Vale!" is used as an interjection meaning "OK!" or "Fine!" *Valeo,* the Latin verb at the root of the word *value,* means both "I am strong, powerful, influential, and healthy," and "I prevail." The imperative "Vale!" meant "Farewell!" at the end of a letter in Rome, a usage echoed by George Moore's witty autobiographical account of the Irish Renaissance, *Hail and Farewell,* when he added a third book entitled *Vale.* Geulincx's "beautiful Belgo-Latin" highlights this ambiguity,[33] while providing a remarkable dialectical weapon: by knowing the whole extent of my ignorance and facing it squarely, I become stronger. The paradox of value lies in the *coincidentia oppositorum* neatly summed up by Beckett's imperative of "Fail better!" Such paradoxes are not dissipated, but rather hyperbolically magnified by literature. Literary value derives thus from the "strength" displayed by an author who overcomes limitations, as Nietzsche argued. It also says farewell, a joyful good-bye, to the conventions of morality.

Nietzsche and Geulincx both reconcile the pursuit of health with a belief in the domination of the Unconscious. Beckett founded his subsequent fiction on a philosophy of a negative consciousness that ushers in a subject who does not know anything while knowing that he does not know. The philosophy of radical occasionalism required as its logical complement the philosophy of the unconscious that emerged in the nineteenth century with Hegel and Schelling, then relayed by Schopenhauer before reaching its pinnacle with Nietzsche, von Hartmann, and Freud. In the middle of the seventeenth century, Geulincx announced Nietzsche and Freud. Schopenhauer was his direct descendant when he reduced the world to a dualism of will and representation, thereby making will, by a calculated misnomer that would reverberate for more than a century, the carrier of the unconscious spirit of the world.

Having reached this foundational point, we can distinguish three moments in Beckett's appropriation of Geulincx's motto of "Where you are worth nothing, you will want nothing." In spite of its negative syntax, the sentence *Ubi nihil vales, ibi nihil velis* entails a positive calculation concerning the objects of the will. The maxim slyly inverts the Golden Rule ("Don't treat people in a way you wouldn't want to be treated"), or twists it by a calculated use of negation. It states something like: Do not invest with desire, volition, and value those people, places, and institutions that treat you as if you had no value. Or, to put it in a more condensed form: Give no value (desire, health) to what gives no value (desire, health) to you.

Geulincx revisited by Beckett, after his meditations on Descartes's doomed horoscope and Proust's recapture of lost time, asserts in clear terms that one should not waste one's time by desiring improper objects. A critique of misdirected energy presupposes that one should know where true values lie. For instance, in Murphy's case, the plot of the novel demonstrates that his mistake was to try and make money by finding a job. From the start, Murphy knew that he stood outside the quid pro quo of economics and social exchanges. When he found a job in a mental hospital, this economic triumph brought about his downfall. He followed not his own desire but that of the woman he loved. Had he applied his Occam's razor (his "surgical quality"[34]) to the choice of values, Murphy would have remained a "seedy solipsist." He let himself be raped by love. His contrarian and irresponsible absurdity was more rational than the efforts to fit the norms of common sense. Having caved in to the promptings of a prostitute's love—the beautiful Celia who was, in the end, responsible for his demise—he could not avoid turning into the subject that a capitalist economy requires, a "responsible" person endowed with erotic and productive values streamlined by the social machine.

Marcel Duchamp, a proficient chess player who preferred to meditate on future moves (playing chess with Beckett during World War II, he would beat him each time), elaborated a similarly minimalist ethical position facing the market of art. Duchamp, who made a precarious living by selling and buying art in the 1930s, insisted that any given artist worthy of the name should remain immune to the capitalist seductions of excessive surplus-value. This calls up the interruption of Belacqua facing Dante's ascension, this stark and sudden reassessment of the value of any heroic quest. Dante could convince himself of the absolute value represented by the contemplation of the mystical rose of paradise. Belacqua prefers his passive enjoyment, with or without a sandwich, with or without a burned toast, stuck as he is in "Nothing doing."

Here is a question I find myself asking my students now and then. Are they really sure that working as a banker or a trader on Wall Street will correspond to their highest values? If this is not where their most precious wishes lie, should they then really want to excel there? The *Ubi nihil vales, ibi nihil velis* motto can serve as a healthy reminder that if workplaces organized by big companies are not necessarily modern hells, they are not "intermediary sites" either. No purgatorial gain is to be expected from a daily immersion in their cubicles. Workplaces embody values for which one pays for a long time. I am not, of course, talking about paying off students' loans. Brecht's cynical realism in *The Threepenny Opera* made him state once and for all "Erst kommt das Fressen, und dann die Moral" whose rough paraphrase might be: "First get the food, and then try to be good." However, in a world of hoagie-eaters, Beckett's ethical caveat should give us more food for thought. Beckett reminds us that "positive" values depend upon what one first "posits" as value. Inevitably, if one questions whether power and value overlap, one will need to know *where* exactly one wields power and where one's wishes can come true.

A second meaning takes the negative as an end point and makes an absolute of the reiterated "nothing" of *Ubi nihil vales, ibi nihil velis*. This is the discovery of Murphy when he falls into dereliction and existential despair at the end of the novel, when he finally understands the true nature of psychosis with Mr. Endon; then Murphy finds himself unable to connect images; the linking function has vanished: "He could not get a picture in his mind of any creature he had met, animal or human. Scraps of bodies, of landscapes, hands, eyes, lines and colours evoking nothing, rose and climbed out of sight before him, as though reeled upward off a spool level with his throat."[35] This regurgitation leads him to seek peace by rocking himself to sleep until he dies in a gas explosion. Is this the triumph of a pure Nothing? Not entirely, at any rate because the narrative goes on after Murphy's death. The nothing become less an object than a whole libidinal discharge, which corresponds to the famous *nihilism* that often has been reproached to Beckett, a term well explored by Shane Weller.[36] However, Adorno understood that Beckett's negations were in fact positive affirmations, as we will see from the discussion in chapter ten. This reversal fits with the second lesson of psychoanalysis that Beckett learned from Bion. Psychoanalysis teaches that desire requires an empty space to acquire objects. Lacan, Bion, and Winnicott have all stressed the importance of a void in which objects appear so as to recharge subjective desire. The nothing is one of Lacan's four fundamental objects.[37]

A third meaning of *Ubi nihil vales, ibi nihil velis* leads to a decentering of the subject by staging a confrontation with the outside. Having absorbed pure nothingness as a total deflagration destroying the mind and the world, the subject discovers his or her constitutive dehiscence, and thus learns to hear language as it speaks from elsewhere. This is a creative passivity thanks to which one lets culture echo in resounding words through us. In that moment, one appreciates the law differently: the imperative to hear language comes close to a conflation of Kant's imperative to do one's duty no matter what, and of Sade's radical negation of good will in the name of a perverted divine enjoyment. This moment can also be thought via Emmanuel Levinas's insistence that the other subject is less an interlocutor in a dialogue than a radical other—the other of ethics, the other of whom the subject becomes a willing hostage.

In all these stages, Geulincx's universal declaration of impotence provides the foundation for an ethics of courage. The maxim addresses a second person within, a *you* ushering in an inner dialogism within the sphere of the subject's mind. Hence, the voice of the nothing as a thing continues dividing the subject from himself or herself. Yet, by stressing impotence, Beckett's texts call up even more forcibly another type of potency—Beckett's recurrent depiction of sexual scenes that are hilarious and grotesque point out that sexual health will be reached *a contrario*, by its opposite end, as it were. We have to find true values by discovering what remains after one has destroyed even the ruins, as Alfred Jarry once quipped; that is what is really *worth* in life and language, after we have reduced our objects to bare essentials. Here is the root of what has been misconstrued as minimalism, as if it was only a matter of style. The main issue in Beckett's late modernism is ethics, but it takes form into account because beauty cannot be divorced from value.

The sequence of three articulations of negative value corresponds to what Beckett had learned from Proust. The proximity of Beckett's reading of Proust with that of Levinas has been noticed.[38] Levinas was writing extensively on Proust's *The Captive* when he was a prisoner in Germany during World War II. He condensed his views in 1947 with "The Other in Proust."[39] Unlike Sartre, Levinas refused to reduce Proust to psychology. *À la recherche* is a philosophical novel whose narrative is cut by digressions offering theories about art, jealousy, homosexuality, music, travels, memory, perception, and so on. Such proliferating theories bypass ethics— one should not read Proust ethically. Proust's investigations explore the spiraling abyss of human perversion, but once Sodom and Gomorrha have been crossed, no ethical system remains intact. For Levinas, the lesson of Proust is that no moral value survives unscathed once common sense has been pierced through:

> It is curious to note the extent to which Proust's amorality fills his world with the wildest freedom, and confers on definite objects and beings a scintillating sense of possibility undulled by definition. One would have thought that moral laws rid the world of such glittering extravaganzas more rigorously than natural laws and that magic begins, like a witches' Sabbath, where ethics leave off. The change and development in characters, some of them highly unlikely, feel completely natural in a world that has reverted to Sodom and Gomorrah, and relations are established between terms that seemed not to permit them. Everything is giddily possible.[40]

Levinas argues that Proust's amoralism goes beyond the antimorality of Sade and Nietzsche. The key lies in the lesson brought home to the narrator by Albertine, in the ethical revelation of existence as otherness.

Beckett, too, presented an amoral Proust when he completed the first English monograph on Proust in 1931. In this remarkable book, Beckett highlights the absence of any moral sense in Proust's world: "Here, as always, Proust is completely detached from all moral considerations. There is no right and wrong in Proust nor in his world."[41] Like Levinas, Beckett offsets this lack of moral concerns with the emergence of a radical otherness embodied by Albertine in the last part of the novel; another sexuality (not reducible to jealousy or lesbianism) allegorizes the radical otherness of subjects. He notes that in Proust's novel, humans are compared with plants and not animals because they have absolutely no shame: like flowers, they exhibit their genitals openly. They stand outside any moral condemnation of sin: "There is no question of right and wrong. Homosexuality is never called a vice."[42]

Such a revelation is provided most clearly by the "novel of Albertine" at the end, a section of the novel to which Beckett devotes a long running commentary in his *Proust*. He notes that there are so many versions of Albertine that her "*pictorial* multiplicity" evolves into a "*plastic* and moral multiplicity."[43] Albertine's dizzying contradictions are an effect of structure. They are not "an effect of the observer's angle of approach" but "a multiplicity in depth, a turmoil of objective and immanent contradictions over which the subject has no control."[44] What the narrator loves in the fickle and mendacious Albertine is not a disappointing body or a limited intellect that bores him, but the potential for infinite otherness that it holds. For Levinas, similarly, Proust's fiction acquires exemplary philosophical value in that its opening to otherness achieves a radical break with classical ontology. Proust "breaks definitively with Parmenides," when he opens the field of an ethics of otherness beyond morality.[45]

This shows that the lesson of Proust's *À la recherche* can also be condensed by Geulincx's motto: *Ubi nihil vales, ibi nihil velis.* What the narrator discovers slowly and painfully throughout the novel is that he was wasting his time in social snobbism, in loving partners who did not reciprocate his affections, and even in dallying with belletristic art criticism as Swann had done. He had to convert radically to the only "worthwhile" task, the completion of the literary work to come. Such a conversion entails a general rethinking of the links between aesthetics and ethics. It leads ultimately to a paradoxical ethics of nonrelation that finds its most adequate or "worthwhile" expression in painting, music, and literature, and all that is captured by the domain of aesthetics.

CHAPTER 6

From an Aesthetics of Nonrelation to an Ethics of Negation

Following Joyce's example, Beckett decided to become an "artist," and not an academic as his parents and professors had hoped. Art in general would allow him to be free, to express a singular vision of life. However, it took Beckett a long time to elaborate an original aesthetic program. His thought was slowly evolving, with references shifting from Vico and Descartes to Dante and Geulincx, soon focusing on the visual arts as a possible alternative to literature. One sees this clearly in a letter from October 1933, more than a year after Beckett had resigned from his teaching post at Trinity College, in which he announces that he has applied for a post of assistant at the National Gallery in London. If he mentions self-deprecatingly his poor "conoysership that can just separate Ucello from a handsaw,"[1] it is certain that, in the next decade, he did all he could to improve his knowledge of Italian Renaissance art, of Dutch painters, and of German expressionism, to name just a few domains in which his firsthand knowledge is undeniable. Already by the time Beckett took his tour of Nazi Germany from September 1936 to April 1937, he had become an expert in art if not yet an art critic per se; one of the explicit aims of his tour was to document the masterpieces of modernist art that were going to be destroyed as "degenerate art" under the Nazi rule.[2]

The letter written to Axel Kaun in German from Dublin after his return insists that literature is trailing behind music and painting: "Or is literature alone to be left behind on that old, foul road long ago abandoned by music and painting? Is there something paralysingly sacred contained within the unnature of the word that does not belong to the elements of the other arts?"[3] Much has been made of that letter already quoted in chapter 2 because this is the main document in which we see Beckett announce his decision to break with the Joycean "apotheosis of the word." It seems that the visual expertise acquired by visiting museums in Dublin, Paris, London, and then all over Germany, was a strong component of his refusal both to write in "formal English" (Joyce had been there before) and to cultivate the word as if it could contain the world. His deeply felt despair over the limits of literary language was evidently buttressed on his expert familiarity with the most varied schools of painters. This would suggest that the famous illumination that Beckett had in December 1945—when he discovered that his way would be via poverty, impotence, and darkness[4]—had been slowly prepared all those years of wandering by silently contemplating pictures.

The final formulation of Beckett's aesthetic theories is provided by the series of dialogues that he had with Georges Duthuit, when both were collaborating and launching the second *Transition* magazine. At the time, Beckett was finishing *Malone Dies*, beginning *Waiting for Godot*, and planning *The Unnamable*, and these discussions of paintings generate countless echoes in the trilogy and the first plays. I will tackle one of the three dialogues with the wish to understand how a notion of aesthetic failure can lead to expressive freedom, a freedom displayed as much in his novel trilogy as in the play *Waiting for Godot*. Thus in the second dialogue, Beckett can assert that the French painter André Masson "failed" above all because he did not have the courage to "fail" as perfectly as Bram van Velde, who was, according to Beckett, the world champion of failure. In these discussions, it is clear that artistic failure does not preclude expression; on the contrary, it demands it.

Masson's work provided a good launching pad for Beckett's terse formulations about art and negativity in the second dialogue with Duthuit. Duthuit was a friend of Masson and fully conversant with the discourse and artistic practice of the French painter. Duthuit had endorsed Masson's new manner after the war, a more fluid and spare technique by which Masson attempted to "paint the void" after having oscillated between several styles (he had been a Cubist first and then a neo-Surrealist).[5] Masson's Cubist works from the 1920s struck the knowing eye of Gertrude Stein who started collecting him.[6] Masson then spent the war years in America, where he again revolutionized his technique and he ushered in a French version of Abstract Expressionism. One can argue that Masson influenced American painters in the 1940s: he allowed them to see how the practice of automatic painting brought a greater degree of freedom in improvisation. Also, while living in Connecticut between 1941 and 1945, Masson had discovered Asian calligraphy and painting at the Boston Museum of Fine Arts, and he used this art as a new model for his creation.[7]

Masson's Void

Duthuit understood Masson's new departure not as a rejection of Surrealism but as a sublimation of its wildest impulses. Masson tamed his images and turned into ethereal forms the teeming monsters and relentless massacres of his earlier work, those shocking images blending sexual aggression and natural catastrophes. Whether the softening of his touch marked a return to figuration under the sign of social concerns, a materialist engagement with texture, a Zen-like contemplation of the void, or a specifically French version of American Abstract Expressionism, Masson's new transparency attracted a lot of critical attention. Before World War II, Masson had adopted the radical theses of his brother-in-law and role model, Georges Bataille. Masson tirelessly featured dramatic figures of sacrifices of male or female victims and castrated and headless men, as in the naked male figure that stands headless and sexless on the famous cover that he had designed for *Acéphale*, Bataille's infamous review that lasted from 1936 to 1939.[8] As mentioned previously, Beckett immediately felt a proximity with Bataille after the war; he, too, had participated in a neo-Surrealist avant-garde before the war. Why then was Beckett so resistant to Masson's aesthetics when their points of departure were so close?

This very proximity posed a problem. When Beckett stated, "Here is an artist who seems literally skewered on the ferocious dilemma of expression,"[9] he exposed his own dilemma, as has been noted.[10] Beckett's reservations were at first subjective intuitions, but soon, given Duthuit's prodding, he had to make them cohere into something looking like a systematic aesthetic. First came the question of abstraction, which was brought to the fore by Pascale Casanova;[11] it was followed by a dialectical exchange between aesthetics and ethics, a theme about which Duthuit and Beckett agreed, up to a point; Masson's role in this dialectics of discovery and definition was crucial.

Clement Greenberg, a tireless advocate of abstraction in painting, also eager to promote American artists and denigrate the Paris school, paid homage to Masson alone, which confirms the latter's eminence in the history twentieth-century painting: "André Masson's presence on this side of the Atlantic during the war was of inestimable benefit to us. Unfulfilled though he is, and tragically so, he is still the most seminal of all painters, not excepting Miró, in the generation after Picasso's. He, more than anyone else, anticipated the new abstract painting, and I don't believe he has gotten enough credit for that."[12] Most art historians have accepted Greenberg's judgment; however accurate the assessment may have been, it would not have swayed Beckett or brought him closer to Masson—on the contrary.

A point not broached by Greenberg, who hated Surrealism with a passion, was that Masson had been a Surrealist, even if he had been a dissident Surrealist. Considering Masson's evolution over three decades led Beckett to reexamine his own involvement in Surrealism. Most of its practitioners had gone in exile during the war. While Beckett's investment in *transition* before the war had made him a fellow traveler of Surrealism, the situation had changed drastically after 1945.[13] Even Breton wondered whether Surrealism could continue. Masson had broken with Breton a first time to follow Bataille and his group of dissidents at the end of the 1920s; he made peace with Breton in the late 1930s, collaborated with him in Martinique in 1941, only to have a terrible dispute in America when Breton objected to his "patriotic" painting, *Liberté, Egalité, Fraternité* from 1942.[14] The second break was final. Beckett evinced a similar animus against Breton; the latter's smugness during World War II irked Beckett five years later. When Breton wanted to help a Czech poet about to be executed by the Communists, Beckett countered that this was "enough to make you want to join the Party."[15]

The question of a second avant-garde frames the dialogues with Duthuit. Duthuit, I mentioned in chapter 1, had revived the journal *Transition* (then with a capital *T*) after the review launched by Eugène Jolas had folded in 1938. Beckett reminisces about his earlier investment in a letter to Duthuit from June 1949: "Here in the loft I find an old copy of *transition* (1938), with a poem of mine, the wild youthful kind, which I had quite forgotten, and an article (also by me) on a young Irish poet (young then) who had just published a volume of poems in the same series as *Echo's Bones*."[16] The poem, "Ooftisch," typical of Beckett's *transition* first manner, flaunted its Yiddish title; the Irish poet mentioned was his old friend Denis Devlin.

Already when *transition* was under Jolas's leadership, it had brought together Beckett and Masson. The June 1930 double issue (19–20) featured "For Future Reference" by Beckett and "La Rencontre" by Masson. Beckett knew Masson as a neo-Surrealist given his proximity with Bataille: Bataille had married the actress Silvia Maklès while Masson married her sister, Rose Maklès.

Beyond the nostalgia one detects in Beckett's comment, there is the issue of repetition, especially if we consider the radical pronouncements made in the 1930s by the Surrealists and the first *transition* group. Could one still believe in any avant-garde after the war? Could there be a revolution of the word while Europe was in the throes of an incipient Cold War? The same letter makes fun of André Breton's intervention to sponsor a young protégé. Immediately after, Beckett asks Duthuit whether Masson had been commissioned to make a medal of André Malraux's face, then minister of culture in de Gaulle's government. Indeed, Masson crafted the medal in 1949. Beckett was annoyed by artists who played at being rebellious while profiting from their connections.

Duthuit, connected by marriage to Henri Matisse, did not see anything wrong in this official recognition. Taking the flame from Eugene Jolas (Jolas was invited to contribute to *Transition*, which he did in the first issue when he published an excellent survey of the evolution of experimental poetry[17]), Duthuit promoted a different program. No more than Beckett did he believe in a universal mythos ushering in a "language of the night" whose models were James Joyce and Gertrude Stein. Names that recur in the new *Transition* are those of Jean-Paul Sartre, Georges Bataille, René Char, Jean Wahl, André Malraux, Maurice Nadeau, and Jean Genet. Joyce remained a fixture: the fourth issue of *Transition* announces the publication of the *James Joyce Yearbook*, which was edited by Eugene Jolas and included Stuart Gilbert, Louis Gillet, and Paul Léon as contributors to the first series. Its frontispiece and cover were by Masson. The second *Transition* belongs to a postwar mentality and promotes discussions polarized by Existentialism, Marxism, and a revived left-wing Catholicism; it showcases emerging poets like René Char, André du Bouchet, and Antonin Artaud next to more established writers like André Gide.

Duthuit, a respected art critic, had written about Matisse and Byzantine art. Masson painted his portrait in 1945. Duthuit would visit him in Provence. Beckett's information on Masson came from Duthuit and from articles by Masson published in *Les Temps Modernes*.[18] Duthuit explained Masson's career in a letter mailed on February 28, 1949, from Le Tholonnet, near Aix-en-Provence, close to the Montagne Saint-Victoire painted by Cézanne.

Masson had a house there and Pierre Tal-Coat lived nearby, as did the philosopher Henri Maldiney who wrote excellent essays on Tal-Coat.[19] The poet André du Bouchet was a frequent visitor, and one talked about the "Aix school." Here is how Duthuit explains their theories:

> [T]hey claim that, rather than putting down forms, they are setting them free from one another, creating between them zones of silence, fields of non-movement. The word "void" often crops up in their conversations. On the edge of this void stands a sign, a value just set that offers a key to it, opens it up, breathes life into it. One tries, while working, not to be paralysed by the idea of the picture that has to be made. One stops when there's no more to say, when one can no longer lighten, aerate the masses more than already done. One tries to untangle the vipers' nest of space and allow the mind to move more easily into this blankness set out, set moving by infinitely discreet, almost faded tones of grey, of ochre. Remain intense though, but with a light touch.[20]

This empty space meant to "aerate" painting was the outcome of Masson's diligent study of Chinese painters and Japanese Zen masters. One should first find the void in oneself before reaching an open space. Here is how Masson summed up his ideas: "The Chinese painter, acquainted with the infinite, cuts all mooring ropes. The layered ascent, succession, fluidity, cosmic breathing: locus of all dilatations, sanctuary of the OPEN."[21] He developed the idea in an essay published in *Les Temps Modernes* of June 1949 in which one finds most of the terms thrown to Beckett by Duthuit. Duthuit mentioned "inner emptiness, the prime condition, according to Chinese esthetics, of the act of painting,"[22] whereas Beckett suspected that the problem of expression could not be solved by an appeal to Eastern aesthetics.

Masson's fascination for the void and for abstract primitive forms found an echo in Duthuit's main thesis about aesthetics, that Western art after Cézanne ought to return to abstract art. For the Byzantines and the Japanese, art was not to be exhibited in museums but to facilitate collective contemplation. These theories were expounded in a special issue of *Transition* on painting. Duthuit's manifesto compares Matisse and Byzantium, both illustrated by Venice whose famous basilica San Marco keeps Byzantine forms alive. Its architecture bridges the gap between religion and paganism, a point missed by Nietzsche, according to Duthuit, who wrote this: "Nietzsche strangely undervalued this religion, yet it seems to have accomplished as nearly as possible, through its etiquette and pomp, what he himself on the threshold of madness dreamed of achieving: the absorption of all anguish in joy and the alliance of the sun-god and the god of the cross."[23] Mason agrees that, if contemporary painters could just agree to relinquish their individuality, they would blend collective myth and personal ecstasy in a productive fashion: "To situate oneself beyond the measurable world ineluctably leads whoever is there to the heart of a problem—the problem of being—or, if one prefers, to come close to mysticism."[24] Such a new mysticism would offer a way out of the "crisis of the imaginary," a crisis that would have been triggered jointly by Cubism and Surrealism.

Modernism and Abstraction

In *Transition 49*, no. 5, André du Bouchet proposes a similar analysis of the renewal of Masson's art, which "loses weight and is granted a gift or air and light."[25] With Masson's new concern for transparency, diaphanous landscapes replace bloody mythological battles, and animals and humans look lighter and move under a radiant sun. Du Bouchet agrees with Clement Greenberg who analyzed how Masson overcame his previous *terribilità*. Before, he was obsessed by "the monstrous, the epically brutal, and the blasphemous."[26] Now, "Self-control, elimination, and simplification would seem to be the solution for Masson."[27] If there is a risk of "impoverishment, not simplification," nevertheless Masson will "surprise us in the future."[28] For Greenberg, Masson's evolution toward "elimination and simplification" would enlist him automatically in the modernist program, a program that he defines with reference to Kant:

> Modernism . . . covers almost the whole of what is truly alive in our culture. It happens, however, to be very much of a historical novelty. Western civilization is not the first civilization to turn around and question its own foundations, but it is the one that has gone furthest in doing so. I identify Modernism with the intensification, almost the exacerbation, of this self-critical tendency that began with the philosopher Kant. Because he was the first to criticize the means itself of criticism, I conceive of Kant as the first real Modernist.[29]

The work of Masson seems to exemplify Greenberg's idea that modernism requires an art struggling against its own limits. However, Beckett goes further by distinguishing Masson's effort from that of Bram van Velde. To sum up his position, van Velde's work exemplified an attempt to paint the impossibility of painting. The Dutch painter did not attempt to find technical solutions that would bypass or overcome the formal limitations inherent to painting. Van Velde would *be* at the limit of art whereas Masson attempted to paint the limits of painting because his program expressed a modernist ideology corresponding to the main precepts of Greenberg's modernism.

Beckett responded to this program skeptically, preferring van Velde's art, an art that would move within and not beyond; because it strove to present a condition of impossibility, it would limn the contours of an ethical domain. Modernist abstraction was never an aesthetic ideal for Beckett. He disagreed with Duthuit's condemnation of Italian Renaissance painting as illusionistic. On the whole, Duthuit shared Greenberg's beliefs, whereas Beckett was wary of a modernism reduced to abstraction. In July 1948, Beckett praised a painting that he had seen in Dresden in 1937. It is a Saint Sebastian by Antonello da Messina whose geometrical composition "would draw moans from you."[30] Beckett writes in French: "Espace pur à force de mathématique, carrelages, dalles plutôt, noir et blanc, en longs raccourcis genre Mantegna . . . tout ça envahi, mangé par l'humain";[31] "Pure space by dint of mathematics, tiling, flagstones rather, black and white, with long, Mantegna-style fore-shortenings . . . the whole thing invaded, eaten into by the human."[32] Indeed, Sebastian is called the "lapidated," which alludes to the saint's second death, not to the four arrows one sees here stuck in his body. Beckett was transfixed by the saint's hieratic hesitation between two deaths; here, the "human" returns because it is caught up in a rigorous architectural perspective. The saint has become pure form, he has blended with or morphed into a landscape drawn as a geometrical frame. Sebastian's pierced body turns into a column or merges with the arcades visible in the background. Thus Beckett's phrase of "eaten into by the human" suggests above all that the saint's body and the ambient buildings have exchanged their qualities.[33] Such a "human" statue is a far cry from Sartre's humanism or Breton's poetic hope that art will rebuild wholeness and hope after the war.

Beckett's letter quotes Duthuit's essay "Sartre's Last Class" (I will return to it in chapter 13) in order to increase the distance taken both from Breton's and Sartre's humanism: "From your Sartre-Breton equation one may indeed emerge, I think, into a pure air of grandeur, distinguished conation and utilitarian splendor, in which an end is made of the pernicious illusion [*duperie*] in which they are at one, in which people everywhere have always been at one (I can hear you groaning), the illusion [*duperie*] of the human and the fully realized."[34] "Illusion" is *duperie* in the French original, which stresses the "lie" of a "realized" or achieved humanism. In the second part of his essay, Duthuit had made the surprising suggestion that, despite their recent quarrel over the value of poetry in general and of Surrealism in particular, Sartre had become a Surrealist![35] Duthuit argues very cogently that Breton had ultimately similar positions facing art, history, and politics; they have the same atheism, the same sentimental love for the underdog; they believe that literature can redeem humanity, they believe that monuments can save: "We must not be free of the object, Breton stoutly declares, and he finds in this complete submission a maximum of liberty. For Sartre also liberty is the outcome of a spell, but he prefers not to insist. Consider, admire, and adore the incomparable beauty of this immense illumination! The God of Descartes has become an object."[36] Neither Breton nor Sartre ever questioned "the autonomy of artistic activity," an issue that had become problematic for Duthuit. For Surrealism as for Existentialism, art is granted an "absolute sovereignty" over its particular dominions.[37] This arrogant and unfounded domination is based on an unconditional preeminence granted to the "human," a presupposition with which both Beckett and Duthuit disagreed.

The epistolary conversation with Duthuit had been under way for a while, for the three dialogues condense in eight pages more than fifty pages of correspondence. When Beckett left for Dublin where he visited museums and galleries, he meditated on the worth of representative painting. He let Duthuit know that for him, abstraction, even of the most "inhuman" kind, offered no solution. Having admired a Dublin show with Renoir, Matisse, Manet, and Derain, he joked about critics who had declared that abstract art was their "only hope."[38] In a letter in which he asks Duthuit to say "tu" to him, he derides the "pure manstuprations of Orphic and abstract art." Such masturbations have to be stopped, he adds: "What if we simply stopped altogether having erections?"[39] This bawdy humor barely concealed a wish to move in another direction. When Beckett explained his concept of "relation," he had to criticize abstract art: "Thus terebrated, to speak like Fénéon, the artist can wallow untroubled in what is called non-figurative painting, assured of never being short of themes, of always being in front of himself and with as much variety as if he had never left off wandering idly along the banks of the Seine. And here again we see triumphing the definition of the artist as he-who-is-always-*in-front-of*."[40] Beckett had translated Félix Fénéon's descriptions of paintings in which the word *terebrated* described rocks hollowed out by the sea. Here it is the artist who is hollowed out. The painter refuses the mastery of forms as in classical painting because he is "precipitated" into the waves, the storms, the natural dynamism, in a Romantic interpenetration of subject and object. Even if this is still a worthwhile effort, Bram van Velde breaks with the repetition of this Romantic gesture: his refusal is total, hence totally new. "For my part, it is the *gran rifiuto* that interests me, not the heroic wrigglings to which we owe this splendid thing."[41] Beckett blends Dante's doomed pope of *Inferno* (Canto 3:60), and van Velde. Finally, he rejects the heroic posture of a Masson pretending to be a "visionary exile."[42]

Beckett evokes a longer history. Why should the second abstract school of the forties be presented as new if it merely repeats the first abstract school from the 1920s? Here, Beckett echoes Marcel Duchamp's worries facing modernism; both question the naïve belief that there has been a progress in technique, or that artists who overcome obstacles evince more competence than their predecessors. Beckett refuses the teleology that presents modernism as a step forward in the historical evolution from representation to abstraction. Identically, Duchamp opposed the "purity" of an abstract medium at that time. However, Beckett is more radical than Duchamp in his wish to rethink the whole representational mode of painting. Form is nothing if it is not underpinned by a preliminary questioning and should never be taken as an end in itself. This entails a rejection of the heroic struggle with the world and provides an opportunity to state a certain disagreement with Bataille about "destruction."

Beckett's meditation on art led him to propose a theory of aesthetics as second to ethics, a theory that found its roots in Kant but also relied on Bataille's concept of the impossible, as we have seen. Moreover, like Bataille, Beckett sounds like a deviant Freudian, for curiously, in *Three Dialogues*, Kant appears through Freud. Several times, Freud had made fun of Kant's comparison of the beautiful starry sky at night with the moral law. He would query Kant's optimistic combination of ontology and psychology, and Beckett duly recorded this critique in the psychology notes that he typed between 1933 and 1935. He then used these notes for his discussions with Duthuit in 1948.

Freud and Kant: Starry Heavens

Freud's *New Introductory Lectures on Psychoanalysis* was published in 1933 in German and in English.[43] One finds the facsimile of the relevant page in *Notes Diverse Holo* (*Samuel Beckett Today/Aujourd'hui* 16). The notes Beckett took come from Lecture 31, sketching "The Anatomy of the Mental Personality." Freud explains the division of the subject between ego, superego, and id:

> Id, Ego & Superego.
> The philosopher Kant once declared that nothing proved to him the greatness of God more convincingly than the starry heavens and the moral conscience within us. The stars are unquestionably superb . . .
> *Super-ego*: heir to Oedipus complex. A special function within the ego representing demand for restriction & rejection.[44]

Freud summarizes his topology of the subject in a neat little diagram reproduced by Beckett; in an oval shape looking very much like an eye, the ego straddles the border between the preconscious and the unconscious; the id lurks below while the superego provides a vertical border to the left of the schema. Beckett quotes Freud who quotes Kant. Freud would always refer to Kant when discussing the issue of morality; he had done so when he wondered whether there were "moral feelings" in dreams at the beginning of the *Interpretation of Dreams*. Thus once more in his 1933 lectures, Freud quotes Kant's famous statement from the end of the *Critique of Practical Reason*: "Two things fill the mind with ever new and increasing admiration and awe, the oftener and more steadily they are reflected on: the starry heavens above me and the moral law within me."[45] As Kant adds, one can have a direct experience of both; such an experience is associated with a consciousness of one's existence. The vision of the starry heavens brings about a sense of the sublime; one experiences one's puny nature facing the infinity of the world: "The former view of a countless multitude of worlds annihilates, as it were, my importance as an animal creature, which must give back to the planet (a mere speck in the universe) the matter from which it came, the matter which I for a little time provided with vital force, we know not how."[46] The consideration of the moral law raises the idea of another infinity, a positive infinity this time. Awe in front of the natural Sublime leads to Respect for the moral law. Here is the argument that dominates the analysis of the Sublime in the *Critique of Judgment*.

This was an argument known to Beckett; he had found it presented in Windelband's *History of Philosophy*, with its terse but competent summary of Kant's notion of the sublime: "In the presence of the immeasurable greatness or overpowering might of objects, we feel the inability of our sensuous perception to master them, as an oppression and a casting down; but the supersensuous power of our reason raises itself above this our sensuous insufficiency," so that "the superiority of our moral worth to all the power of Nature comes to consciousness."[47] Finally, Windelband's commentary links this well-known dialectical reversal with the concept of sublimation: "In both cases the discomfort over our sensuous inferiority is richly outweighed and overcome by the triumph of our higher rational character. And since this is the appropriate relation of the two sides of our being, these objects have an exalting, '*subliming*' effect, and produce the feeling of a delight of the reason, and this feeling, again, because it is based upon the relation of our ideational Forms, is universally communicable and of *a priori* operation."[48] All these terms are relevant even when Beckett argues for an absence of relation and insists on a formlessness that is not communicable or rational. For him, Kant would be too rational in erecting his system of aesthetics.

This is why Beckett could not but endorse Freud's ironical debunking of Kant: "Following a well-known pronouncement of Kant's which couples the conscience within us with the starry Heavens, a pious man might well be tempted to honour these two things as the masterpieces of creation. The stars are indeed magnificent, but as regards conscience God had done an uneven and careless piece of work, for a large majority of men have brought along with them only a modest amount of it or scarcely enough to be worth mentioning."[49] As previously shown, in his notes, Beckett stopped typing after "superb": "The stars are unquestionably superb . . . // *Super-ego*: heir to Oedipus complex."[50] We can guess why: the ending of Kant's sentence is so clunky that Beckett must have struggled against the impulse to rewrite it.

Instead, Beckett completed or rewrote Kant's sentence with the famous joke of the tailor praising his trousers and comparing it with a botched divine creation in his first essay on van Velde's art, "Le Monde et le Pantalon."[51] The same joke was later used in *Endgame*. Beckett's English tailor, in the joke narrated by Nagg, looks like an Italian Pantalone, the stock character of the commedia dell'arte: an older curmudgeon railing at the others while being the butt of greater ridicule. Nevertheless, he holds his ground, disparages God's creation of the world while lauding the unsurpassable perfection of his trousers. Terms like *pantalonade, buffoonery*, or *pantaloon's dance* apply to God's creation. It was a "caricature," as Nietzsche said when he walked in the streets of Turin, crying and screaming that he himself was the author of that farce. If God's creation of the stars finds a poor equivalent in the gift of conscience to humans, the messy creation of the world is brought down to size by the tailor's trousers, a neat synecdoche for Heraclitus's *panta rhei* (all things flow): all things may flow, but let my *pantalon* stay rigid and neat. Anyway all things end up in the drain, except, perhaps, for the perfect phallic crease of my trousers. Moral conscience finds a refuge in impeccable clothes, a thesis that flirts with nineteenth-century dandyism, although inverted in the tattered rags proudly worn by Beckett's tramps.

Freud saw a kernel of truth in the idea that conscience has a divine origin, but immediately added: "the thesis needs interpretation."[52] His interpretation is that God condenses paternal attributes that cohere as a superego with its harshly repressive role. In a lecture on "visions of the world," God is once more a severe father figure:

> I may remind you of Kant's famous pronouncement in which he names, in a single breath, the starry heavens and the moral law within us. However strange this juxtaposition may sound—for what have the heavenly bodies to do with the question of whether one human creature loves another or kills him?—it nevertheless touches on a great psychological truth. The same father (or parental agency) which gave the child life and guarded him against its perils, taught him as well what he might do and what he must leave undone, instructed him that he must adapt himself to certain restrictions on his instinctual wishes.[53]

Beckett's enduring love for his father, often evoked and pared down to one image in later texts, brings a moving testimony to this Freudian thesis.

The Limits of disfazione

The recurrent image of father and son holding hands as they walk together, the leitmotiv of *Company*, emphasizes the fragile dependence of the child, still afraid and in need of support. By contrast, Masson appears as too heroic and too self-possessed to recognize the depth of man's helplessness. Masson displays the kind of blustering male arrogance, the typical *braggadocio* of which Beckett makes fun in his plays—he would quickly turn into a French Pozzo! At the other extreme, van Velde keeps his singularity as an artist while leading viewers to crucial questions about the generic by forcing them to move from his quasi abstract canvasses to a vision of humanity stripped bare: not a gendered subject, but the power of resilience in weakness. Beckett developed the argument when recycling Leonardo da Vinci's concept of *disfazione*: "[Masson's] so extremely intelligent remarks on space breathes the same possession as the notebooks of Leonardo who, when he speaks of *disfazione*, knows that for him not one fragment will be lost."[54]

Earlier, the term *disfazione* had served Beckett in his analysis of Proust's concept of habit. It occurs in one of the most convoluted sentences of the little book. Beckett opposes the superficiality of habit to depths hidden in our "dungeons" in his *Proust*. He quotes Baudelaire's "The Balcony" with the powerful image of an "unfathomable abyss":

But here, in that "gouffre interdit à nos sondes," is stored the essence of ourselves, the best of our many selves and their concretions that simplists call the world, the best because accumulated slyly and pain-fully and patiently under the nose of our vulgarity, the fine essence of a smothered divinity whose whispered "disfazione" is drowned in the healthy bawling of an all-embracing appetite, the pearl that may give the lie to our carapace of paste and pewter.[55]

These "unfathomable abysses" of the Freudian unconscious contain what is most true in us. What remains our "best" part derives from a patient accumulation of refined impressions. If the little gods hidden in us are manifested not by their creation but by their "decreation" (*disfazione*), the decreating process cannot last, it has to be relayed by the positivity of our appetite to live and enjoy. There may be too many mixed metaphors in this sentence, but Beckett manages to retrieve the Proustian pearl hidden in the deeps.

The key term is Leonardo's *disfazione*, a word now obsolete in Italian, but then used to mean ruin and destruction.[56] In Leonardo's *Notebooks*, *disfazione* describes catastrophes, tempests, or the deluge,[57] while it appears in the disputation on the question of whether the law of nature is tanta-mount to a law of universal destruction:

Behold now the hope and desire of going back to one's country or returning to primal chaos, like that of the moth to the light, of the man who with perpetual longing always looks forward with joy to each new spring and each new summer, and to the new months and the new years, deeming that the things he longs for are too slow in coming: and who does not perceive that he is longing for his own destruction (*E' non si avveda che desidera la sua disfazione*).[58]

One of the issues debated was whether animals and humans should live by killing each other. There are two voices in this disputation, the stron-ger one belonging to the materialist camp; it asserts confidently that man is caught up in a natural rhythm of creation and destruction. In all this, Leon-ardo seems intent on capturing the signs of pain caused by catastrophes. As Beckett writes, "for him, not one fragment will be lost."[59] Leonardo gloats over the panic of men and animals, the ruins of cities commingling with the ruins of mountains and offers a hyper-realistic fantasy in which no detail gets lost, up to eddies whirling in lakes into which palaces have collapsed.

If Masson and Bataille have the right to enjoy *disfazione*, their frantic acquiescence to universal destruction undermines itself, and, what is worse, ends up sounding glib. Beckett appears wary of ready-made disasters: "Greatly enjoyed your lack of enjoyment of the all-purpose disaster, à la Bataille."[60] This ironical phrase, *désastre à tout faire*, offers an apt semantic comment of Leonardo's *disfazione*. Beckett sees in this "unworking" an all too easy attitude, a compliant *Schadenfreude* facing cosmic annihilation. Against this, he requires a zero-point of values that will lead to a Nietzschean "transvaluation of all values."

The concept of *disfazione* presupposes an ontology of disaster (Nature loves disasters), but neglects to think about the creation of values; the risk is that disaster turns into a set of clichés. Leonardo and Bataille meditate on the substance of the world; they imagine the recombination of atoms after the dissolution of matter; they ponder the power of time, since as we saw Leonardo highlights the dramatic irony that the more we desire the return of the spring, the closer we are brought to our dissolution. True to his ethical impulse, Beckett refuses to transform this nihilistic enjoyment into an illusion of omnipotence. Such an illusion was driving Leonardo's creativity. As Freud had noted, Leonardo, who was fastidiously clean and amused himself by freeing caged birds, never betrayed compassion for other people. He would follow without any qualm criminals led to their executions and study faces distorted by fear for his sketches. "He often gave the appearance of being indifferent to good or evil, or he insisted that he should be measured by different rules."[61] Leonardo evinced no sense of ethics: everything fell under the domination of knowledge or beauty. This double *libido sciendi* and *libido pingendi* elicits no admiration from Beckett. He cannot condemn it in the name of positive ethical rules but brings to bear his motto: *Ubi nihil vales, ibi nihil velis.*

What Beckett reproaches Leonardo for is also what irritates him in Masson and in Bataille: a dialectical sleight of hand by which loss automatically becomes the artist's gain. Heroic efforts deployed by these artists lead to a vain posturing:

> Masson could perhaps be told that it is time to stop these pointless hostilities, to make peace with the wood from which he will never emerge. . . . What you and I have managed to get hold of, Georges my old friend, is very simple and not the least bit metaphysical or mystical; indeed it is common sense, good and round, like d'Alembert's back. It is all in the old sentence from Geulincx quoted in *Murphy*, admittedly a little hastily: *Ubi nihil vales ibi nihil velis.* The only point is to be clear about the domain in which one is worth nothing.[62]

True to his central intuition based on Geulincx's *Ethica*, Beckett's aesthetics presupposes a revision of the theory of values via the doctrine of "humility." The point is not to conquer the world but to assess its relative worth or worthlessness by comparison with the magnitude of subjective dispossession.

The core of this thesis lies in a paradoxical ethics of nonrelation, which alone can reject the myth of the romantic creator ready to fight until the bitter end in a heroic struggle with his material, a masculinist myth of the artist still dominant in the 1950s—from Jackson Pollock to Ernest Hemingway, from Norman Mailer to Robert Lowell. Against this romanticism, Beckett opts for an *aerte povera* underpinned by an ethics of poverty and alterity, an ethics that looks very much like the ethics of the other elaborated by Levinas exactly at the same time. What is paradoxical indeed is that the relation to the other is predicated on a nonrelation: the face of the other subject reveals first of all an infinite distance.

The key term *nonrelation* destroys from the outset the humanistic illusion that we are alike, or that human reciprocity should be taken as a given. On the contrary, it is because we are all infinitely different that a true rapport can be posited.[63] To heroic gesticulation lashing blindly at the void, Beckett prefers the austere humility of Bram van Velde, whose sayings are recorded in *Transition 49*: no. 5: "Painting is man face to face with his débâcle." Or: "I have nothing in my pockets, nothing in my hands. Where shall I find what I need?" Finally, in a statement almost echoing Geulincx's *Ethics*: "I do not know what I do. What I put into a picture is not the result of any act of the will. I do not know myself what it means."[64] Like Murphy, like Geulincx, we see van Velde discovering his *cogito* (I think) via a *nescio* (I don't know). He reiterates something like: "I do not know, therefore I paint." A deliberate poverty of expression fits the ideal of "an art unresentful of its insuperable indigence and too proud for the farce of giving and receiving."[65] It is only insofar as one feels dispossessed, helpless, and worldless, that one can be called an artist. The absence of a world as a totality leads to a duty of saying because it never presupposes a "relation." Paul Celan expressed this superbly: "Die Welt ist fort, ich muss dich tragen [The world is gone, I have to carry you]."[66] Such a duty ultimately relies on an ethical imperative—a loaded term that brings us back to Kant's *Critiques*.

CHAPTER 7

Beckett's Kantian Critiques

Kant often figures as a point of reference when philosophers engage with Beckett. Philosophers like Adorno, Badiou, Deleuze, Cavell, or Martha Nussbaum believe that Beckett's oeuvre can stand on its own as philosophy, whether it be called critical philosophy, ethical philosophy, existentialism, ontology, nihilism, cynicism, or negative dialectics. To produce original readings, they tend to discard the guides written by specialists. They focus on the texts themselves that they read with fresh eyes and a different vocabulary. This attitude is illustrated by Nussbaum's 1988 essay "Narrative Emotions: Beckett's Genealogy of Love."[1] I want to engage with her reading for what it reveals about the issue of values and ethics in Beckett. Nussbaum's contention is that we learn from our emotions; emotions are not instinctual expressions but socially constructed by narratives telling us how to behave and feel. A renewed dialogue between philosophy and literature attempts to answer to the age-old question: "How should one live?"[2] Nussbaum finds in Aristotle a concept of practical wisdom that will be fine-tuned by paying attention to particular cases. She does not discard literary models for she thinks that form and content are inseparable;

we learn truths about life from their interaction. I fully endorse such a reading program—how Beckett fits in it, is my question.

Reading Beckett with Kant

Nussbaum starts her investigation with *Molloy*; one sentence serves as a point of departure: "It is in the tranquility of decomposition that I recall the long confused emotion which was my life, and that I judge it, as it is said that God will judge me, and with no less impertinence."[3] Her commentary revolves around these words. She provides a paraphrase of the novel in which the dominant theme is Moran's overdetermined relation to religion, which leads to this generalization: "We could summarize the emotion story that is Molloy's life by saying that it is the story of original sin, of the feat of God's judgment, and of the vain longing for salvation."[4] Nussbaum conflates two approaches, the religious one and the psychoanalytic one. Molloy's obsession is anal birth; he and Moran share a similar disgust for bodily functions, the body is reduced to shit. The Mother is indeed "Countess Caca," we will never go further than that. One might contend that Nussbaum barely misses the possibility of seeing that the combination of an "excremental vision" with a postreligious one is not necessarily Calvinist but can be read as an Augustinian trope via Augustine's famous "Inter urinas et faeces nascimur [We were all born between urine and shit]." Joyce paved the way for Beckett when he borrowed from Augustine the idea that corruption is a proof of the innate goodness of what was corrupted: only "good" things decay.

Nussbaum states that Beckett's solution is similar to Proust's: both end up asserting that there is no salvation outside art. She compares Beckett with two other philosophical deniers of God, who, according to her, have the merit of being more consistent—Lucretius and Nietzsche, who aim at destroying religion in order to assert the possibility of a truly human life. They want to get rid of the nihilism perpetuated by religion. Nussbaum concludes that Beckett's view of emotions, in which guilt and disgust dominate, is not healthy—one cannot recommend it to impressionable children: "it is in part because Beckett sees society as single and monolithic that he is able to omit the presence of argument, criticism, and change. In all this we sense, I believe, a deeply religious sensibility at work."[5] This is, obviously, a reductive reading. Nussbaum makes unwarranted jumps or interpretive errors: she thinks that Molloy speaks of "finality without end" whereas it is Moran who mentions the famous Kantian tag; she assumes that the entire novel is written by Jacques Moran (if this were true, he would have had to write *Watt* and other texts by Beckett). She thinks that Youdi's name means "You die." Such misreadings are not devastating and mostly show that she has read the text without relying on too many guides.

What is more worrisome is her reading program; because it is deployed in the name of emotions, her attempt at reading literature and philosophy together fails to identify obvious literary references and misses relevant philosophical references. She writes:

> There is a peculiar movement in Beckett's talk of emotions . . . from a perception of human limits to a loathing of the limited, from grief to disgust and hatred, from the tragedy and comedy of the frail body to rage at the body, seen as covered in excrement. It is as if Beckett believes that the finite and frail can only inspire our disgust and loath-ing—that life (in the words of Youdi) can be "a thing of beauty" and a joy," only if it is "for ever." And this is because, as we said, mortality in Beckett's world is seen not as our neutral and natural condition but as our punishment for original sin. The complete absence in his writing of any joy in the limited and the finite indicates to us that the narrative as a whole is an expression of a religious view of life.[6]

It is not the first time that Nussbaum evokes the Keatsian reference mentioned by Gaber—"He said to me, said Gaber, Gaber, he said, life is a thing of beauty, Gaber, and a joy for ever"[7]—but at no point does she acknowledge its intertextual status as a quote from Keats. Neither does she seem to latch on the pervasive irony of Moran's comment: "Do you think he meant human life? . . . Perhaps he didn't mean human life," a remark that we have already encountered. She only mentions this sentence to con-nect Beckett's supposed critique of religion with Epicurus's idea that ani-mals offer models for men:[8] indeed, animals "show us what it could be to be alive without hope or fear or disgust or even love."[9] Bataille would query all these presuppositions.

Nussbaum's mistake appears in her failure to acknowledge the presence of "joy" in the text, which is made manifest by her decision to see no refer-ence to Kant or Keats in *Molloy*. She does not seem to recognize Kant when she asserts: "Molloy feels always, in this world, that he dwells in an atmo-sphere of finality without end,"[10] but had she identified him, she would have waxed all the more critical: Kant is her bête noire because of his alleged "hostility to emotions."[11] In a 1997 essay, she promoted the idea of "compassion" as a key to ethics, and as a counter-model opposing Kant's formalism.[12] A philosophy of affects and cognitive emotions, albeit replete with good intentions, cannot be the pretext for bad literary criticism. What is clearly bad is a reading that is reductively religious or moralistic, based on a psychobiography rehashing platitudes about the mother and the father. The conclusion is sweeping: Beckett has to be rejected wholly as having no value whatsoever; and if we have a taste for the negative, even there he is wanting for he falls short of Nietzsche's invigorating nihilism.

Typically, the two passages of *Molloy* that have been mentioned deal with beauty. Why is Moran suddenly seized by a Kantian sense of the beauty of the world just when Gaber arrives and orders him to find Molloy? Why does Gaber sum up Youdi's teachings with the famous quote from Keats's *Endymion*? Martha Nussbaum's moralistic analysis was immediately rebuked. In 1997, Simon Critchley attacked her interpretation in *Very Little . . . Almost Nothing*.[13] He noted that silence was not the "goal" of Beckett's work, as Nussbaum assumes because she obsesses about religious readings, but rather a "*desecration* and *desacralization* of silence" as he said to Adorno.[14]

Critchley is ferocious: "The consequence of Nussbaum's reading of Beckett is depressingly familiar (not to mention being pre-Nietzschean), namely, that Beckett's 'search for silence' is a 'nihilism.'"[15] In another note, he contrasts J. M. Coetzee's sense that Beckett's prose gives "sensuous delight" with Nussbaum's rejection of Beckett as being joyless. For Critchley, Beckett's style may be cruel but it remains humorous, it exhibits a joyous relation to finitude, "a celebration of human limitedness that is replete with sardonic, side-splitting, antidepressant comedy."[16] Critchley debunks the mixture of neo-Aristotelianism and classical psychoanalysis which underpins Nussbaum's analyses: "Despite the undoubted felicities offered by a psychoanalytic interpretation of *Molloy*, I find Nussbaum's use of psychoanalytic categories a little too easy and fluent. . . . There is, I feel, the danger of a *hermeneutic literalism* there."[17] Attempts at combining literature and philosophy should be attentive to the reflexivity of the text and avoid reducing the literary to the philosophical or the reverse.

Sensing that the debate had nevertheless not been satisfactorily solved, Bjørn Myskja attempted to reconcile the positions of Nussbaum and Critchley in *The Sublime in Kant and Beckett* (2002; volume 140 in the *Kantstudien* series). Myskja favors a philosophical approach to literature, thus his point of departure is identical with Nussbaum's. He wonders how *Molloy*, which is so full of reprehensible or disgusting actions and is also hard to comprehend in a rational manner, can be morally significant. His answer is to suggest that Kant's concept of the sublime provides a key: "The novel is sublime in the sense that its systematic negation of the meaning of the text denies the reader a coherent meaning, which gives rise to the complex

feeling described by Kant as the main element in a judgment of sublimity."[18] Myskja distinguishes three levels of application of the sublime: first,
it can be produced by hermeneutic contradictions that prevent any interpretive closure for the reader; then it can derive from the way Beckett's
characters are seen striving toward a purpose, even though it may appear
absurd to all others; finally, it can be generated by a poetic style, by the
creation of a verbal "murmur" in which one can recognize an ontological
category.

Myskja's book, whose bulk is made up of a reading of Kant's third *Critique* (*Critique of the Power of Judgment*), effectively mediates between Nussbaum and Critchley. Myskja takes his bearings by looking back to an older
critical disagreement: the debate opposing Martin Esslin's neo-existentialist
reading (Esslin saw Molloy as a hero confronting the absurdity of human
fate) and Georges Bataille's heterological reading of *Molloy* already discussed. Since one of Bataille's main concepts is the formless, Myskja links
it with the sublime. Both would offer a key to Beckett. Indeed, Bataille's
awe facing *Molloy*—his mixture of terror and pleasure when reading the
novel in which he saw the portrayal of a new form of human abjection—
could easily fall under the heading of the sublime, a term that "explores the
agony and the pain of the powerless."[19]

However, even if a Kantian analysis of the sublime can indeed make
sense of Beckett's shifts between ethics and aesthetics, the concept of the
sublime looks out of place when applied to Bataille. The attempt to establish a connection between Bataille's *informe* (formless) and Kant's sublime
looks forced or misguided, moreover one can hardly call Bataille a Kantian,
as he always tends toward Hegelian or Nietzschean discourses. If indeed
Molloy questions the limits of the human by exploding the legitimacy of the
term as Bataille asserts, then by going back to the positive ethical significance of moral values defined by the sublime in *Molloy*, one goes against
the grain of Bataille's program. Myskja is aware of this and admits that he
is "taking the risk of turning it into something more or less contradictory
to Bataille's aesthetic theory."[20]

As we have seen, Bataille understood the philosophical project of Beckett as a debunking of humanism in the name of an abjection coming close
to animality. Against Sartrean humanism, Bataille, who, as Sartre brilliantly
said, had "survived the death of god," ushered in an antihumanism that
played with nihilism in order to maximize the negative energy it still contained. Thus both play with philosophy to undo it, subvert it, parody it, in
a debunking that generates a conflicted affirmation. The process can be
observed in Beckett, too, which accounts for the clash between abundant

philosophical references and their offhand treatment. This point was stressed by Critchley but missed by Nussbaum and Myska. If Beckett drops philosophical concepts on almost every page, they function more like booby traps for reference hunters. It is impossible to say whether Beckett was Kantian, Cartesian, Wittgensteinian, or Heideggerian. This indecision explains why Beckett flaunts his immersion in minor philosophers—all important in their contexts, but not "heavy-weights" like Plato, Aristotle, Kant, Hegel, Nietzsche, Husserl, or Heidegger—to give shape to his most important insights. Beckett preferred to use Geulincx rather than give a refutation of Descartes, who could be treated rather offhandedly in "Whoroscope." He praised Schopenhauer to his friends at the time they were discovering Husserl and Heidegger. He preferred Mauthner's diluted version of *Sprachkritik* to Nietzsche, Wittgenstein, Russell, or Carnap. On the issue of matter and materialism, he would quote Democritus more than Marx or Bergson.

Beckett repeated to friends and journalists that he did not know any-thing about philosophy and had never read Wittgenstein or Heidegger. We have nevertheless evidence that he read Wittgenstein late in life.[21] His dismissal was intended to avoid inquisitive prying, or to ward off the temptation to find too many neat "identifications." In the late 1920s, his friendship with Jean Beaufret, who became the leading commentator of Heidegger after World War II, had brought him into contact with the texts of the pre-Socratics, the works of Descartes, and many other phi-losophers. If in the 1950s Beckett read Blanchot and Sartre and in the 1960s Husserl and Wittgenstein, then he had no regard for fashionable or canonical authors. He was struggling with Schopenhauer in the summer of 1930 as he was completing his monograph on Proust. For his *normalien* friends, the name of Schopenhauer called up *fin de siècle* nihilism and was *passé*. Beckett did not care: "I am reading Schopenhauer. Everyone laughs at that. Beaufret & Alfy etc. But I am not reading philosophy, nor caring whether he is right or wrong or a good or worthless metaphysician. An intellectual justification of unhappiness—the greatest that has been attempted—is worth the examination of one who is interested in Leopardi & Proust rather than in Carducci & Barrès."[22] In line with Proust's deni-gration of abstract intelligence, Beckett insists that he is not "reading phi-losophy" as such. He delves into those texts in order to justify his main affect, unhappiness. He does not care whether Schopenhauer is not a seri-ous enough thinker, as long as he brings food for thought or the imagina-tion; this was not just because he was a pessimist but also because he held that philosophy should be as well written as literature. Schopenhauer's attacks on Hegel targeted the latter's opaque sentences. Nietzsche, who claimed to have been "educated" by Schopenhauer, continued the same crusade against turgid philosophical writing.

The main exception among those philosophers is Kant, even though he was not, admittedly, a great stylist. Let us return to Myskja's contention that the Kantian sublime makes sense of Beckett's radical departures, self-contradictions, and parodies, thus to his main question: "How can this form of self-negation give rise to the feeling of the sublime?"[23] We may agree that the sublime presupposes that the imagination is unable to form a picture of plot or characters while enjoying something that comes close to sacred terror. There is a lot to gain from the sublime—and Myskja's thesis is consistent: "The claim I want to make is the following. The sublime is experienced by a feeling connected to a 'reality' beyond the empirical world. This feeling indicates human freedom from the regularity of causal laws and social norms . . . because we are self-legislating as Kant says."[24]

The Sublime and the Bathos

To examine whether Beckett's references to Kant and the sublime warrant such assumptions, we should start from the notes on philosophy kept at Trinity College. As we have seen, Beckett copied extensive passages from textbooks by Archibald Alexander, Wilhelm Windelband, and John Burnet. With Kant, however, something different happened. When in 1933 Beckett was taking notes on Kant from Windelband's *A History of Philosophy*, once in a while, he would erupt in scorn or anger. This happened mostly when Windelband discussed Kant's moral philosophy. Beckett copied:

> The problem arises whether there is a *practical synthesis a priori*, i.e. *necessary ad universally valid objects of willing*; i.e. anything which the reason makes its end *a priori, without regard to empirical maxims*; i.e. a *moral law*.
>
> This activity of the reason, if there be any such, must appear as a *command*, in the form of an *imperative*, distinct from the empirical maxims of will and action. The true rational will cannot be determined by the particular objects and relations of experience but by itself only. *It is necessarily directed toward something other than the natural impulses*, and this something, required by the moral law as over against the inclinations is duty.[25]

And then, just under, he added: "Tarataratata!" A little later, he inserted an exclamation mark in parenthesis, following: "Man does his duty *out of reverence for himself.*"[26] Beckett did not quote the end of the sentence: "and in his intercourse with his fellow-man he should make it his supreme maxim, never to treat him as a mere means for the attainment of his own ends, but always to honour in him the *worth of personality.*"[27] This was the type of glib and well-meaning morality that his Sadism would debunk. After that sentence, Beckett decided to abbreviate Kant, abbreviating "Categorical Imperative": "Essence of this system *the contrast between duty and inclination.* Only that will done, only man's duty is moral. Empirical impulses ethically indifferent, but become bad as soon as they oppose C. I. Hence life of man consists in his realising C.I. in its warfare against his inclinations"[28] Another note juxtaposes "Good Lord" with "C.I." Beckett adds in brackets: "But what the G. L. *are* the maxims?" Beckett's reading was attentive, for indeed, nowhere in Windelband can one find a definition of these maxims.

Frustrated with this summary, Beckett continued bravely until he reached the underlined statement; "*Virtue alone is worthy of happiness.*"[29] He copied the following sentence: "Since this has no counterpart empirically, the *reality of highest good* requires another skip into the supersensuous and the postulate of *extra-empirical personality, immortal life, moral order of the universe,* grounded in a Supreme *Reason—in God.*"[30] after which he added the sarcastic remark in French: "Rien que ça [Just that]." The deflation is wonderful. The word *skip* sums up and sends up drolly Windelband's ponderous "beyond the order of Nature, on into the supersensuous."[31]

After that point, Beckett's note-taking becomes spotty. He has only two pages of notes for Kant's third *Critique.* Windelband, like all nineteenth-century neo-Kantians, considered the third *Critique* as a superfluous addition. Nevertheless, as discussed earlier, he could explain cogently the distinction between the beautiful and the sublime. In spite of these clear definitions, Beckett showed no interest in these at the time, which suggests that in the early 1930s at least, the Kantian sublime was not a theme that attracted his attention. As he saw it then, the sublime would entail a "jump" into another "reality" beyond the empirical world. Such an unaccountable leap of faith left him sniggering: he objected that this constituted an unwarranted switch from aesthetics to ethics. On the other hand, Beckett was hugely interested in Kant's theory of freedom, and took copious notes on it. The gist of it was Kant's thesis that considerations of freedom make us forget "the regularity of causal laws and social norms." This rang true for Beckett, who agreed with the argument that such bracketing off of causality can make us become aware of ourselves as autonomous self-legislators.

Why had Beckett been reading Kant—via Windelband—so attentively and so critically? His London psychoanalyst, Bion, knew Kant well, and later introduced all his books with a Kantian grid of schemes and concepts. Beckett's carping and caviling did not prevent him from acquiring the collected works of Kant in German in 1938. This purchase concluded his tour of Germany. Beckett announced to McGreevy on January 5, 1938: "The entire works of Kant arrived from Munich. I had to go away beyond Gare de l'Est to collect them. I haven't had time to open them, two immense parcels that I could hardly carry from customs to taxi."[32] Having struggled with these eleven volumes myself, I can conclude that Beckett was a very strong man.

On the night of January 6, Beckett was stabbed and almost killed on the spot by a pimp armed with a knife as he was walking on Avenue d'Orléans, not far from Alésia. There is no connection between the two events, except that the life-threatening wound and the subsequent recovery prevented Beckett from opening Kant's volumes for a while. The edition that he bought was the standard *Immanuel Kants Werke*, edited by Ernst Cassirer, Hermann Cohen, and others and published in Berlin from 1921 to 1923. In May 1938, fully restored to health, Beckett wrote: "I read nothing and write nothing, unless it is Kant (*de nobis ispsis silemus*) and French anacreontics."[33] Indeed, Kant's epigraph to the *Critique of Pure Reason*, taken from Bacon: "Of our own person we will say nothing,"[34] will be claimed by the Unnamable: "*De nobis ipsis silemus*, decidedly that should have been my motto. Yes, they gave me some lessons in pigsty latin, too."[35] Of course, this particular narrator will no more be able to keep silent about himself than Cousse's pig chatting on endlessly in his deathsty. The proud motto of *De nobis ipsis silemus* was to announce a new departure, free of subjective prejudice, an impersonal beginning, leading to the form of the law. Hence Beckett's subsequent immersion in Kant's works was intense: "I read an average of an hour a day, after an hour the illusion of comprehension ceases, Kant, Descartes, Johnson, Renard, and a kindergarten manual of science."[36] He alludes often to Kant in the "Whoroscope" notebook, which was composed in 1938. We find thus: "das fruchtbare Bathos der Erfahrung (Kant)/Bathos: deep (Gr.),"[37] soon to be quoted in *Watt*'s addenda.[38] "Das fruchtbare Bathos der Erfahrung ["the fruitful bathos of experience]" comes from the *Prolegomena to any future metaphysics*. Kant attacks a reviewer who had misunderstood his first *Critique*, and for this uses "Bathos" in its literal sense of "low place," meaning simply "experience."

Beckett was conversant with the term *bathos*, a word that Pope flaunted to debunk the "ridiculous and failed sublime" of poets.[39] He uses it when Belacqua prepares his famous toast, whose consistency has to be dry and hard, hence quasi charred, in order to avoid a soft mulch in the middle: "If there was one thing he abominated more than another it was to feel his teeth meet in a bathos of pith and dough."[40] A little later, Belacqua appears caught up in a sadistic fantasy facing the remainder of flabby and deliquescent breadcrumbs that the French call "la mie": "He laid his cheek against the soft of the bread, it was spongy and warm, alive. But he would very soon take that plush feel off it, by God but he would very quickly take that fat white look off its face."[41] As discussed in chapter 4, these images evoke the little drama in which Cain's rueful countenance appears on the moon surface, a surface replicated by a singed toast that has barely avoided being consumed in a holocaust offering to the gods.

Indeed, the pathos unleashed by the sublime often turns into its contrary, the pathetically ridiculous. Similarly, Kant explains that one should avoid unnecessary flights into the heights of metaphysical speculation: "Note: High towers and the metaphysically-great man resembling them, around both of which there is usually much wind, are not for me. My place is the fertile *bathos* of experience."[42] In January 1782, Kant had been taken to task by Christian Garve who attacked the *Critique of Pure Reason* in a very confused manner. Kant responded pithily, concluding his defense in this way: "my would-be judge has not correctly understood the least bit of it, and what's more, has not correctly understood himself."[43] Beckett rephrased it in his notes: "Not only did he know nothing, but he was ignorant of the fact."[44] This is to be found in the "Whoroscope" notebook, in which Beckett duly copied Kant's satirical barb—the statement carries its lesson with respect to Geulincx: for the Flemish philosopher as for Socrates, it was crucial to *know* that one does not know anything—Geulincx, Kant, and Socratic irony thus meet.

Just before this sentence, there was a quote from the last volume of the Kant set, volume 11, which consists in a general introduction to Kant's life and philosophy by Ernest Cassirer, *Kants Leben und Lehre* (1923): "Socrates. Tí Èsti (Kant XI 294)."[45] Here, Beckett quoted page 294 of Cassirer's volume; Cassirer explained how Kant's *Critique* rephrased the Socratic question about the essence of a thing, concept, or virtue. Kant would ask: "What is this?" differently; instead of a question about the essence, he posed a question about the conditions of possibility of knowing anything.

This is why, in his *Prolegomena*, Kant can reject all accusations of idealism; he insists that his system is distinct from Descartes's skeptical idealism or Berkeley's dogmatic idealism; his philosophy could be called a "formal idealism," provided one adds the mention that it is a "critical idealism." The polemic asides on the reflexivity of ignorance amused Beckett, which led him to a second commentator. Thus, after several notes taken from Cassirer, there is a long series of quotes from Fritz Mauthner. After this, references to Kant are interspersed with passages from Mauthner's second volume of the *Sprachkritik*, in which Mauthner offered an original assessment of Kant. One might say that Mauthner played for Beckett the role that David Hume played for Kant: both helped the previous thinker break with a "dogmatic sleep" by introducing skepticism. For Kant, dogmatic sleep was precritical metaphysics, for Beckett it consisted of his uncritical endorsement of an avant-gardist *mythos*, the Jungian term that Eugene Jolas kept using about the later Joyce.

Mauthner was the object of intense discussions between Joyce and Beckett when they were working together in Paris.[46] What the Austrian philosopher of language brought to the Irish exiles was *Sprachkritik*, or the critique of language, an expression implying a radical skepticism facing language. Mauthner's influence on Beckett was first explored in depth by Linda Ben-Zvi, and more recently by Matthew Feldman.[47] Mauthner saw Kant as paving the way to his own work. Kant's sad fate was that, like Moses, he could not enter the promised land of *Sprachkritik*. The following passage comes in the context of an analysis of the effects of metaphors in philosophy:

> In Kant we see the fusion of the astuteness of the most honest Schoolmen and the matter-of-fact doubt of the English. Kant has guided the world up to our present. He knows—admittedly only from the point of view of the critique of language—that human concepts are always attached to pictorial representations and that we will never reach the knowledge of the real world, of the thing-in-itself, because our thinking—as we can have him say without any violence to him—is metaphorical and anthropocentric. It is to be put to Kant's credit that he managed to harness the ambitious pronouncements of Locke's representations and make them serve a newer investigation of the sensory organs, thereby paving the way for us. From Kant's work, one could deduce an unassailable critical epistemology of the "not-knowing" (*eine unangreifbare kritische Erkenntnistheorie des Nichtwissens*) that would be even freer than the once famous *docta ignorantia* of Nicolas of Cues. In his negative thinking, Kant already destroys everything (*der Alleszerstrümmerer*); we bow before the intellect that in its strongest moments began such a gigantic work, which it was necessary to per-

form as a self-deconstruction of language or thought (*als Selbstzerset-zung der Sprache oder des Denkens*).[48]

Mauthner's encomium stops short, and then he proceeds to explain why Kant failed to realize such a sweeping critical program:

> But Kant's final worldview nevertheless still stems from a transition period; or perhaps it was the awareness of his gigantic powers that misled him into the transformation of the negative action into a positive system. No matter how, he stands in relation to absolute reason as Count Mirabeau stood facing absolute monarchy. He wants to bring it back to definite limits, he wants to destroy its misuse, he wants to throw it down from its throne in order to prevent it from using an illogical right of veto.[49]

The metaphors are loaded and politically charged: Kant is a revolutionary destroyer who then drew back, frightened by the consequences of his radical gesture. Kant could not help restoring if not absolute reason at least practical reason, but from there, all the rest would follow. Kant is the philosophical Moses who stays outside the paradise of critical semantics opened by Mauthner: "Kant remained in front of the portals of truth. Only the critique of language can open these portals."[50] We find echoes of this tension in Beckett's "Whoroscope" notebook, when the reference to Kant's *Bathos* is followed by another quote from the second volume of the *Beiträge*. It concerns the issue of animal language and freedom: "We should not think that we are freer than animals with our language. Surely, animals are under the yoke of necessity in their orientation. The chain can be longer or shorter, according to whether the senses of perception carry far or not; it is by this chain that necessity drags the amoeba exactly as it does with the intelligent dog. And the chain of man who is richly endowed with sense is so long that he thinks he is free."[51] Then the notebook follows Mauthner who shifts to a discussion of writing, calling man a "reading and writing animal." Mauthner splices together the critique of language, the critique of freedom, and the centrality of metaphorical writing. But he does not give its due importance to a central Kantian concept, that of freedom.

Eleutheriologies

Thanks to Cassirer, Beckett became interested in the Kantian word for freedom, the Greek word of *eleutheria*. *Eleutheria*, which happened to be the title of Oscar Wilde's first collection of poems, also suggested for Beckett a strong passion for freedom. In Beckett's works, this concern bridges the gap between a first period defined by *Murphy* and other English prose texts, and the second period marked by plays, stories, and novels written in French.

Kant was led into heady debates about the difficulties generated by his belief in an unconditional freedom. One of his first detractors, Johann August Heinrich Ulrich, wrote a book entitled *Eleutheriology*, an aggressive pamphlet in which he severely criticized Kant's main concepts, mostly attacking Kant's idea of freedom.[52] *Eleutheriology, or On Freedom and Necessity*, published in 1788, tried to oppose a modern (that is, post-Cartesian) idea of science to Kant's moral idealism. Ulrich, himself a disciple of Leibnitz, combined scientific determinism and philosophical rationalism. For him, Kant's mistake had been to stray away from the safe path of the *"Bathos der Erfahrung."* Kant, he argued, contradicted scientific determinism by postulating that reason requires freedom as a principle, as he did in the second *Critique* (*Critique of Practical Reason*) in which freedom intervenes as an a priori concept. Ulrich refused the idea that there would be no morality without absolute freedom and moreover rejected timeless and abstract categories like the categorical imperative. If freedom was not rejected as an idea by Ulrich, at least it would have to be measured by psychology. Ulrich wanted to find a middle ground between categories based on principles and daily experience marked by chance, contingency, and randomness.

The objection was serious. Kant took notes that he gave to his friend from Königsberg, the legal theoretician Kraus.[53] Kraus had then to battle with *Eleutheriology*. He tried to prove that Kant paid close attention to the link between the practical and the theoretical, but the question remains: how can one reconcile natural necessity with its deterministic laws and the unconditional principles of understanding leading us to morality? A third critique was needed to reconcile incompatible postulations of teleology, determinism, and unconditional principles. In *Eleutheriology*, Ulrich thought that a limited determinism was enough to account both for moral actions and for scientific progress. Against this, Kant and Kraus assert that nothing can be known of freedom: freedom cannot be measured; it is not an object of the world; it can only be understood as a pure principle. Indeed, freedom is "absolute" because it is constitutive, exactly as time and space provide a constitutive framework enabling our perception of the empirical world. Even scientific determinism could not be founded rigorously in a vague Providence or thanks to the laws of a limited determinism.

Beckett discovered that controversy and heard in *eleutheria* echoes of a further excess. The word carried a whiff of "elation" while bringing along something darker, closer to mania or hysteria. We hear of this affection as a specific Irish malady thanks to a nice joke in *Murphy*: "The turf was truly Irish in its eleutheromania, it would not burn behind bars."[54] The disease of eleutheromania is an ethical disease with political overtones since it means craving for freedom, and trying to get it at any cost.[55] Eleutheromania is given a new lease of life in Kant's theory of freedom. Here is the root of the serious philosophical debate underpinning Beckett's first French play, a true farce, *Eleutheria*. Beckett was wondering how to stage the Kantian dead end of unconditional freedom.

Beckett's original answer to the question was by creating a rhythmical division of the space. *Eleutheria*'s innovative conceit presents its stage as divided in two. If we only read the text and forget the detailed stage directions preceding it, we may miss the fact that Victor Krap, the absent character who attracts the passions (whether for love or education) of all the others, exactly the way Murphy is situated at the core of *Murphy*, is in fact present on the stage. He is quite visible all the time, on stage but silent, a shadowy figure from the other side. The Note on the stage setup poses the inevitable question of how it may be possible to "convey scenically the sense of a dualistic space less via transition effects than through the fact that Victor's room takes up three quarters of the stage and by the flagrant disharmony between the two sets of furnishings."[56] What is more, each act changes the perspective: in the first act, Victor's room is on the left; in the second act, it is on the right; and in the final act, it occupies the entire space. This spatial juxtaposition generates less a neat Cartesian division between mind and body, or between bourgeois order and the rebellious chaos belonging to Vicor, than a deliberate imbalance that literalizes the riddle of the play. Victor, about whom his well-off parents seem worried, refuses to talk to them, to see them, or to live a normal life. The key to the riddle, we discover, lies in the hero's symptom, his eleutheromania.

The difference with the plot of *Murphy* is that Victor's statements are hopelessly muddled, contradictory, and self-canceling: "If I was dead I wouldn't know I was dead. I want to squeeze pleasure out of my death. That's where freedom lies: seeing oneself dead."[57] His name, Victor Krap, enhances the atmosphere of scatological farce, well relayed by the name of Doctor Piouk, but confirms that he can only be entitled to a Pyrrhic victory. His eagerly sought and obtained freedom discloses only a death wish; but it is a social death wish only, and Victor in the end decides that he does not even want to die, only agonize slowly as long as he can. Besides, his absurd or empty "victory" as a dropout eager to leave the entire social system behind triggers mounting aggressions from all the others.

Whereas Murphy was the universal object of desire, Victor's stubborn resistance even to meaning and humanity (the play ends when he remains alone on his bed and turns his "scrawny back" on "mankind"—"*le maigre dos tourné à l'humanité*"[58]) only brings about loathing or belligerence. Thus the Spectator enlists a Chinese torturer called Tchoutchi to force Victor to speak. It is only because the Glazier warns Victor that he is about to be tortured that he explains his position, which he does, but weakly, badly, and confusingly. *Eleutheria* demonstrates that when Kantian and Mauthnerian categories merge in a nihilistic rejection of the human—in a savage debunking of the humanism professed by well-meaning but stupid or sadistic petty bourgeois, workers, and rich philistines alike—the result is an excremental farce combining torture and bathos.

The term *bathos* captures rather well the tone of Beckett's first completed play; *eleutheria* overlaps partly with the Kantian sublime when the latter gives access to moral freedom, but it remains a farce that takes its point of departure in the pathetic aftermath of a young man's decision to be absolutely free, without any consideration of consequences for his parents or for his lover. Here, bathos is not just a "bad pathos," as Pope would have it, but also a "low pathos." Pathos evokes a whole spectrum of emotions ranging from the lofty to the obscene. Beckettian bathos works by exhibiting the body caught in its baser functions. This is not the tragic awareness of Sophocles's "*pathos mathos*" (one learns after one has suffered, one has to suffer in order to learn anything), but an original "*bathos mathos*": one will learn only by going to the heights *and* to the depths of anything.

Before writing *Eleutheria*, Beckett had used the term *bathos* in a letter from 1935 in which he made fun of Balzac's style: "Am reading the Cousine Bette. The bathos of style & thought is so enormous that I wonder is he writing seriously or in parody. And yet I go on reading."[59] Even when rejecting Balzac's realism, Beckett confesses that he cannot stop reading the text. He was discovering that the most entrancing page-turners are often written badly (the novels of Ayn Rand come to mind). Beckett's negative assessment is not arbitrary—Balzac dashed this sprawling novel in less than two months. He did not care for style but aimed at writing as fast as the *feuilletonnistes* of the period. He was the first to be surprised when the novel became a classic. The point of his exaggerated bathos—this will not be lost for *Happy Days*—is that one may wonder whether any sentence is serious or a mere parody; hence the added power of the novel. The unleashing of the terrible violence of "Bette," whose ominous name sounds like "beast" in French, is only one instance of this productive hesitation between a savage comedy of manners and a laughably pathetic attempt at early naturalism. Such a hesitation will impact Beckett's sense of the comic for good.

Given all these cross-references, one might say that Beckett's intellectual evolution duplicates Kant's passage from the first to the third *Critique*. For Beckett, a first critique consisted in rejecting the representational mode of classical fiction—this was a critique of representative reason in the name of the unconscious or productive unreason. This defines the trajectory of the prewar Beckett works, when Beckett was still an avant-gardist in the *transition* mode who preferred the dark mythos of irrational expression to clear plots and all-around characters. Expression entailed scouring the depths of a divided subjectivity, leading to an excavation of the most obscure recesses of the self. A second moment corresponded to an ethical mode of thinking art, moving an ethics of nonrelation. Here was the root of Beckett's critique of practical reason: the question about the truth of art leads to the ethical positioning of absolute freedom. Eleutheromania, the madness of freedom, had to be reconciled with truth as Aletheia. Finally, a third moment led to a third critique by pushing the critique of judgment beyond its limits until it turned into a critique of the imagination.

With *How It Is* and the later texts, the serial death and rebirth of the imagination is achieved by staging a dominantly sadistic fantasy. It is by traversing the perverse fantasy of unceasing torture that Beckett can release an imagination that is not private or singular but collective, conflating the hell of life and the remaining images of a lost paradise. If both imaginary worlds are founded on an absolute freedom, a limit will come from the suffering of the others; then the expression of freedom will lead to penury, poverty, and parsimony.

CHAPTER 8

Dialectics of Enlittlement

In *Eleutheria* as in *Murphy*, the central issue is the dead end created by the insistence on the free possession of one's self—thus Murphy is split between his mind and his body, his sexual desire and his regressive wish to become a psychotic. Victor's autistic refusal leads him to a strange levity, as sort of levitation over the world of social contacts, which describes his own freedom of the void. He does enjoy the unbearable lightness of being, doing all he can to push away the heaviness of his family and love entanglements. Such a nihilism is given the most consistent voice by Doctor Piouk who launches an impassioned tirade against generation and birth. Piouk has found a radical solution to solve the problems of the human species:

> I would ban reproduction. I would perfect the condom and other devices and bring them into general use. I would establish teams of abortionists, controlled by the State. I would apply the death penalty to any woman guilty of giving birth. I would drown all newborn babies. I would militate in favour of homosexuality and would myself give the example. And to speed things up, I would encourage recourse to euthanasia by all possible means, although I would not make it obligatory.[1]

Listening to this and beaming, Madame Krap just adds: "I was born too early."[2] Halfway between Malthus and Sade, Piouk wants to stop the propagation of the "abominable" species of the humans. As Borges's philosopher had it, mirrors and paternity are abominable because they reproduce the human species.[3] One could add the imagination to the list.

Against such a nihilist drift, the moral law formalizes what is humanly possible to do and know. In *Watt*, the mysterious Mr. Knott, who calls up Kant in many ways, reminds us of this law by naming what one cannot do. The project of *Watt* is comparable to Adorno's and Horkheimer's *Dialectic of Enlightenment*, a book coincidentally written by two exiles from Nazi Germany at the same time. Like the refugees from the Frankfurt school, Beckett aims at a questioning of the "madness of Reason," a madness that he evoked in an interview with Michael Haerdter: "The crisis started with the end of the 17th century, after Galileo. The 18th century has been called the century of reason, *le siècle de la Raison*. I've never understood that; they're all mad, *ils sont tous fous, ils déraisonnent*! They give reason a responsibility which it simply can't bear. . . . The Encyclopedists wanted to know everything . . . But that direct relation between the self and—as the Italians say—*lo scibile*, the knowable, was already broken."[4] Beckett guessed that Sade's cruelty was the exact reverse of Kant's formalism, a point made recently—even violently and obscenely—by Jonathan Littel in *The Kindly Ones*.[5]

Watt's Rats

Watt was written when Beckett was hiding from the Gestapo between 1942 and 1945 in Roussillon. This beautiful village in the South of France is within eyesight of the neighboring village of La Coste—a mere fifteen miles away, in fact. Sade's castle, at that time fully in ruins, now partly rebuilt, is visible from certain ridges above Roussillon facing the slightly higher Lubéron chain of mountains. What would have Beckett thought of this ominous proximity, at a time when history seemed to present the possibility of unleashing wholesale sadism with all its attendant torture chambers, and when, as Pasolini demonstrated in his *Salò* film, Sade's cruel fantasies had come back to life with a vengeance? One may pose the question knowing that Beckett had taken to Sade's works. He had accepted to translate Sade's *Hundred and Twenty Days of Sodom* for Jack Kahane who had founded the Obelisk Press in 1938. Here is the passage from a letter to Thomas McGreevy in which he discusses the book: "I have read 1st and 3rd vols. of French edition. The obscenity of surface is indescribable.

Nothing could be less pornographical. It fills me with a kind of metaphysical ecstasy. The composition is extraordinary, as rigorous as Dante's. If the dispassionate statement of 600 'passions' is Puritan and a complete absence of satire juvenalesque, then it is, as you say, puritanical and juvenalesque."[6]

Beckett insisted that he would write a preface for his forthcoming translation. The comparison with Dante is illuminating because it throws a bridge between the links we have analyzed between Dante, Proust, and Joyce, and Beckett's later work. It is not too fanciful to imagine a puritan Sade. The insight anticipates the theses developed a few years later by Klossowki and Blanchot, as we have seen. Beckett distinguishes between "surface obscenity" and pornography, because Sade's conception was "metaphysical," the creation of an antitheology. Beckett perceived from the start Sade's rivalry with God. Sade the writer wanted to show everything, including whatever exceeds the "stage," in which we find the root of "obscenity," while attempting to seduce the reader by erotic images and the use of reason. Reason, contaminated by obscenity, leads to its undoing, which coincides with an exploration of the limits of ethics.

This starting point helps us understand Beckett's deployment of sadist fantasies in *Watt*. They appear most clearly in the third chapter of *Watt*. At that point of the novel, we find ourselves in a curious asylum. Its inmates include Sam, who looks very much like the author, and Watt, who has already left Mr. Knott's house. We are told that the previous chapters were narrated by Watt to Sam in this institution. One of the favorite pastimes of Sam and Watt during their daily conversations is to play with young rats by the river:

> But our particular friends were the rats, that dwelt by the stream. They were long and black. We brought them tidbits from our ordinary as rinds of cheese, and morsels of gristle, and we brought them also birds' eggs, and frogs, and fledglings. Sensible of these attentions, they would come flocking round us at our approach, with every sign of confidence and affection, and glide up our trouserlegs, and hang upon our breasts. And then we would sit down in the midst of them, and give them to eat, out of our hands, of a nice fat frog, or a baby thrush. Or seizing suddenly a plump young rat, resting in our bosom after its repast, we would feed it to its mother, or its father, or its sister, or to some less fortunate relative.
>
> It was on these occasions, we agreed, after an exchange of views, that we came nearest to God.[7]

Here, all the characteristics of Sadian mischief are on display. The pastoral Rousseauism is turned upside down. Just before, Watt and Sam were frolicking in lush meadows, enjoying the charms of Nature. Like Sade, Sam and Watt forge a conflicted relationship to this "mother," demonstrating that its basic law is that of reciprocal murder. And the object of Sade's transgressive gestures is always parenthood. Similarly, Beckett subverts here the foundational notion of the family as the site of morality. Not unlike the Libertine's endless exactions and tortures, Sam's and Watt's actions shift vertiginously from a sham goodness for animals to cruelty, surprising the poor creatures who had believed in their benevolence. Like Sade's hyper discursive torturers, the two friends "reason" upon their actions.

Another passage from the same chapter adds to this fundamental sadism a series of oblique allusions to Nazi death camps. The institution in which Watt and Sam have become friends looks less like a mental hospital than a concentration camp. "This garden was surrounded by a high barbed wire fence, greatly in need of repair, of new wire, of fresh barbs" (*W*, 156). Gardens surround little houses, the houses being connected by a dense network of hedges; whoever wants to pass from one house to another risks being caught in barbed wire, a fate comically evoked by the language of serial lists:

> While persons at once broad-shouldered and big-bellied, or broad-basined and big-bottomed, or broad-basined and big-bellied, or broad-shouldered and big-bottomed, or big-bosomed and broad-basined, would on no account, if they were in their right sense, commit themselves to this treacherous channel, but turn about, and retrace their steps, unless they wished to be impaled, at various points at once, ands perhaps bleed to death, or be eaten alive by the rats, or perish from exposure, long before their cries were heard; and still longer before the rescuers appeared, running, with the scissors, the brandy and the iodine. (*W*, 157)

Here is one instance when rats have been allowed to take their revenge on humans!

For Beckett as for Sade, the foundation of the cruel fantasy is an inverted theology. Sade's libertines have such a hatred of religion that in the *120 Days of Sodom* the most severely punished violation is to mention God. This point had not been missed by Beckett, who rewrites Pascal's maxim about man who wants to be an angel or god but who ends up being a beast; in *Watt* man is not even able to be a rat. Animality is not a solution for men, even though we know that rats are intelligent, curious, and even theological, creatures. Indeed, they happen once in a while to eat a consecrated host. As Mr. Spiro lectures to Watt in a train, this predicament poses a problem concerning the transubstantiation of the host:

> A rat, or other small animal, eats of a consecrated wafer.
>   1. Does he ingest the Real Body, or does he not?
>   2. If he does not, what has become of it?
>   3. If he does, what is to be done with him? (*W*, 28)

The attempt to provide a solution generates a sublimely serial textuality:

> Mr. Spiro now replied to these questions, that is to say he replied to question one and he replied to question three. He did so at length, quoting from Saint Bonaventura, Peter Lombard, Alexander of Hales, Sanchez, Suarez, Henno, Soto, Diana, Concina and Dens, for he was a man of leisure. But Watt heard nothing of this, because of other voices, singing, crying, stating, murmuring, things unintelligible, in his ear. With these, he was not familiar, he was not unfamiliar either. So he was not alarmed, unduly. Now these voices, sometimes they sang only, and sometimes they cried only, and sometimes they stated only, and sometimes they murmured only, and sometimes they sang and cried, and sometimes they sang and stated, and sometimes they sang and murmured, and sometimes they cried and stated, and some- times they cried and murmured, and sometimes they stated and mur- mured, and sometimes they sang and cried and stated . . . (*W*, 28)

These endless verbal permutations make *Watt* recognizable, and their idiomatic signature launches the whole writing into a serial exhaustion by enumeration. A semantic vertigo parallels the absurdly rational knowledge of theologians. Here, logical exhaustion leads to a hollowing out of mean- ing. No doubt Watt understands almost nothing in Spiro's verbiage, and while he shuts off his mind, he announces the perverse couples of later plays, as when Lucky is forced to think on command in *Waiting for Godot*. This passage is followed by a paragraph in which, for the first time in the novel, a device appears that will recur systematically—the mimetic render- ing of a lacuna: "The racecourse now appearing, with its beautiful white railing, in the fleeing lights, warned Watt that he was drawing near, and that when the train stopped next, then he must leave it. He could not see the stands, the grand, the members', the people's, so? when empty with their white and red, for they were too far off" (*W*, 29). Syntax has given up, the non sequitur of the perceiving subject's perspectivism has been replaced by a network of gaps and silences that signals a deviant textuality.

The isotopy of the rat, an animal posited as a limit to the human, functions as a red thread in these complex devices. If man cannot even aspire to the dignity of a rat, according to Beckett, it is that he never raises himself above the level of the termite: "For the only way one can speak of nothing is to speak of it as though it were something, just as the only way one can speak of God is to speak of him as though he were a man, which to be sure he was, in a sense, for a time, and as the only way one can speak of man, even our anthropologists have realized that, is to speak of him as though he were a termite" (*W*, 77). A philosophy of the "as if" is the only access to a true definition of man. Given the limits of language previously sketched, one can say that if man is not a metaphor, man can be man only by catachresis, that is to say by an abuse of language.

The idea recurs when Watt tries out names on things as if they were old rags found in an attic. "Not that Watt was in the habit of affirming things of himself, for he was not, but he found it a help, from time to time, to be able to say, with some appearance of reason, Watt is a man, all the same, Watt is a man, or, Watt is in the street, with thousands of fellow-creatures, within call" (*W*, 82). Troubled, Watt can no more say of a pot that it is a pot than of a man that it is a man:

> And Watt's need of semantic succour was at times so great that he would set to trying names on things, and on himself, almost as a woman hats. . . . As for himself, though he could no longer call it a man, as he has used to do, with the intuition that he was perhaps not talking nonsense, yet he could not imagine what else to call it, if not a man. But Watt's imagination had never been a lively one. So he continued to think of himself as a man, as his mother had taught him, when she said, There's a good little man, or There's a bonny little man, or There's a clever little man. But for all the relief that this afforded him, he might just as well have thought of himself as a box, or an urn. (*W*, 83)

By a curious slippage, this linguistic dereliction calls up the crisis of language experienced by Lord Chandos in Hugo von Hofmannsthal's famous "Letter," a text dating from 1902. In his letter, young Lord Chandos announces to his friend Bacon that he has resolved to abandon writing because of a paroxystic crisis he experienced when drowning rats: suddenly he felt empathy with the rats that he was killing. A similar crisis produces in Watt a feeling of despair that nevertheless inverts itself in ultimate relief. For Watt at any rate, bliss comes when there is nothing to do, when all is lost, that is when even the rats have abandoned the sinking ship of language:

> Not that Watt longed at all times for this restoration, of things, of himself, to their comparative innocuousness, for he did not. For there were times when he felt a feeling closely resembling the feeling of satisfaction, at his being so abandoned, by the last rats. For after these there would be no more rats, not a rat left, and there were times when Watt almost welcomed this prospect, of being rid of his last rats, at last. It would be lonely, to be sure, at first, and silent, after the gnawing, the scurrying, the little cries. (*W*, 84)

These metaphysical rats traverse all the layers of pseudohumanity, moving from a voracious greed for godlike transcendence to animal panic facing death throes. In that sense, rats are more human than men, which explains this vignette of Beckett saving rats, after he had been shocked by the violence evinced by the farmers for whom he was working in Roussillon: "Josette Hayden could remember one occasion being with Beckett on the farm when the Audes discovered a rat and were about to kill it. Beckett rushed to intervene, picking the rat up and running across a field to let it run free into a ditch."[8]

Sade's Ataraxy

Indeed, we have moved away from Sam's and Watt's cruel games, but not so far away. It is because of the tension between an "unnamable" humanity and a sizable animality, a tension giving expression to the worst perversions humanity is capable of, that an ethics is all the more needed. Beckett's sadism inverts the transcendent Law posited above humanity. His drift in *Watt* echoes the thesis about Sade developed by Adorno in *The Dialectic of Enlightenment*.[9] For Adorno, who actually wrote the Sade essay alone, Kantian reason leads to the calculating rationality of a totalitarian order. Its counterpart is the systematic mechanization of pleasures in Sade's perverse utopias. Kant's *Critique of Practical Reason* has stressed the autonomy, purity, and self-determination of the moral subject: the only condition set to define an ethical action is conformity with the form of practical reason. In Kant, the philosophy of Enlightenment meets global capitalism with a vengeance: any human concern has to be ruled out; what matters is merely the conformity of Reason with its own laws, a Reason that must then appear abstract and devoid of any object. All "human" affects are pushed further away from an independent and all powerful Reason. Juliette draws the conclusions that Kant denies: the bourgeois order of society justifies crime provided crime is regulated by a Reason controlling all activities and pleasures.

The Sadean goal of reaching apathy stressed by Blanchot—which entails sexual excess and horrible pain inflicted to others—functions like an equivalent of Kant's disinterestedness. Both are underpinned by the "brutal efficiency" of the bourgeois reordering of the world according to its own laws. Sade's vaunted "right to enjoyment" will imply a limitless and unstoppable extension of its field, up to a right to enjoy the bodies of others, and to do with them as one likes. The counterpart of this globalized rationality is the systematic mechanization of perverse pleasures in Sade's orgies; indeed, it was Roland Barthes who had astutely noted that the orgy functioned as a perfectly oiled mechanism; the orgy is not play but work, it is an erotic machine in which everyone has a precise function, and in which nobody can be idle.[10]

This dire image sends us on a new track with respect to *Watt*. We know how overdetermined the eponymous hero's name is; once we focus on its particular spelling, it may evoke less the old metaphysical question, the "What is x?" or the Socratic "Ti esti?" already hinted at, than point simply to the name of James Watt, the inventor of the steam engine. James Watt (1736–1819) was a contemporary of Kant (1724–1804) and of Sade (1740–1814). His name is synonymous with the launching of the industrial revolution in Europe. His principal invention presupposed the interaction of pistons, rods, and cylinders transforming energy into work. A psychoanalyst would recognize here a sexual mechanism: the steam engine emblematizes the way human bodies "work" to produce enjoyment in repetitive actions.

Similarly, when Kant's *Metaphysics of Morals* discusses the role of ownership in sexuality, it offers surprising and revealing definitions: "For the natural use that one makes of the other's sexual organs is *enjoyment*, for which one gives itself up to the other. In this act a human being makes himself into a thing, which conflicts with the right of humanity in his own person. There is only one condition under which this is possible: that while one person is acquired by the other *as if it were a thing*, the one who is acquired acquires the other in turn."[11] Such involuntary parody of marriage had amused Walter Benjamin. A dried-up vision of love as mutual commodification derives from Kant's relentless formalism. Benjamin paved the way for Adorno's later strictures in *Dialectic of Enlightenment* when he wrote in the mid-1920s: "Kant's definition of marriage in *The Metaphysics of Morals*, which is now and again remembered solely as an example of a rigoristic stereotype or a curiosity of his senile late period, is the most sublime product of a *ratio* that, incorruptibly true to itself, penetrates infinitely deeper into the facts of the matter than sentimental ratiocination. . . . From the objective nature of marriage, one could obviously deduce only its depravity—and in Kant's case this is what it willy-nilly amounts to."[12]

Benjamin notes the derisive sublimity of such a law, and quotes an even more revealing sentence by Kant, which is the beginning of the section: "*Sexual union* (*commercium sexuale*) is the reciprocal use that one human being makes of the sexual organs and capacities of another (*usus membrorum et facultatum sexualium altrius*). This is either a *natural* use . . . or an *unnatural* use, and unnatural use takes place either with a person of the same sex or with an animal of a nonhuman species."[13] One is tempted to ask whether sexual union with an animal that might be called "of a human species" like a house pet would be authorized by Kant.

For Kant, however, the law is the law only if it is devoid of content. The animal marks just a certain limit or a border, next to what he calls "perversion"—all the activities that delight Sade in fact. The irrepressible giggles that will greet these passages come from the fact that Kant tries very hard to exclude purely "human" considerations; what matters is the conformity of practical reason to maxims that turn into universal axioms. Following Blanchot's quote discussed in chapter 1, Lacan formulates Sade's law as: "Lend me the part of your body that will give me a moment of satisfaction and, if you care to, use for your own pleasure that part of my body which appeals to you."[14] Indeed, such a "reason" is undistinguishable from madness—a drift perceptible in Kant as well. Sade went further than Kant by giving free rein to his fantasies of tortures, the ultimate aim of which was to approximate the enjoyment that he imagined to be God's own. Sade's God is thus the *Dio boia* of *Ulysses*, a "hangman god," a supreme being presented as unsurpassable in evil, with a touch of Descartes's "porca Madonna" added in the novels promoting female Libertines like *Juliette, or Vice Amply Rewarded.*

Both Sade and Beckett deploy a negative theology with the aim of "excavating" the human subject; this antitheology also aims at transforming the practice of writing, a point made forcibly by Pierre Klossowski's book on Sade, which Beckett read with great interest in 1950.[15] Klossowski insists on the writerly aspect of the process, assuring that Sade could not be called a "pervert" or a monster: Sade was above all a writer, a rather boring and repetitive writer, for sure, but an author in the strong sense. Here is how Klossowski defines this "non-language" transforming the practice of

writing: "The parallelism between the apathetic reiteration of acts and
Sade's descriptive reiteration again establishes that the image of the act to
be done is re-presented each time not only as though it had never been
performed but also as though it had never been described. This reversibility of the same process inscribes the presence of non-language in language; it inscribes a foreclosure of language by language."[16] On this view,
Sade's writing hesitates between the repetitive fantasy of an outrage to a
Mother Nature and a question about the quintessence of God's enjoyment.

Sade's predatory transgressions question the limits of humanity by
deriding a law that presides over its limits. If it is this derision that requires
a different writing, we see the same postulation at the limit of the human
underpinning the serialist writing invented by Beckett in *Watt*. *Watt* trans-
forms Sade's infantile rage facing the mother's body into the hilarious
serenity of an unleashed pseudorationality. This writing takes its bearings
by combining Mr. Knott's name as both "no" and a "knot." Finally embody-
ing the figure of Descartes's dream who says: "Est et Non," Knott's incompatible attributes make him less a god of parody than a living node of
negations. Facing him, Watt can only experience "ataraxy," a solid numb-
ness destroying all affects:

> Watt suffered neither from the presence of Mr. Knott, not from his
> absence. When he was with him, he was content to be with him, and
> when he was away from him, he was content to be away from him.
> Never with relief, never with regret, did he leave him at night, or in
> the morning come to him again.
> This ataraxy covered the entire house-room, the pleasure-garden,
> the vegetable garden, and of course Arthur. (*W*, 207–8)

Ataraxy combines the Sadian ideal of impassibility in the most extreme
enjoyments and the Kantian idea of an autonomous regulation of Reason
by itself. Thus the central question of *Watt* is a Sado-Kantian interrogation: "But what was this pursuit of meaning in this indifference to meaning?" (*W*, 75). Thus the post-Kantianism *Watt* is the effect of a linguistic
machine that stages Reason as torture, for rational knowledge barely hides
relations of fear and domination: "Too fearful to assume himself the onus
of a decision, said Mr. Hackett, he refers it to the frigid machinery of a
time-space relation" (*W*, 21). Sade and Beckett denounce the seamy side of
universalistic ethics. If man is defined as such by the unconditionality of a
rapport to the law, the Sadian subversion reminds us of the reverse of the
subject by pointing to an extreme law of enjoyment, and both find a quasi
purpose in the process: "And what is this coming that was not our coming

and this being that is not our being and this going that will not be our going but the coming and being and going in purposelessness" (*W*, 58).

The parallels between *Watt* and Sade's magnum opus are confirmed when we realize that the Addenda inserted by Beckett at the end of *Watt* find their model and origin in the Addenda appended by Sade at the end of *The 120 Days of Sodom*. In these supernumerary insertions, Sade invents, among other refined torments, the torture that so fascinated Freud's patient: his main obsession was about a rat forced to dig a passage into a victim's anus which gave him the Freudian nickname of "the Ratman." In Sade's huge roll of paper, the new tortures are added as frenzied afterthoughts; meanwhile, Sade does not forget to address himself:

> Under no circumstances deviate from this plan, everything has been worked out, the entirety several times re-examined with the greatest care and thoroughness.
>
> Detail the departures. And throughout the whole, introduce a quantity of moral dissertation and diatribe, above all at the suppers.[17]

Then he adds:

SUPPLEMENTARY TORTURES
—By means of a hollow tube, a mouse is introduced into her cunt, the tube is withdrawn, the cunt sewn up, and the animal unable to get out, devours the entrails. (*120 Days*, 673)

Watt's Addenda parody symbolical or allegorical interpretations by ending with "no symbols where none intended" (*W*, 255). However, Beckett hilariously insists on the serious intention of a novel that must be studied with attention: "The following precious and illuminating material should be carefully studied. Only fatigue and disgust prevented its incorporation" (*W*, 247). Many supplementary entries are parodies, like the rewriting of Faust's famous "Die Erde hat mich wieder" as "Die Merde hat mich wieder (*W*, 250)." Goethe's Faust had exclaimed: "The earth [*Erde*] claims me once more." Here, the text says simply, half in English, half in French: "Shit claims me once more." Moreover, it is in those endnotes that we find the precious reference to Kant's "fruchtbare Bathos der Erfahrung" discussed earlier (*W*, 354).

Beauty and Torture

We have seen in the discussion of aesthetics that there is just a step from *Watt*'s serial verbal permutations to the contemplation of Beauty, a step that was taken when Kant's "purposiveness without a purpose," the definition of beauty, appears in the second part of *Molloy*. Even if it acquires an ironic ring, the expression asserts a principle according to which meaning is granted to the world, even in the most innocent forms of beauty like flowers in the mountains. Beckett wants to query such assurance. He uses Moran's wish to work for serious motivations "more serious and imputable less to pleasure than to business."[18] Moran adds: "For it was only by transferring it to this atmosphere, how shall I say, of finality without end, why not, that I could venture to consider the work I had on hand."[19] First, Moran needs to withdraw from the "spray of phenomena," because he can only see his true goal when allowed to reach a purely disinterested activity. The Kantian paradox works better in the French text of *Molloy* with "finalité sans fin." This passage asserts that the aim of Moran's quest is not the object, that is Molloy, but the establishment of a link. This link is both a *report* and a *rapport*, which is the same word in French, both a narrative and an intellectual connection. The establishment of such a double *rapport* implies that we consider natural beauty as defined by Kant's judgment on the beautiful.

The judgment attributing beauty to *Zweckmässigkeit ohne Zweck*, "the form of purpose without a purpose" is an oxymoron meaning that a reflective judgment stemming from my perception of beautiful objects can give me an idea that the world containing such beautiful objects has the form of teleology. If I see beauty in the world, the world acquires the form of a purpose, without necessarily being teleological in itself. Whenever I perceive beauty, I sense that the world is not absurd, even if it is replete with absurd people, situations, and commands. Thus, the relation without a relationship, to translate a *rapport sans rapport*, again offers a key, as we have perceived in reference to Levinas: "For where Molloy could not be, nor Moran either for that matter, there Moran could bend over Molloy. And though this examination prove unprofitable and of no utility for the execution of my orders, I should nevertheless have established a kind of connexion, and one not necessarily false. For the falsity of the terms does not necessarily imply that of the relation, so far as I know."[20]

If the link between beauty and duty is not probed further in *Molloy*, a neo-Kantian appreciation of beauty as quasi teleology resurfaces in *Three Dialogues*, written more or less at the same time. When Freud smiles at Kant's naivety facing the beauty of stars at night, he makes room for the argument that the beauty of the world justifies the intervention of God, even though no divine handiwork is discernible in the distribution of moral conscience among human beings. Beckett follows Freud's skeptical lead: he, too, pokes fun at Kant's philosophy. However, the question about the form of teleology contained in aesthetics leads to an ethical principle entailing a duty to represent what cannot be represented. Like Mr. Knott, here is the knot tying up aesthetics and ethics in Beckett, and it keeps a Kantian ring even if it avoids the concept of the sublime.

When Beckett deployed his third critique, the critique of the imagination, in the later Fizzles and fragments, he implied that even when the imagination reproduces the torture of thought, it can bypass the finality of death. To understand what such a program entails, one would have to compare texts such as "Imagination dead, Imagine"[21] with its dry formalization of eroticism, and *Rough for Radio II*.[22] In the second text, a young and sexy Stenographer reads to an Animator a previously written "exhortation," after which they continue the torture of Fox, a poet. She rereads what had been noted: "Thus rigid enforcement of the tube feed, be it per buccam or be it on the other hand per rectum, is [']absolutely'—one word underlined—'essential. The least word let fall in solitude and thereby in danger, as Mauthner has shown, of being no longer needed, [']*may be it*'— these words underlined."[23] Mauthner devotes some space to considerations of the crucial link between language and power: "*Sprache ist eine Macht*"—an insight developed when he surveys philosophers of language and ends with Nietzsche.[24] Such considerations barely justify the sordid torture that is enacted in Beckett's play, culminating when Fox passes out after having rambled away poetically but incoherently. The stenographer's kiss fails to revive him; what remains of him are poetic fragments of a journal extorted by violent torture. In the end, the Animator inserts the words "between two kisses" in a passage that originally was not erotic—it merely evoked the death of an infant at the mother's breast, which gave some substance to the fantasy of an imaginary twin.

In a section of Mauthner's book devoted to the essence of language, one finds the maxim: "*Sprache ist Sprachgebrauch* [Language is the use of language]."[25] When words are not used or used in isolation, they die out and disappear. No solipsism is possible in language since it is fundamentally a social or collective activity. Language implies a natural communism— there is no private property in language.[26] In the play, the Animator enacts Mauthner's theories with a vengeance: if nothing belongs to anyone in particular, he is free to create meaning. He has absolute power, and yet, his attempt at making Fox reveal a secret fails because the tormentor remains romantically attached to the idea of an individual truth hidden in the folds of a metaphorical language. The torturer frantically searches for the "least word," for any hint betraying a secret. The torturer conflates speaker and speech in a Sadian version of Mauthner's skeptical nominalism. Beckett's Sadian fascination for torture derives from his meditation on the structure of language.

Developing the idea that torture is linked with language in her Nobel Prize acceptance speech, Elfriede Jelinek said: "Language should be tortured to tell the truth." Slavoj Žižek developed her insight, adding that language should be twisted, denaturalized, extended, condensed, cut, and reunited, and finally made to work against itself because most of the time language is the site of cruelty, indifference, and stupidity.[27] This insight suggests an important link between Beckett and an Austrian tradition going back to Thomas Bernhard and Elfriede Jelinek, and including the director Michael Haneke. The assimilated Austro-Hungarian Jew Fritz Mauthner would be its predecessor. Such a context makes sense of the idea launched by Beckett that he had taken the opposite road from that of Joyce—whereas Joyce believed in his power over language, Beckett would work only with ignorance and impotence. In fact, the choice of impotence and dispossession is a classical *topos* of Austrian thinking. It begins with Hugo von Hofmannsthal's "Letter" by Lord Chandos. A reenactment of Hofmannsthal's "Letter" appears at the end of Coetzee's novel, *Elizabeth Costello*, thanks to whom the Lord's letter is rewritten in the feminine, bringing a testament wrung out of the hell of nonlife.[28]

The Austrian idea that form—often allegorized as music by Bernhard or Jelinek—provides access to freedom by launching a bridge between ethics and literature has its relevance for Beckett. When he stated energetically that he was no philosopher, he implied that, for him, the experience of thinking was closer to music than ratiocination. Such a musical thinking would be determined as much by form as by content. It displays "brilliant" forms almost at will, it seems, yet these convey dark or dire truths. These truths act on us because they open holes in what we take to be our knowledge of the world. Beckett's texts think via performative perforations that play with philosophical axioms culled from authors like Kant or Descartes, then transform them, and finally make them radiate with a dark glow combining laughter and a heightened sense of form. Thus they do create formal beauty while questioning our usual values and meanings and dig deeper into the mind's darkness. Form leads to the creation of new values; a new aesthetics capable of piercing the opacity of language is unleashed thanks to the unbridled power of the Imagination. Beckett's texts always think even when they pretend that they don't, even that is, when they play the game of empty formalism.

A crucial lesson that Beckett learned from Kant is that even when formalism is empty, it is never pointless. What is more, Beckett's texts always lead to the postulation of values like courage, endurance, or resilient humor, even when they pretend that such values won't prevail in the world. We see this everywhere; here is a passage from *Molloy* in which the ethical quandary is once more examined: Molly has been invited to stay in Lousse's house even though he has run over and killed her dog (by staying with her, he will end up as her dog). Not sure what to do, he wonders whether he can appeal to a principle or to a "sense of values": "And how can you want to know? No, all that is not worth while, not worth while bothering about, and yet you do bother about it, your sense of values gone."[29] The French text says more pointedly: "inconscient des valeurs,"[30] thus suggesting that a nonknowledge about ethics is linked to the unconscious.

Molloy's rumination goes on until it exhausts itself and peters out: "And the things that are worth while [*qui valent la peine*] you do not bother about, you let them be, for the same reason, or wisely, knowing that all these questions of worth and value have nothing to do with you, who don't know what you're doing, nor why, and must go on not knowing it, on pain of [*sous peine de*], I wonder what, yes, I wonder."[31] The English version introduces an ambiguity not present in the French original, since one can introduce a pause after "go on" and parse: "must go on, not knowing it." Beckett's ethics is an ethics of "going on" while not knowing where, or knowing anything about the values underpinning the itinerary. It is precisely because one knows nothing that the ethical position gets stronger: because they are "unconscious of values," subjects keep on walking and living, even if higher principles are not available.

What stands out in the original is a balancing act carefully paralleling the "*choses qui valent la pein*e [the things that are worth while]" and a hidden transcendent law met as a limit, "*sous peine de*"—Pain of what? One might supply the missing word and assume that it is "on pain of death." But is it? Are we really discussing life and death issues? Whose death? The death of whose soul, if no one is quite sure of being a responsible subject? How can one be subjected to death if one cannot present oneself as an autonomous subject? Once we reach this point of subjective dissolution, the very thought of a "pain of death" only produces laughter, a weak laughter no doubt; it is laughter mixed with consternation, the low laughter of the dispossessed who muster strength enough to deride those famously absent principles and the sempiternally identical causes of pain.

We will have to examine this ethical laughter whose hums and titters never leave Beckett's split subjects in their endless and pointless quests, assuring them of one single certitude, that one can go on laughing: thanks to a certain laughter, life will appear as worth living even if it is full of pain and misery.

CHAPTER 9

Bathetic Jokes, Animal Slapstick, and Ethical Laughter

Is life worth living if it is but a brief interval full of misery, an anguished gasp exhaled between birth and death, as in the very short play *Breath*?[1] The question is reiterated in various modes and tones throughout Beckett's texts, as Christopher Ricks's breezy survey, *Beckett's Dying Words*, amply shows.[2] The recurring trope is enunciated most forcibly by Pozzo in a last speech before he disappears for good from the scene of Waiting for Godot: "One day, is that not enough for you, one day he went dumb, one day I went blind, one day we'll go deaf, one day we were born, one day we shall die, the same second, is that not enough for you? (*Calmer*) They give birth astride of a grave, the light gleams an instant, then it's night once more."[3] Not only is the subject of "give birth" *Elles* in the French version, which refers to women as mothers, but also pronouns keep shifting from I to he, and from we to they. Isn't this highly rhetorical tirade an example of the pathos that Beckett is trying to contain via parody, sarcasm, or mindless jokes? Here is the place to meditate on Beckett's use of the comic: what is comic here is the site of birth, provided it be linked with a deflated pathos that we have already encountered under the name of bathos. In short, my hypothesis is that Beckett's laughter derives from the bathos of birth.

When discussing Beckett's specific sense of humor, most critics begin by referring to Henri Bergson's influential *Laughter* (1900), a book whose central insight was that laughter is triggered by the combination of the mechanical and the human. We laugh, Bergson argues, when we see someone slip on a banana peel because that person suddenly becomes an automaton, a mere machine. He could have added that this works as well when we see the person as an animal, a recurrent resource of political satire and topical cartoons. Thus we smile when we see Molloy replace Lousse's dog after killing it by becoming her house pet. What was perceived as living, organic, and dynamic, suddenly becomes a grotesque puppet, or also, by another distortion, an animal instead of a human being. Caught by the sight, we forget our shared humanity and disregard pity. Here is the root of why we often laugh in a hostile manner, often as part of a group, or a collective ideology.

There is no lack of Bergsonian laughter in Beckett's works, if by this we refer to the powerful mechanism of slapstick. We find it at the beginning of *Krapp's Last Tape*: two finely printed pages document the details of the old man's routine, finding the keys, opening the drawer, peering into tapes, pulling a banana, peeling it, dropping the skin, treading on the skin, nearly falling, and so on.[4] A competent actor will make the most of these promptings, and with a measure of talent, will have the entire audience roaring with laughter in five minutes. In a similar mode, we have the hilarious scene of *Film* when Buster Keaton takes out the dog and forgets the cat, takes it out while the dog reenters, and so on.[5] This is a scene often seen in silent movies from the twenties. The stylized variation on the logics of slapstick will not necessarily generate howls of laughter but it triggers a second-degree hilarity. We laugh when we recognize the dated nature of the genre and the sources of the mechanical comedy. In those moments, the machine-like element of Bergson's formulation derives from a Cartesian belief that animals are soulless machines, or that humans seen from a distance behave exactly like automata.

These automata are nonetheless desiring machines—thus Bergson's idea of vital dynamism in those plays, films, or videos will be recalibrated as a Freudian resource. Thus in *Film*, we understand that Buster Keaton is getting rid of his past by tearing off, one by one, his family photographs. The aged king of American slapstick may not have had an inkling of what he was representing in Beckett's wicked contraption, but viewers could not miss that the final shots of the film stage a confrontation with his double, the ghostly image of himself that he cannot evade. This redoubling of the gaze sends us in the direction of the Uncanny, much more than of Freud's analysis of jokes and humor.

In a series of notes taken in 1913 about Bergson's *Laughter*, the Hungarian psychoanalyst Sándor Ferenczi compared Freud's theses on jokes with Bergson's theory. Ferenczi questioned the French philosopher's sociological bias so as to enhance the distance between psychoanalytical and philosophical theories of laughter, and added the following corrective:

> The pleasure and unpleasure mechanism of laughter: a repetition of the pleasure and unpleasure in being born.
>
> Bergson (p. 26): Bergson recognizes, not laughing, but only being laughed at.
> Bergson: The laughter laughs at what is dead (the mechanical).
> Bergson: Because he is disgusted by it. Ferenczi: Because he longs for it (*cliché*).[6]

Although those notes on laughter never explain why laughter triggers an unconscious mechanism that repeats our pleasure and displeasure at being born, it seems that Beckett's entire work should exemplify the theory. Neither Beckett nor Ferenczi will take Bergson's clash between the "living" and the "mechanical" for granted. Both question Bergson's reliance on an idealist conception of life as spontaneity, plasticity, and untrammeled movement. By insisting that a true theory of laughter should not limit itself to the objects of laughter but begin with the act of laughing itself, Ferenczi understands laughter as a gesture uniting body and psyche. Laughter can be triggered by any object, word, or situation, anything can become the pretext for a good guffaw, because the body is the site of a radical downsizing of abstract or sublime ideas.

The problematic of "laughing in itself"[7]—a laughter free of any object— echoes with the conception of Bataille who insists upon the abjection and filth associated with base matter. As we have seen, Beckett had read closely a few pages from Bataille's preface to *Madame Edwarda*. He underlined words and sentences pertaining to the issue of laughter about sexuality and to its opposite, the tragic seriousness linked with death. Bataille had pitted against each other our embarrassed laughter facing eroticism and the gravity required by a tragic conception of life. Making a call to the awareness of a "rift" (*déchirure*) in the spirit itself, he argues that laughter that does not respect anything can lead us astray. We all laugh, Bataille says, at the sight of reproductive organs.[8] That said, laughter should not make us believe that sexual prohibitions are artificial prejudices or obstacles artificially erected by society and that they should be destroyed at once, for, if "laughter knows no respect" indeed, nevertheless "it is the sign of horror."[9] Laughter, in this dialectical conception, is both a salutary reaction to any kind of sacred awe, and the dangerous moment when the "spirit," here defined by a tragic awareness of the link between sexuality and death, can turn into its own caricature. Eroticism should then keep this anguished spirit alive. Bataille's preface goes on:

> What the hearty laugh screens from us, what fetches up the bawdy jest, is the identity that exists between the utmost in pleasure and the utmost in pain: the identity between being and non-being, between the living and the death-stricken being, between the knowledge which brings one before this dazzling realization and definitive, concluding darkness. To be sure, it is not impossible that this truth itself evokes a final laugh; but our laughter here is absolute, going far beyond scorning ridicule of something which may perhaps be repugnant, but disgust for which digs deep under our skin.[10]

Hence, for Bataille as for Beckett, it will be crucial to distinguish between types of laughter, from the silly titter barely hiding social embarrassment at the mere mention of basic bodily functions to an "absolute" laughter strong enough to outstare at once death and the sun in the ecstatic leap into cosmic destruction.

Laughter was a serious matter for Bataille, as it was for Beckett, which has been confirmed by excellent syntheses like Anca Parvulescu's book or Laura Salisbury's reading of the comic gamut in Beckett.[11] Laughter is no less serious for Ferenczi, who presented it as an activity that takes us back to the experience of being born, an idea that he owed to Otto Rank's *The Myth of the Birth of the Hero* (1909). Rank wrote that what distinguished Jesus's birth from any other was the fact that he had laughed immediately after being born. One finds an echo of the idea of a short-lived postnatal hilarity in the quatrain that Mrs. W. extemporizes in the first scene (it is the only one we have) of *Human Wishes*:

> Madam, for mirth, for my part,
> I never had the heart;
> Madam, for my part, to mirth
> I have not been moved since birth.[12]

In the play, Mrs. W. is a witty but cantankerous old woman who resents the presence of the young Polly, an ex-prostitute, in the household of Mrs. Thrale at Bolt Court. What was it that triggered such laughter at her birth? Was it the old joke that we are born naked, wet, and hungry, and that then everything gets worse?

Freud's book on the *Witz* quotes a joke about the mirth generated by the idea of being born. It is in fact a quote from Sophocles's famous statement in *Oedipus at Colonus*: the best thing for man is never to have been born. Freud twists this conceit by reminding us that this nonbirth happens rarely: "'*Never to have been born would be the best for mortal kind. But,*' add the philosophers of the '*Fliegende Blätter, that scarcely happens to one in 100,000.*'"[13] This exaggerated use of calculation is a constant feature of Beckett's comedies. We can also remember the title of his enigmatic short story "A Case in a Thousand," in which the mystery concerns the death of a child and the obstinate refusal to mourn him by the narrator's old wet nurse. We can think of the delirious series of numbers at the end of *How It Is*, when the narrator attempts to imagine crowds of other crawlers in the mud like him. Such "jokes" can be pathetic or tragic, but they all imply an exaggeration, which, in the end, presupposes an implicit calculation whose mounting expectations are suddenly baffled. Its paradigm is given in a dialogue between a psychoanalyst and a patient quoted by Ferenczi: "'Doctor, if you help me, I'll give you every penny I possess!' 'I shall be satisfied with thirty kronen an hour,' the physician replied. 'But isn't that rather excessive?' the patient unexpectedly remarked."[14]

The subtraction of one type of excess from another inevitably affects the body and creates the phenomenon of laughter. However, one can cry when seized by sudden happiness, or laugh when overwhelmed by disheartening sights. A cartoon of the *New Yorker* represents a medieval fool showing a group of destitute serfs dressed in rags to the king sitting on his throne. The fool says: "It's sad, but it's not laugh-aloud-sad."[15] Similarly, Beckett's laughter is never far from tears. Ferenczi adheres to Freud's theory of the comic as an unconscious economy, but stresses the cathartic function of laughter: "In laughing we feel ourselves into the physical condition of the comic and get rid of the superfluous provision of affect by means of laughter."[16] For Ferenczi, seriousness derives from repression: one should indulge one's childishness, which entails allowing oneself to laugh irrepressibly as often as possible: "Laughter is a failure of repression. A defense symptom against unconscious pleasure."[17]

The final resolution of the tension between lack of repression and the expulsion of negative affects is the utopia of a smiling baby: "Happiness.

Smiling (the child after being quieted; absence of all needs)./Laughter = defence against excessive pleasure."[18] If postnatal bliss results in a satisfied smile, laughter, by contrast, remains ambivalent: it reenacts both the pleasure and the pain of being born. One might say that laughter points to a lost enjoyment of which we have almost no memory. Christ would hold both ends of the arc of pain and pleasure while he kept on laughing. But then a question arises: do we know whether Christ laughed at all? In *Molloy*, Father Ambrose and Jacques Moran agree on the fact that he may not have felt mirth. Moran worries that his hens will die if he leaves his house (they will). Ambrose compares the despondent grey hen with Job and laughs weakly, which triggers a weak laugh in Moran. One needs to hear the whole passage to grasp Beckett's devious strategy generating this weakened laughter:

> What a joy it is to laugh, from time to time, he said. Is it not? I said. It
> is peculiar to man, he said. So I have noticed, I said. A brief silence
> ensued. What do you feed her on? he said. Corn chiefly, I said.
> Cooked or raw? he said. Both, I said. I added that she ate nothing any
> more. Nothing! he cried. Next to nothing, I said. Animals never
> laugh, he said. It takes us to find that funny, I said. What? he said. It
> takes us to find that funny, I said loudly. He mused. Christ never
> laughed either, he said, so far as I know. He looked at me. Can you
> wonder? I said. There it is, he said. He smiled sadly. She has not the
> pip, I hope, he said.[19]

Depending on tone and utterance, this exchange can sound banal and boring, or hilarious and philosophically self-reflexive. When Ambrose asks "what?" he wants Moran to tell him what "that" refers to—that is, what was the cause of laughter—whereas Moran thinks that Ambrose has not heard him well. The main comedy derives from the splicing of questions about the animals' diet and their failing health and questions about the metaphysics of laughter as reserved to human beings, but perhaps unknown to Christ.

This example of Beckett's strategy of *rire jaune*, the hollow laugh that laughs at laughter itself, corresponds to the famous delineation of three modes of laughter in *Watt*. Arsene, the previous servant, departs from Mr. Knott's house, and gives precious warnings to Watt, which include a whole philosophy of laughter: "The bitter laugh laughs at that which is not good, it is the ethical laugh. The hollow laugh laughs at that which is not true, it is the intellectual laugh. . . . But the mirthless laugh is the dianoetic laugh, down the snout. . . . It is the laugh of laughs, the *risus purus*, the laugh laughing at the laugh, the beholding, the saluting of the highest joke, in a word the laugh that laughs—silence please—at that which is unhappy."[20]

Arsene, who later sounds like a neo-Kantian when he rehearses the concept of finality without purpose,[21] is here evoking Aristotle. His categories borrow from the list of Aristotelian virtues, the dianoetic virtues. Beckett learned this from Windelband who had stated: "The *dianoëtic* virtues are the highest, and those which bring complete happiness."[22] These virtues concern themselves with pure thought; here, because pure laughter replaces pure thought, it seems logical that happiness be inverted into unhappiness. The sentence reverberates through Beckett's later work, as we see with Nell's famous assertion of *Endgame*: "Nothing is funnier than unhappiness."[23] An excellent analysis of Arsene's theory of laughter has been provided by Simon Critchley in *On Humour*.[24] We may be alerted by the curious fact that, in *Watt*, the theory of the modes of laughter is developed by Arsene, a minor character who vanishes from the plot; meanwhile, the eponymous hero of the novel remains a strict "non-laugher."

If laughing is never a natural reflex for Watt, smiling is an even more outlandish operation:

> Watt had watched people smile and thought he understood how it was done. And it was true that Watt's smile, when he smiled, resembled more a smile than a sneer, for example, or a yawn. But there was something wanting to Watt's smile, some little thing was lacking, and people who saw it for the first time, and most people who saw it saw it for the first time, were sometimes in doubt as to what expression exactly was intended. To many it seemed a simple sucking of the teeth.[25]

On the other hand, as soon as he appears on the stage, Watt's grotesque behavior becomes the pretext for endless tall tales about giving birth. In the first chapter of *Watt*, the irruption on the scene of the eponymous antihero is framed by a conversation between Goff, Tetty, and Mr. Hackett. Their hilarious exchange accumulates Johnsonian witticisms and Sternian double entendres. For instance, Goff explains that Tetty had to cut the umbilical cord with her teeth, which leads Mr. Hackett to meditate:

> That is a thing I often wondered, said Mr. Hackett, what it feels like to have the string cut.
>
> For the mother or the child? Said Goff.
>
> For the mother, said Mr. Hackett. I was not found under a cabbage, I believe.
>
> For the mother, said Tetty, the feeling is one of relief, of great relief. As when the guests depart.[26]

Since Hackett was born from a mother, he assumes that he must have kept a precise memory of having *his* side of the cord severed! Such "delivery jokes" (here, too, enunciation is the key to the comic effect) confirm Ferenczi's hypothesis that laughter is irremediably haunted by a lost memory of the birth trauma. The thesis would account as well for the choice of a reflexive laugh laughing at itself or laughing at unhappiness. What has been irremediably lost is the innocence of a baby at birth, or its bliss at the mother's breast. Pure contemplation of the mind will either erase traces of painful feelings of loss, or fall into desperate longing for the lost paradise. However, whatever remains of the old laughter will be mediated by the world of culture, therefore will look old or conventional, adding to the huge repertoire of exhausted clichés.

We can now put together Beckett's recourse to low or clownish forms of slapstick and his concept of a pure laugh laughing at itself—or at us, as in one of the best gags of *Endgame*. The blind Hamm asks Clov to look through a telescope and tell him what he sees outside. Clov points the telescope at the audience and says slowly, for better effect: "I see . . . a multitude . . . in transports . . . of joy."[27] Another example is the exchange about fatherhood between Hamm and Nagg:

HAMM: Why did you engender me?
NAGG: I didn't know.
HAMM: What? What didn't you know?
NAGG: That it'd be you.[28]

Adorno, one of the sharpest commentators of *Endgame*, perceived the necessity of these clownish elements; he sees them as compatible with Beckett's refusal of the facilities afforded by popular comedy. For Adorno, clownish humor ought to be understood both historically and psychoanalytically:

> Psychoanalysis explains the clown's humor as a regression to an extremely early ontogenetic stage, and Beckett's drama of regression descends to that level. But the laughter it arouses ought to suffocate the ones who laugh. This is what has become of humor now that it has become obsolete as an aesthetic medium and repulsive, without a canon for what should be laughed about, without a place of reconciliation from one could laugh, and without anything harmless on the face of the earth that would allow itself to be laughed at.[29]

According to Adorno, Beckett enacted a most scathing philosophical critique of philosophy. Philosophy is reduced to clowning; it is debunked

by a gesture akin to the lifting of the veil: "The philosophy that calls everything radically in question by confronting it with the void stops itself from
the outset—by means of a pathos derived from theology—from reaching
the frightening conclusion whose possibility it suggests."[30] As revealed in
my discussion of Kant in chapter 7, this pathos quickly turns into bathos,
and the hilarity that this bathos generates does not prevent negativity from
remaining within the confines of a comedy.

Adorno constantly aligns Beckett and Kafka as two dark humorists with
similar mindsets, and thus presents *Endgame* as "heir to Kafka's novels."[31]
For Adorno, Kafka's story of "Hunter Gracchus" provides a paradigm
shared by Beckett. As Kafka narrates, Gracchus was a man who had missed
his own death by accident. Even though he has died, he is condemned to
roam the earth as an immortal being in spite of himself. In Adorno's
politicized reading, Gracchus is compared with the bourgeoisie that has
failed to die, but he also introduces the more sinister meaning of "between
life and death" that the death camps of the Nazis have enacted with a vengeance.[32] As we will see in chapter 10, for Adorno the horror staged in
Endgame does not come from the likeliness of the death of Hamm at the
end, as would be the case in a classical tragedy, but from a deeper "abortion
of death." This impossibility of dying—which is paradoxically bathetic and
funny—corresponds to the text's position in a post-Holocaust historical
context. The idea would be that the only possible denunciation of the
Holocaust would consist in a dramatization of the nondeath of the subject.
Hamm's vainglorious stoicism ("Peace to our . . . arses," he blurts out at the
end[33]) combined with his reiterated announcement that he will be silent in
Endgame does not betray a fear of death but a deeper "terror that death
itself could miscarry."[34]

The bathetic pathos of *Endgame* derives from the sense that after all is
over, one has to go on. Such a reading had been slipped early enough by
Beckett himself when he gave a tip to the director Alan Schneider: "'The
end is the beginning and yet we go on.' In other words, the impossibility of
catastrophe. Ended at its inception, and at every instant, it continues, ergo
can never end. Don't mention this to your actors!"[35] In the same letter,
Beckett tells Schneider that when the actors say: "Keep going," it means
keeping the ball rolling at any cost, and adds: "I think the whole passage . . .
should be played as *farcical parody of polite drawing-room conversation*."[36] We
have to combine a double point of view: the parody of polite conversation
is also the depiction of a post-Holocaust hell. This is indeed a "comedy" in
Dante's sense—it includes hell and all its tortures, but can also be said to
be hilariously low, therefore funny.

We are back to the aborted project of *Human Wishes*, the unfinished play revolving on Doctor Johnson. One reason why Beckett could never complete it was that he was trying too hard to present the famous English wit as the victim of sexual impotence. The sexual theme proved difficult to handle. Moreover, Beckett was uncertain about the exact nature of Johnson's personal crisis when he found himself rejected by his long-time lover Mrs. Thrale. She had become free to marry Johnson at the death of her rich husband. Instead, she married her Italian music teacher. The overarching idea of depicting the folly of human wishes underpinned by a fear of death akin to madness proved too much for the stage. As Beckett wrote to McGreevy in 1937, Samuel Johnson had such a terror of death that he said that he preferred an eternity of torment: "His horror at loving her I take it was a mode or paradigm of his horror at ultimate annihilation, to which he declared in the fear of his death that he would prefer an eternity of torment."[37] Beckett's way of getting out of the dead end of horror was to wonder whether an eternity of torment might not be more funny than tragic.

If horror may not immediately trigger a guffaw, it can elicit a strained laughter that the French call *rire jaune* (forced laughter), a quality that Beckett loved in the French humorist Jules Renard, whose diary he often quoted, as with this witty but sad note: "When he looked at himself in a mirror, he was always tempted to wipe it."[38] Beckett's translation of the French idiom is more literary: he calls it "xanthic laugh" in the second of the *Texts for Nothing*: "What exactly is going on, exactly, ah old xanthic laugh, no farewell mirth, good riddance, it was never droll. No, but one more memory, one last memory, it may help, to abort again."[39] If abortion is not by itself a funny topic, the idea of keeping on aborting again and again may prove to be more mirth than birth. At any rate, this will be a key issue for Adorno.

CHAPTER 10

Strength to Deny: Beckett between Adorno and Badiou

The strength to deny, that most natural expression of the human
fighting organism, ever changing, renewing itself, reviving as it
decays, this strength we possess always, but not the courage; and yet,
life itself is denial, and therefore denial affirmation.

—Franz Kafka, "He"[1]

Adorno was the thinker who understood best the source of Beckett's dark comedy, its constant self-renewal, its inexhaustible resources playing with exhaustion, even if it is likely that he did not laugh so much when reading his texts. Which is why I want to compare him with a laughing philosopher, Alain Badiou, who also takes Beckett's laughter seriously.[2] In Adorno's system, Beckett played the role that Kafka had played for Walter Benjamin, or that Schönberg played in his own essays on music, whereas for Badiou, Beckett replaced both Maoist Marxism and his favorite French poets, Rimbaud and Mallarmé. Adorno and Badiou presuppose that self-standing intellectuals should be conversant with Beckett's *oeuvre* if they want to find their bearings in matters of ethics, dialectics, considerations about the relationship between art and society, theories of love and power, the role of images, and the place of truth in culture, before addressing eschatological questions such as whether life is worth living. Their efforts aim at producing a speculative accompaniment to literary readings and are therefore quite demanding.

If one compares their interpretations of Beckett, one notes an almost complete reversal in their starting points; it seems that their general evaluations evince a dramatic shift from the negative to the positive. Spanning half a century of philosophical discussions of Beckett, their points of departure stand at antipodal ends while emphasizing the exemplarity of Beckett's work. Adorno, writing at the end of a long career in the late 1950s and 1960s,[3] began by tackling Beckett's negativity, a dialectical negativity that should not be confused with nihilism; for him, Beckett exemplified a negative aesthetics.[4] Badiou writing in the late 1980s and 1990s quickly brushed aside any suggestion of nihilism or negativity so as to stress the affirmative character of Beckett's philosophy.[5] Both Badiou and Adorno provide systematic readings that deal with the entire Beckettian canon grasped in its most general problematics, but they manage not to be reductive. Beckett's texts do not turn into mechanical exemplifications of their concepts or hermeneutic programs. In both cases, the philosophical starting point does not elide a certain specificity of art and literature, while working with abstract concepts and not just playing with the signifiers of the texts in a psychoanalytic or deconstructive mode. Adorno and Badiou never allow themselves to be impressed by the mystical autonomy of the text that one finds in Blanchot, for instance. Nevertheless, their interpretive procedures are bolstered by sustained exercises in close reading— Adorno with *Endgame* and later with *The Unnamable*, Badiou with the later texts *Lessness* and *Worstward Ho*.

The change of tone noticeable in their philosophical discourses has to do with the fact that they belong to different generations. Badiou, born in 1937, thirty-four years after Adorno (1903–1969), is more aware of the historicity of his own reading. Badiou never mentions having met Beckett in the flesh but he begins his book on Beckett with an autobiographical account of how he first encountered the works. Beckett's texts left a strong impression on him, and were caught in the Sartrian context of his youth, since he was originally a disciple of Sartre. Interestingly, Sartre is mentioned by Adorno in his essay on *Endgame*, but it is to argue that the play provides a parody of Sartrian themes. If Adorno begins by acknowledging that Beckett's oeuvre "has many things in common with Parisian existentialism,"[6] he sees it as a Trojan horse debunking existentialism.

Badiou explains that he discovered Beckett when he was a young man and a devoted Sartrean. The encounter with Beckett's first works in French left on Badiou an indelible mark: it was a blow as one can only receive when one is young. Badiou expatiates on the unique characteristics of youth:

> This is the principal task of youth: to encounter the incalculable, and thereby to convince oneself, against the disillusioned, that the thesis

"nothing is, nothing is valuable" is both false and oppressive. . . . Being young is a source of power, a time of decisive encounters, but these are strained by their all too easy capture by repetition and imitation. Thought only subtracts itself from the spirit of the age by means of a constant and delicate labor. It is easy to want to change the world—in youth this seems the least that one could do. It is more difficult to notice the fact that this very wish could end up as the material for the forms of perpetuation of this very world. This is why all youth, as stirring as its promise may be, is always also the youth of a "young cretin." Bearing this in mind, in later years, keeps us from nostalgia.[7]

The fine translation provided by Nina Power and Alberto Toscano, in their invaluable collection of Badiou's essays on Beckett, for once glosses over Badiou's active participation in what came before and after the students' unrest in 1968. A more literal rendering of the ending of this passage would be: "Thought can only avoid being reduced to Zeitgeist by strenuous and delicate labor. It is easy to want to change the world, as at this time this was *for us* the least one could do. It is more difficult to realize that this very wish may be nothing but material used by the forms of the same world's perpetuation." Badiou is alluding to his political commitment, and to his sense of belonging to the generation that came of age in May 1968. Until recently, he would declare that he was a Maoist philosopher. The passage quoted contains a discreet admission that he recanted his earlier leftist theories.

Using the Aristotelian opposition between form and material, Badiou implies that the students' demonstrations in 1968 were nothing but a way for France to catch up with the world at large, that the young and idealist revolutionaries only realized later that they had been propelled by a historical necessity forcing France to enter the homogeneous space of globalized, if not Americanized, culture. This is relevant in the context of a discussion of Adorno's politics and aesthetics (for, similarly, Adorno did not refrain from using the dialectics of form and material), especially at the end of his life. Then, thanks to Beckett, we will catch a glimpse of the philosopher's dismay at being called a "reactionary mandarin" by the Frankfurt students to whom he had taught Marxism, critical thinking, and negative dialectics.

Adorno's Negative Aesthetics

Beckett and Adorno met a few times; their first meeting was in November 1958, when Adorno went to Paris to give a series of lectures at the Sorbonne. He called up Beckett and they had a long discussion on *Godot* and *Endgame* at the Coupole and later in a Montparnasse restaurant. On this occasion, Adorno jotted down a few condensed statements that gave, as it were, keys for his reading. Among these, he heard Beckett making unspecified "reproaches" against Kafka, which tempered his earlier decision to develop a systematic comparison between the two writers. One of the most revealing notes is this: "Beckett (after Godot). Not abstraction but subtraction."[8] This led to Adorno's idea that Beckett debunks existentialism, mostly by reducing existentialist philosophy to meaningless clichés. By doing so, Beckett radicalizes an attempt at finding a sure and certain foundation in the subject whether it be provided by Descartes, Geulincx, or Husserl. Adorno argues that Beckett's work clashes with an "existentialist jargon" that gives a mystified image of the human condition by essentializing in a "process of abstraction that is not aware of itself." Here is Adorno's dig at Martin Heidegger. For him, fundamentally, Beckett opposes such an abstract vision of man: "To this kind of unacknowledged process of abstraction, Beckett poses the decisive antithesis: an avowed process of subtraction."[9] Beckett's work functions as an antiformalist machine even when it requires a new concept of form.

We need to pay attention to this reversal. When Adorno evokes existentialism, he has in mind less Sartre than Heidegger, whom he was preparing to attack frontally in *The Jargon of Authenticity* (1963–1964).[10] Beckett's "subtraction" is directly opposed to the fake "abstraction" of those who negate concrete life and its historical determination in the name of a reified concept of existence. Beckett's process of subtraction works with a reduced subject. This subject then reduces even more the abstractions of existentialism and gives them an utterly laughable quality. Beckett derides philosophical abstraction and what remains of a late modernism by showing us a dead end. One can be saved by a laughter that spares nothing.

However, it would be a mistake to refuse this process in the name of the plenitude of life, as Lukács had attempted to do. "True to official optimism, Lukács complains that in Beckett human beings are reduced to their animal qualities. . . . Just as it is ridiculous to impute an abstract subjectivist ontology to Beckett and then put that ontology on some index of degenerate art, as Lukács does, on the basis of its wordlessness and infantilism, so it would be ridiculous to put Beckett on the stand as a star political witness."[11] After he had completed this preparatory work, Adorno announced that his essay about Beckett's *Endgame* boiled down to a refutation of Lukács's position. The famous Marxist critic was attacking an "absurdist" theater deemed to be nothing but "petty-bourgeois nihilism." For Adorno,

Beckett's supposed apolitical stance was in fact highly political and it
exposed both the disingenuousness of Marxist humanism and the sterility
of Heidegger's ontological essentialism. In that context, Adorno can be
ferocious: "Adherents of totalitarianism like Lukács, who wax indignant
about the decadence of this truly *terrible simplificateur*, are not ill-advised
by the interest of their bosses. What they hate in Beckett is what they
betrayed."[12] One can follow the transformation from an apolitical Beckett
to a figure of resistance to totalitarianism of any kind, and of salutary cynicism facing the complacent illusions of the bourgeoisie about living well
without a purpose.

In his jottings, Adorno had noted an obvious point of departure: *Endgame* refers to a chess problem. What is specific to this "endgame," is that
even if we guess that all is lost from the beginning, the game must be played
to the end. Adorno saw this as a proof of Beckett's proximity with Kafka,
while registering a factor unknown to Kafka, Beckett's passion for music:
"B. said that his plays were as much music as play, following a purely immanent logic of sequences, not of meaning."[13] This may explain Adorno's habit
of dotting his copies of Beckett's works with marginal F (forte) or FFF
(fortissimo). Here and there, he voices some incomprehension, and often,
quite symptomatically, about the issue of negativity: "Very enigmatic
remark about a kind of positivity contained in pure negativity. In view of
such absolute negativity, one could be said to *quasi* live."[14] This last note
sums up what is most baffling for Adorno. This is a point that he will meditate again and again, teasing out its consequences in various ways. It reappears in the notes that Adorno took in 1960 about *Endgame*. In all these, we
see him pondering the Beckettian paradox of: "Life does not live."

Beckett and Adorno met again in Frankfurt in the spring of 1961 when
Adorno gave a lecture that was more or less the substance of "Trying to
understand *Endgame*." Adorno left a rather mitigated impression on Beckett, always a stickler for linguistic detail and historical precision. Beckett
found to his dismay that although he had explained to Adorno that the
name "Hamm" contained no reference to Hamlet, Adorno imperturbably
developed his thesis on the links between *Hamlet* and *Endgame*.[15] One finds
this in "Trying to understand *Endgame*."[16] From then on, Adorno embodied for Beckett the stereotypical German professor whose watertight
architecture of concepts proved impervious to facts. This probably triggered Beckett's dismissive remark when questioned about *Endgame* in
1967: "*Endgame* will be just play. Nothing less. Don't worry about enigmas
and solutions. For these, we have well-equipped universities, churches, cafés
du commerce, and so on."[17]

In January 1968, Beckett and Adorno met more cordially, for the last time in fact. Adorno had come to Paris to give a lecture at the Collège de France. He talked for two hours with Beckett who gave him the wonderful gem that his work amounted to a "desecration of silence" (in English).[18] This phrase found its way into the unrevised pages of *Aesthetic Theory*: "Whereas each artwork that succeeds transcends the nexus (of guilt), each must atone for this transcendence, and therefore its language seeks to withdraw into silence: An artwork is, as Beckett wrote, a *desecration of silence*."[19] Betraying an incipient minimalism, Beckett confided cryptically that everything that mattered in life depended less upon "man's maximum" than "man's minimum."

After this meeting, Adorno went to Cologne, where he participated in a heated discussion of Beckett with Martin Esslin and others for a German radio network. In the discussion, entitled "It would be criminal to think optimistically," Adorno reiterated the principle of "negative dialectics" or "determined negation" at work in Beckett's oeuvre. The latter phrase is heard repeated at the end when the discussion gets lost in a cacophonic medley of voices. Adorno was not to see Beckett again, but wrote to him in February 1969, announcing the imminent publication of his *Aesthetic Theory*. He mentioned ruefully that he had been shocked at being called "reactionary" by his students. Uncharacteristically, Beckett answered to him so as to reassure him on the issue of leftist politics prevalent among German students: "I have not yet been *conspiré [an obvious misreading for* conspué, meaning "publically heckled"] so far as I know and that is not far, by the *Marcusejugend*. As you said to me once at the Iles Marquises [the Paris restaurant where they had dined together], all is *malentendu*. Was ever such rightness joined to such foolishness?"[20]

Adorno died soon after. *Aesthetic Theory* was published posthumously. Among his unfinished projects was a series of marginalia to *The Unnamable*, a novel that he had come to consider as Beckett's masterpiece, followed by the draft of an essay on it. The notes betray a distinctively German slant, pointing to parallels not only with Kafka but also with Brecht, Benn, Benjamin, Bloch, Wittgenstein, and Hegel. The discussion turns philosophical with the motto: "The path of the novel: reduction of the reduced."[21] A similar idea will be pushed further with Badiou: Beckett's method is to work by a phenomenological reduction of what has already been reduced. Beckett goes back not only to Descartes but also to Proust, as Adorno identifies the speaking *I* of the *Unnamable* with the *I* heard at the beginning of Proust's novel: "The 'I' of the beginning and the 'I' of the beginning of *La Recherche*."[22] Like Proust, Beckett has reached a point of differentiation between narrative and theory.[23] Adorno harps on the dialectics of negativity: "L'innommable is the negative subject-object."[24] "With Beckett, positive categories [such] as hope turn into absolutely negative ones. Here hope goes to the nothing."[25] The last pages of the draft meditate on the specific nature of Beckett's nothing: "Is the nothing only nothing? This is the central issue in Beckett. Absolute rejection, because hope is only where there is nothing to keep. Plenitude of the nothing. This is the explanation of his remaining in the zero-point."[26] At least, this emphasis on negativity should refute any imputation of "absurdist" allegiance in Beckett—who has nothing to do with Ionesco.

The seven pages draft is condensed and testifies to the seriousness with which Adorno dedicated himself to his task. The essay was to constitute the core of the fourth volume of his *Notes to Literature*. Adorno had planned to dedicate his forthcoming *Aesthetic Theory* to Samuel Beckett, which highlights his importance for a book that was to crown his critical *oeuvre*. It can be taken as a point of departure since it condenses Adorno's views on Beckett, and in some passages, like the following, revisits in a more nuanced way the *Endgame* analysis:

> Beckett's plays are absurd not because of the absence of any meaning, for they would be simply irrelevant, but because they put meaning on trial; they unfold its history. His work is ruled as much by an obsession with positive nothingness as by the obsession with a meaninglessness that has developed historically and is thus in a sense merited, thought this meritedness in no way allows any positive meaning to be reclaimed. . . . Artworks that divest themselves of any semblance of meaning do not thereby forfeit their similitude to language. They enunciate their meaninglessness with the same determinacy as traditional artworks enunciate their positive meaning. Today this is the capacity of art: Through the consistent negation of meaning it does justice to the postulates that once constituted the meaning of artworks. Works of the highest level of form that are meaningless or alien to meaning are therefore more than simply meaningless because they gain their content through the negation of meaning.[27]

Adorno rewrites here his earlier essay on *Endgame*, generalizing its conclusions so as to encompass all of Beckett's plays. An Aristotelian opposition underpins the analysis: "The negativity of the subject as the true form of objectivity can only be presented in radically subjective form, not by recourse to a purported higher reality. . . . In all art that is still possible, social critique must be raised to the level of form, to the point that it wipes out all manifestly social content."[28] One finds a similar dialectics of content and form coupled with a Hegelian return of the principle of negativity in the "draft introduction": "In Beckett the negative metaphysical content affects the content along with the form. . . . A relation, not identity, operates between the negativity of the metaphysical content and the eclipsing of the aesthetic content. The metaphysical negation no longer permits an aesthetic form that would itself produce metaphysical affirmation; and yet this negation is nevertheless able to become aesthetic content and determine the form."[29] The terms used throughout remain the same: form determines content and then sublates negativity to another level. What is stressed therefore is the domination of parody (in the realm of ideas) and of slapstick comedy in the realm of the theater. An oxymoronic coupling of immobility with dynamism underpins the whole Beckettian oeuvre, which combines the blocked or stymied movements of his characters with a formal dynamism conjuring up a horizon of disaster, caught up between a past unnamable horror and a distant but looming catastrophe:

VLADIMIR: Where are all these corpses from?
ESTRAGON: These skeletons. . . .
VLADIMIR: A charnel-house! A charnel-house!
ESTRAGON: You don't have to look.
VLADIMIR: You can't help looking.[30]

One of the consequences of Beckett's exemplary restraint is that he keeps a political impact even when he does not explicitly engage with politics. For Adorno, the proof of this political force was given when the fascist junta of colonels who had seized power in Greece decided to ban Beckett's works: "Greece's new tyrants knew why they banned Beckett's plays in which there is not a single political word."[31] Beckett's texts exemplify the spirit of resistance in art, a spirit of obstinate ethical perseverance facing barbarism. Such perseverance does not have to shout its name or be explicit. The idea is developed at the end of *Negative Dialectics*: "Beckett has given us the only fitting reaction to the situation left by concentration camps—a situation he never calls by name, as if it were subject to an image ban. What is there, he says, is like a concentration camp. He spoke once of a lifelong death penalty, implying as only hope for the future that there will be nothing any more. This, too, he rejects. From the rift of inconsistency thus found it is the imagery of the Nothing as Something that emerges, and it will then stabilize his poetry."[32] The particular negativity deployed by Beckett is not a pure "nothing" since it retains its historical value and its dialectical properties: "Such nihilism implies the contrary of an identification with nothingness."[33] Beckett would thus—like Paul Celan but with different rhetorical strategies—provide the only possible answer to Adorno's quandary: how can one write "poetry" (*Dichtung*) after Auschwitz?

Adorno, like Badiou, tends to see Beckett's *oeuvre* as inscribed in the genre of poetry. To write poetry after Auschwitz entails a number of paradoxes. What Adorno praises in Beckett's alleged nihilism is that it appears as the opposite of nihilism: he is a "true nihilist" because he opposes the faded positivities of a post-Auschwitz restoration of older values in which no one believes any longer. Even if Badiou rejects any "negative dialectics," he finds his own starting point here as well.

Badiou's Affirmative Ethics

Badiou starts by rejecting the French doxa in Beckett's reception in the late 1950s: Beckett was portrayed as "a writer of the absurd, of despair, of empty skies, of incommunicability and of eternal solitude" (*OB*, 38). His break with a negativist view is given pride of place in the blurb he wrote for his own Beckett book (on the back cover): "No, Beckett's oeuvre is not what was always said about it—that it was despair, absurdity of the world, anxiety, solitude, decrepitude." Badiou's "No" to nihilism defines the jaunty tone of the slim volume on Beckett aptly entitled *Beckett: L'Increvable Désir.*[34] His short book is a user-friendly guide restating in less technical language the philosophical analyses devoted to Beckett in "The Writing of the Generic" (1989). After this, Badiou devoted a chapter to *Worstward Ho* in his *Handbook of Inaesthetics* (*Petit Manuel d'Inesthétique* [1998])—this dense book can appear as a rejoinder to Adorno's huge and sprawling *Aesthetic Theory.*

Badiou's position had been prefigured in the United States by the groundbreaking essay Stanley Cavell devoted to *Endgame* in 1964, whose main thesis is that Beckett has nothing to do with *Angst* at all but is all constrained by the logics of everyday conversation: "The discovery of *Endgame*, both in topic and technique, is not the failure of meaning (if that means the lack of meaning) but its total, even totalitarian success—our inability *not* to mean what we are given to mean."[35] Cavell approaches Beckett via Wittgenstein and Austin, while Badiou prefers Althusser, Lacan, Deleuze, Dedekind, Cantor, and a few others. Andrew Gibson's book on Badiou and Beckett helps readers who might get lost in Badiou's mathematics and ontology.[36] Gibson is right in assuming that one needs to muster the essentials of Badiou's philosophy to gauge his relevance in the Beckett canon. His book is honest, thorough, and courageous, for Gibson never tries to hush some doubts facing Badiou's treatment of Beckett's texts,[37] but reconstructs each time the framework of Badiou's systemic interpretation. Badiou's specific concepts, such as "subtraction, restricted action, actual infinity, the event, subjectification, the logic of appearance, naming, fidelity, apagogic reason, the waiting subject, investigation, inexistents, patience, vigilance, objectivity; undecidables, indiscernibles, and unnameables, *événementialité* or the event of the event," can all be applied in turn to Beckett's canon.[38] I will focus on one crucial and problematic concept, that event or *événementialité*, to understand better how Badiou thinks through Beckett.

There is a temptation to take the short book on Beckett as a shortcut leading to the heart of Badiou's system with its numerous books replete with technical allusions to mathematical logic and classical philosophy. However, Badiou's point of departure is parallel to that of Adorno: both were woken up, even startled, by Beckett's texts in the late 1950s. Like Adorno in the essay on *Endgame*, Badiou perceived affinities between Becket's works and the theses of existentialism, but since he had been a Sartrean earlier, he treated this proximity more positively. Adorno had often equated Beckett with Kafka and Schönberg, and in a similar manner, Beckett belongs to the heroic artists enthroned in Badiou's canon: he sits next to Mallarmé, not far from Rimbaud, Pessoa, and Celan. These writers designate theoretical issues better broached by artists than by philosophers. More than a poetological reading of the Irish writer, the philosophical readings provided by Badiou and Adorno replace Beckett in a longer discursive tradition. Beckett would be straddling two schools, phenomenology and classical rationalism: he is wedged between Descartes and Husserl, behind whom Heraclitus, Parmenides, Plato, and Kant are present. Badiou, a gifted novelist and playwright himself, does not forget to read as literally as possible the signifiers of Beckett's texts and to pay attention to their baffling rhetorical strategies.

There was little nostalgia in the autobiographical opening of the book. Badiou's first response to Beckett was emblematic of a common misreading. The dominant fashion in the late 1950s and early 1960s was to read Beckett as a nihilist, a pessimist, or an absurdist. Beckett was a dark comedian whose metaphysical clowns wandering under an empty sky were thought to be ruminating on an absent god while expressing tersely and wittily the despair inherent to man's estate. Slightly later, he appeared as a modernist for whom language had become the central concern: he was seen as haunted by the question of a pure writing, endlessly restating the aporia of language's opacity and intransitivity. His Sartrean reading insisting on man as a "useless passion" tended to forget the question of language in the name of ethics, commitment, and politics. Later, this political view was relayed by Blanchot's problematic of silence, negativity, and disappearance of the author: the writer's voice would get dissolved in the neutral space of post-Hegelian negativity. Thus Badiou's philosophical program in the late 1950s aimed at reconciling Sartre's negative ontology with Blanchot's anonymous mysticism of literary space, a space in which language speaks by itself, to itself and about itself. As he sums it up, his juvenile endeavor would have been to "complete the Sartrean theory of freedom through a careful investigation into the opacities of the signifier" (*OB*, 39), a still relevant project. Meanwhile, for Badiou as for Adorno, *The Unnamable* remained Beckett's indisputable masterpiece.

If the project of exploring Sartre's ontology along with Blanchot's Hegelian *neuter* looks like a solid dissertation plan, this would now appear as a mistake for Badiou today, because such a research program would miss what is most crucial in Beckett's trajectory, namely an ethical imperative of courage, a courage to keep on desiring. Such an imperative sustains a whole ethics of desire. This view of desire owes a lot to Lacan's seminar on the ethics of psychonalysis, with its interesting conflation of ethics and aesthetics. Lacan's discussion of Antigone in that seminar posited a strong link between the beauty of the heroine and her ethical position.[39] The desire for truth and the contemplation of beauty condense for Badiou the most vital impulse in Beckett's works.

Badiou remembers that he had memorized Beckett's most cynical, darkest textual nuggets, how he loved quoting these crisp sentences but missed their true irony and the source of their energy. Being too much in love with *The Unnamable*, he forgot that this novel had led Beckett into a dead end, which was paid for by a gnawing feeling of impotence or literary block. It took Badiou a few years to undo the cliché of Beckett the existentialist absurdist, the cynical nihilist. He had also to refuse the opposite version proffered soon after, which was a Beckett viewed as a "thin Rabelais" (*OB*, 40), an author only interested in derision, who would state that everything turned farce in a sending off literature via a postmodern massacre of all values. Badiou felt that he needed to reassert priorities: "Neither existentialism nor a modern baroque. The lesson of Beckett is a lesson of measure, exactitude and courage" (40). It is therefore an ethical Beckett that Badiou wants to portray, a writer who teaches something important—the truth about desire, language, being, and a "generic" humanity, all of which sounds eerily similar to Badiou's main concepts. However, in spite of obvious moralistic overtones, Badiou does not provide a humanistic reading.

Badiou's interpretation owes a lot to Lacan's theories—in Badiou's reading program, Beckett becomes the only writer who knows and says that it is essential never to yield on one's desire, even when everything else collapses, and your life is marked by sexual fiasco, moral perversion, intellectual bankruptcy, and writerly impotence. Beckett's lesson in ethical affirmation offers his readers the courage to keep on living and creating. The lesson is made more poignant and powerful because Beckett multiplies the arguments that show how impossible these affirmations are.

One of the most problematic theses put forward by Badiou is the idea of a break in Beckett's career. He also tends to downplay the importance of Beckett's famous "German letter" from 1937, in which, as he wrote, the ambition of a new literature should be to "bore one hole after another" in language, so as to "see what lurks behind it."[40] In Badiou's timeline, the *Texts for Nothing* mark the end of the first period and signal the termination or the exhaustion of Cartesian solipsism; then, *How It Is* would display a new beginning and show an opening to the other. Moreover, Badiou's reading of *The Unnamable* as pure torture, torment, and despair misses important elements of irony, parody, and aggression. This chronology, which identifies a rupture in 1960 followed by a new departure, does not accommodate important texts on which Adorno insists such as *Endgame*, begun in 1955, *All That Fall*, written in 1956, followed by *Krapp's Last Tape*. For Badiou, one series of works lead to the trilogy, which culminates with *The Unnamable*; this series was followed by a moment of stuttering or quasi silence between *Texts for Nothing* (1950) and *How It Is* (1960). On Badiou's view, the new departure presented by *How It Is* was marked by a newly found minimalism, a practice of subtraction, that allowed for an unblocking, marked by experiments in the theater, and media like film, radio, and television. The second period culminates with the second trilogy of *Nohow On*, which, in Badiou's reading, condenses the highest point reached by Beckett's language and thought.

What is refreshing is that Badiou refuses to treat Beckett's *oeuvre* either as a single block, which is, as we have seen, Adorno's temptation, or as a linear progression leading toward formal minimalism by fulfilling a nihilistic philosophical project (*OB*, 40). Badiou sees Beckett's *oeuvre* as punctuated by hesitations and caesuras. Meanwhile, it is underpinned by original abstractions, a set of concepts that enact a literary equivalent to Husserl's phenomenological reduction. In fact, Beckett would deploy an inverse phenomenology, since it is not just the world and all the objects offered to consciousness that become "reduced" by his texts, but subjectivity in itself and in its relation to the world. Beckett cannot be inscribed in any given genre; he blurs the distinction between novel and short story, theatrical play and performance. His main problematics is underpinned by the answers given to Kant's three fundamental questions: "Where would I go if I could go?" followed by "What would I be if I could be?" and then by "What would I say if I had a voice?" After the alleged hiatus of the 1960s, Beckett would have added a fourth question concerning other people: "Who am I, if the other exists?" (41).

These questions are not meant to remain aporias or dead ends. They do get positive answers: "In a manner that is almost aggressive, all of Beckett's genius of Beckett tends toward affirmation. He is no stranger to the maxim, which always carries with it a principle of relentlessness and advancement" (*OB*, 41). Badiou refuses to take Beckett at his word when the latter stresses negative factors. This was the case when Beckett had accounted for the fact of being a "writer" above all. Just before his demise, Beckett had answered the questionnaire sent to him by *Libération*, which asked: "Why do you write?"[41] The irony is that many minor writers answered in more than a page, whereas Beckett wired back the most condensed statement possible: "*Bon qu'à ça!*" ("Only good for that!" or "That's all I'm good for!"). Following Beckett's qualification in "Enough," "Stony ground but not entirely,"[42] a sentence that he admires and often quotes, Badiou gently rebukes Beckett: "Not completely, Beckett, not completely! That's all, but not completely" (*OB*, 42). Bruno Clément has shown that Badiou adapts a recurring trope in Beckett's texts, the epanorthosis or qualifying modification rhetorically transforming the meaning of a passage, often pushing it from apparent negativity to an almost positive statement.[43]

A passage from *Ill Seen Ill Said* can provide a logical blueprint: "Was it ever over and done with questions? Dead the whole brood no sooner hatched. Long before. In the egg. Over and done with answering? With not being able. With not being able not to want to know. With not being able. No. Never. A dream. Question answered."[44] Even if it seems that the passage concludes that there are no answers, it nevertheless answers, at least insofar as it unleashes the verbal energy that heaps precisions, qualifications, rectifications, double negatives, and tangled contradictions. No, indeed, "it" will never end or reach an absolute period. Here is the site explored by Beckett's later prose, a paradoxical space that Badiou starts describing in terms of basic devices or "operations" (*OB*, 44). For him, the specific beauty of the work forces its readers to feel responsible to truth and to humanity.

Beckett's writerly peregrination toward beauty takes the form of a philosophical investigation. Beckett's operations duplicate a "methodical askesis" going back to Descartes first and then Husserl, with a wish to "suspend" everything that is inessential—the only rigorous path to reach the real and the true. All the trappings of the clownish humor and the nihilistic elements of despair and anxiety are instrumental in that context. When Beckett reduces human subjects to paralyzed cripples, mere ectoplasms or shapes in a jar, fitting Winnie in a hole in *Happy Days* and imagining the Unnamable occasionally as an egg-like sphere with a few apertures, this shows that he returns to a Cartesian and Husserlian *epoché* whose aim is to expose what is "generic" in humanity. Beckett would initiate a systematic and serious investigation of "thinking humanity" (*OB*, 44), and if he proceeds by way of destruction, it is in order to discover what resists, that is what remains absolutely indestructible. Even though Badiou does not mention it, Adorno would have noticed this—Kafka did not proceed otherwise in his own aphorisms; as Kafka famously wrote: "In theory there is a possibility of perfect happiness: To believe in the indestructible element within one, and not to strive towards it."[45] Such a fundamental indestructibility yields the only foundation for ethics, not without questioning what we take as important "events" in our lives. The indestructible is a good lever to rethink the role of the event, of its meaning, and of its links between infinity, truth, and the void.

Watt is for Badiou a sounding board; he shows that it moves from a Cartesian universe still dominant in *Murphy* to a world in which a self-enclosed being does not rule out infinite calculations. *Watt* starkly opposes the infinity of serial proliferation to the unique occurrence of an incomprehensible event, a crucial argument allowing Badiou's to bring his theory of the event to bear on the novel. In a chapter entitled "The Event and Its Name," he lays down the foundations for what is, according to him, Beckett's goal: an investigation of the minimal basis for freedom leading to the conditions of possibility of a true event. Such an event pierces through and hollows out any dominant rationality (*OB*, 55). *Watt* is a novel in which "the prose oscillates between grasping indifferent being and the torture of a reflection without effect" (56).

What saves Beckett from the danger of turning too "Kafkaian" or reaching a theological dead end (unlike Adorno, Badiou is annoyed by Kafkaian parallels and echoes—for him, Kafka is still too religious an author) is the emergence of *events* erupting outside the law. These brilliant events are called "incidents," and the first of these is the arrival of two piano tuners, the Galls, who exchange perfunctory remarks and go about their business. We never know why this event is chosen, yet it provides a conceptual riddle that has to be solved:

The incident of the Galls . . . ceased so rapidly to have even the paltry
significance of two men, come to tune a piano, and tuning it, and
exchanging a few words, as men will do, and going, that this seemed
rather to belong to some story heard long before, and instant in the
life of another, ill-told, ill-heard, and more than half-forgotten.

So Watt did not know what had happened. He did not care, to do
him justice, what had happened. But he felt the need to think that such
and such a thing had happened then, the need to be able to say, when
the scene began to unroll its sequences, Yes, I remember, that is what
happened then.[46]

This passage can serve as a gloss on Badiou's ethics of the event. In
order to be an event, the incident or symptomatic occurrence has not only
to be deployed outside the law but also to question the law. These events
are "paradoxical supplements" (*OB*, 56), defined by "great formal brilliance
and indeterminate purport."[47] Badiou notes that *Watt* still gestures in the
direction of the religious sphere, if one accepts the thesis that the eponymous hero is obsessed by the need to provide meaning when there is none
(57). Indeed, Beckett's texts address the locus of the law and end up mea-
suring themselves with its structural unnamability, which obliges them to
encounter a limit or foreclosure of their language.

As discussed in chapter 8, *Watt*'s foreclosure, along with the disclosure
of this law, would lead to the postulation of a sadistic ethics generalizing to
the others the "torture" that was created by the fight of thought against
itself. Bringing an important element to this discussion, Badiou allows us
to understand how a Cartesian *cogito*, once it is turned against itself, will
clash against the perversion of the Kantian law. Badiou repeats the idea
that Beckett's sadism stages the "torture of the cogito" (*OB*, 49, 51, 52–56,
59, 72). This principle of torture opens up to the question of the other, a
question that Beckett would rediscover in the 1960s according to Badiou's
chronology. This issue is at the core of *How It Is*, less a meditation on
postapocalyptic survival than a parable about everyday-life paradoxes of
love, if we agree that love consists of making a unity of two singularities.

Indeed, the later Beckett often sounds like Badiou, by anticipation, as it
were. In a dense passage of the elliptic and mysterious text "All Strange
Away" from the late 1970s, we find a reference to Greek philosophers, in
which the only specific name quoted is that of Diogenes, which suggests an
affinity with cynicism to which I will return, followed by questions that
eerily correspond to Badiou's concepts and interrogations: "ancient Greek
philosophers ejaculated with place of origin when possible suggesting pur-

suit of knowledge at some period, completed propositions such as, She is not here, the exception, imagine others, This is not possible, there is one."[48] The text evokes those notes on philosophy taken from compendiums by Windelband and others only to pass in review Badiou's theory of exceptions, the Lacanian absence of *the* woman, the theory of the function of love as the site of the one, the function of the impossible in science, and so on.

However, when Badiou approaches *Worstward Ho*, he does not immediately translate the text into statements or propositions that would follow his concepts. Although he compares the last section of the second trilogy with Heraclitus's poetic maxims, Plato's *Sophist*, and Mallarmé's *Un Coup de Dés*, he makes sense of the text in its own terms, via its specific vocabulary and syntax. The essay that Badiou devotes to *Worstward Ho* (or rather *Cap au Pire*, since he works with the French translation by Edith Fournier) in his *Handbook of Inaesthetics* defines Beckett's text as a "short philosophical treatise, as a treatment in shorthand of the question of being" (*OB*, 80). If Badiou's reading is both intensely abstract and philosophical, he nevertheless manages to use words, concepts, and phrases that are already in Beckett's text. As he generally does, Badiou breaks down *Worstward Ho* into a series of theoretical propositions, that I will attempt to summarize (*OB*, 81–96):

(1) "On" marks the imperative of saying, which is the first and only law of the text. A text has to go on, which implies that any new beginning is a continuation.

(2) Pure being is equated with an exercise in disappearance, which has two names: "void" and "dim."

(3) We are all inscribed in being as are the characters of this fiction: the one of a woman, the two of an old man and a child, the three of a thinking head uniting them. The universe is a "void infested by shades." "Dimness" is the condition of being. Whatever or whoever is inscribed in being is defined as that which can "worsen." Existence is a "worsening" brought about by language. It is always possible to say "worse" or "iller" something that has already been said badly before. However, the worst that language is capable of can never be equated to a pure Nothing.

(4) Thought is the recollection of (1) and (3), and is produced by a head, often reduced to a skull, and in whose confines the drama of the Cartesian cogito is replayed endlessly.

(5) The exercises in worsening are of three types, and correspond to three "shades"—they bear on the one, on the two, and on the

head. In these exercises in worsening, which all testify to the sovereignty of language, addition is equal to subtraction.

(6) Worsening is a labor that demands "heart," translated by Badiou as "courage," the courage of truth. Since there will be no termination of saying, this courage is founded upon a strong rapport between words and truth.

(7) If the void is unworsenable as an absolute limit, worsening aims at getting always closer to the void in an asymptotic drift. However, the void can only be crossed in an "event" that remains unspeakable.

(8) What has been gained by exercises in worsening is first a more rigorous definition of the two of love as the root of migration and change, and then a sense of joy and beauty that come from the link posited between words and truth. Beauty surges when we understand that the path of words goes counter to the demand of thought.

(9) Finally, on the last page, we go beyond the setup linking being, existence, and thought because we witness the irruption of an "event." This sudden metamorphosis is similar to the way a "constellation" appears both on the page and in the sky at the end of Mallarmé's poem *Un coup de dés jamais n'abolira le hasard.* Thus terms like "sudden" and "enough" in the penultimate paragraph manifest a rupture with what precedes. The main shape taken by the event is that the old woman has turned into an illegible grave. However, the imperative of language remains, which entails that all will begin again. Mallarmé, the French faun, will meet Beckett the Irish insomniac.

Once more, for Badiou, the main lesson to draw is ethical rather than poetic or ontological: Beckett exemplifies the courage of a truth to which he testifies in his writings (*OB*, 96). Such courage derives from words themselves, insofar as they keep a link with truth. "The courage of effort is always drawn out against its own destination. Let us call this the torsion of saying: the courage of the continuation of effort is drawn from words themselves, but from words taken against their genuine destination, which is to worsen" (97). This justifies Badiou's strategy, which is to quote terms provided by Beckett before articulating them in his schemes and logical categories. His commentary's length is the double of Beckett's prose poem; it includes the text almost entirely, while incorporating it forcibly into his own philosophical system—a rare feat of close reading allied with a radical translation.

The key concept for Badiou is that of the "event," and it is perhaps the most problematic one if one tries to pinpoint its emergence in a text. Badiou's drift suggests a progressive opening of Beckett's work until it can accept the idea of an event rendered all but impossible in *Watt*: "Little by little—and not without hesitations and regrets—the work of Beckett will open itself up to chance, to accidents, to sudden modifications of the given, and thereby to the idea of happiness. The last words of *Ill Seen Ill Said* are indeed 'Know Happiness'" (*OB*, 55). However, when Badiou comments on the moving finale of *Ill Seen Ill Said*, he takes "know happiness" at face value, as if it was a philosophical injunction.[49] One might be tempted to see it as similar to Murphy's end, with a nothing finally reached and engulfing all the rest. Isn't the reference to happiness ironical since it is coupled with death? Could Badiou have missed the latent ironies and the dark humor that pervade Beckett's text?

A similar affirmativeness marks Badiou's decision to see the "event" emerge in the very last page of *Worstward Ho*. He reads this as a recapitulation of the parameters of existence, followed by a sort of explosion: "But once the recapitulation is complete there brusquely occurs—in a moment introduced by 'sudden'—a sort of distancing of this state to a limit position . . . there emerges, in a suddenness that amounts to a grace without concept, an overall configuration in which one will be able to say 'nohow on.' Not an 'on' ordained or prescribed top the shades, but simply 'nohow on'—the 'on' of saying reduced, or leastened, to the purity of its possible cessation" (*OB*, 109–110). Arguably, the penultimate paragraph seems to call up the sudden emergence of something: "Enough. Sudden enough. Sudden all far. No move and sudden all far. All least. Three pins. One pinhole. In dinmost din. Vasts apart. At bounds of doundless void. Whence no farther."[50] However, we may remember that this is not the first time that Beckett uses "sudden." Earlier, we do find: "Next sudden gone the twain. Next sudden back."[51] One could praise Badiou's subtle rhetoric and his intertextual detour via Mallarmé to justify such a forced reading—no doubt brought about by his own philosophical problematic—and leave it at that, were it not for the followers of Badiou who have taken seriously his notion of an extra-textual event that somehow percolates into the text and leaves a "hole" for the emergence of truth.

The Vanishing Event

In his book on Beckett and Badiou, Gibson equates modernity with the event: "The event defines modernity."[52] Badiou has insisted on the paucity of historical events, of which Gibson lists a few: the French Revolution,

Kant, Wordsworth, and, of course, Beckett. Gibson seems to accept Badiou's reading of the last page of *Worstward Ho* but then hedges and retreats, qualifying Beckett's intentions by suggesting that the end of the text describes simply the "evenementiality of the event." In a cautious move, Gibson writes that "Beckett's commitments to aporetics is precisely a commitment to a writing that, in the absence of events, produces and sustains a consciousness of *événementialité*."[53] He argues that in *Fizzle 3*, Beckett "holds the event at several removes," but in his conclusion, still refers to "the passage about the event in *Ill Seen Ill Said*," as if this point has been accepted.[54]

A reader not familiar with Badiou's thought might want to ask: of what event are we talking? Badiou would refuse the promise of Derrida's hospitality to the other, or his concept of a "to come" defined by a "messianicity without a Messiah" as too religious. The event entails for Badiou a type of fidelity; it is often linked with either a political revolution or with a qualitative jump in science. Does it help to put it at a remove, as Gibson does when he talks of the *Unnammable* for instance: "the arduous fidelity of the Unnamable . . . is to *événementialité*, the event of the event?"[55] It is here that Adorno could help Badiou, even though it would run against the grain of Badiou's own *Ethics*, a book that staunchly refuses to talk of the Shoah as an absolute event or a state of "exception" that embodied radical evil. For Adorno, indeed, one event has taken place, and it is what he calls "Auschwitz." As we know, Beckett has been decidedly discrete on the topic. Nevertheless one text at least comes as close as possible to a direct naming of this event, *The Lost Ones*. The ending of the French text of *Le Dépeupleur* is more explicit; it quotes Primo Levi's *Si c'est un homme* in the last lines: "Voilà en gros le dernier état du cylindre et de ce petit peuple de chercheurs dont un premier si ce fut un homme dans un passé impensable baissa enfin une première fois la tête si cette notion est maintenue."[56]

Surprisingly, Gibson never mentions Primo Levi in his discussion of *The Lost Ones*, whereas the allusions to Levi's *Se quest'un uomo* in *The Lost Ones* have been analyzed in convincing detail by Antoinette Weber-Caflisch in *Chacun son dépeupleur*.[57] Weber-Caflisch begins by glossing the astonishing mistakes made by Beckett when he calculates the surface of the cylinder within which men and women are shown moving around. Why such an apparently deliberate perversion of mathematical exactitude? Weber-Caflisch explains that the phrase "si c'est un homme," used twice in the last part of the text, quotes the French title *Si c'est un homme* used to translate Primo Levi's moving memoir *Se quest'un uomo*.[58] Indeed, the questers called the "vanquished" by Beckett's text resemble those concentration camp inmates who had abandoned all hope and who, as Levi narrates, were dubbed "muslims" by those who still had the will to survive. If this can be called an "event," and if it has something to do with literature, as Adorno states, this event cannot be named directly but only evoked obliquely, silently, by effects of torsion created on language. Beckett's stilted and jerky minimalist sentences in *The Lost Ones* would approximate the position occupied by Paul Celan's tortured German syntax.

This is a point better seen and better said, it seems, by Adorno when he describes a paradoxical silence at work in *Endgame*. For him, the play had less to do with the cold war and the fear of universal atomic annihilation than with "Auschwitz," an event so extreme that it cannot be named: "The violence of the unspeakable is mirrored in the fear of mentioning it. Beckett kept it nebulous. About what is incommensurable with experience as such one can only speak in euphemisms, the way one speaks in Germany of the murder of the Jews."[59] The restraint of Beckett's muted reproach impressed Adorno all the more: "Beckett too could claim what Benjamin praised in Baudelaire, the ability to say the most extreme things with the utmost discretion; the consoling platitude that things could always be worse becomes a condemnation."[60] Could the event whose conditions of possibility are sketched in Beckett's later prose happen both in the future and in the past?

The answer to this question depends upon the kind of subjectivity that we imagine behind the condemnation. Badiou and Adorno meet when they see this subjectivity as the end product of a long "torture" associated with Western rationality. Adorno formulates this cogently in his notes on *The Unnamable*: "The sovereign *ego cogitans* is transformed by the *dubitation* into its opposite. And that is what it always was. For in order to retain itself as absolutely certain it had to turn itself into ever less. Sovereignty and filth belong together already in Kafka; in B[eckett] they become one. The Western process of subjective reduction calls itself by its proper name."[61]

Moreover, Adorno seems to have anticipated Agamben when he talks of reducing subjects to mere existence or "bare life" in "Trying to Understand *Endgame*": "He extends the line taken by the liquidation of the subject to the point where it contracts into a 'here and now,' a 'whatchamacallit,' whose abstractness, the loss of all qualities, literally reduces ontological abstractness *ad absurdum*, the absurdity into which mere existence is transformed when it is absorbed into naked self-identity."[62] Or, again, in *Aesthetic Theory*, about Beckett's novels: "they present the reduction of life to basic human relationships, that minimum of existence that subsists *in extremis*."[63] Finally, if one is to speak of an event, or of the mere possibility of an event, Adorno makes better sense, at least insofar as Beckett's *oeuvre* is concerned.

Can one approach Beckett by splicing Badiou and Adorno together? I
have indicated points of convergence, like the concept of reduction or
subtraction, the antidialectical dialectics of a nothing that reverts to a
positive affirmation, the insight that Beckett bridges the gap between
ontology and ethics. Looked at from another angle, Adorno's critical legacy
is severely tested if we focus on the later Beckett. Adorno praised the hero-
ism of modernist artists who rejected the bourgeois mass culture dominated by kitsch, and Beckett occupied a place of honor in this pantheon,
next to Schönberg and Kafka: all their works debunk the shallowness of
late capitalism and its commodified culture. However, this view has led to
a misunderstanding about modernism still prevalent in German culture. A
common myth is that high modernism is by nature opposed to popular
culture, hence is always elitist, thus potentially reactionary. Still adhering
to Adorno's point of departure, the socio-critical attack on modernism
blamed for its elitism became the hallmark of German-oriented critics like
Peter Bürger and Andreas Huyssen. If their analyses are more relevant
when dealing with German culture, the "great divide" that they see split-
ting high modernism from a feminized mass culture loses its edge as soon
as we deal with Anglo-American-Irish modernism, as any reading of *Ulysses*
and *The Waste Land* can show, not to speak of Beckett's trilogy.

In this context, we cannot bracket off the discussions between Adorno
and Walter Benjamin on the topic of mass culture, film, and trash. Benjamin's task had been to redeem the trash of history—especially of Paris in
the nineteenth century—via his own brand of "magical materialism." In
fact, Beckett appears closer to Benjamin than to Adorno. He still stands
out as a defiant bearer of negativity who debunks a world dominated by the
ethical entropy of late capitalism, *and* he identifies his characters with the
trash of a debased culture. He moves between the remnants of a tattered
classical culture that he mercilessly parodies *and* he may well be compared
to a Platonist giving us reasons to believe in the Good and the Beautiful, as
Badiou states. If *Aesthetic Theory* leaves us with a portrait of Beckett as a
paradoxical negativist, it is because Beckett had allowed Adorno to reconcile posthumously with his estranged friend Walter Benjamin. Such reconciliation should include Badiou:

> The "*Il faut continuer*," the conclusion of Beckett's *The Unnamable*, con-
> denses this antinomy to its essence: that externally art appears impossi-
> ble while immanently it must be pursued. . . . The political significance,
> however, which the thesis of the end of art had thirty years ago, as for
> instance indirectly in Benjamin's theory of reproduction, is gone; inci-
> dentally, despite his desperate advocacy of mechanical reproduction, in

conversation Benjamin refused to reject contemporary painting: Its tradition, he argued, must be preserved for times less somber than our
own. . . . But the function of art in the totally functional world is its
functionlessness; it is pure superstition to believe that art could intervene directly or lead to an intervention. The instrumentalization of art
sabotages its opposition to instrumentalization; only where art respects
its own immanence does it convict practical reason of its lack of
reason.[64]

Adorno identified in Beckett's work a refusal of the idea of progress—a
refusal duly allegorized by the lack of movement in his plays. Here is a
passage announcing Agamben's idea of a "bare" life that would be deployed
in *Waiting for Godot*:

The fulfilled moment reverses into perpetual repetition that converges
with desolation. His narratives, which he sardonically calls novels, no
more offer objective descriptions of social reality than—as the widespread misunderstanding supposes—they present the reduction of life
to basic human relationships, that minimum of existence that subsists
in extremis. These novels do however, touch on fundamental layers of
experience *hic et nunc* which are brought together into paradoxical
dynamic at a standstill.[65]

Adorno, for all his insistence on dialectics and negativity, agrees with
Badiou on this point. It is not a coincidence that this should occur at a
moment when the expression "dialectics at a standstill," which had been
used repeatedly by Walter Benjamin to define his method in the *Arcades
Project*, is echoed by Adorno in his evocation of Beckett's program. Moreover, Adorno, like Badiou, understands that the act of thinking is similar to
music for Beckett, which does not entail an adherence to Schopenhauerian
mysticism.

If the "music of thinking" stresses form more than content, it will be a
"brilliant" form capable of opening holes in knowledge, to combine
Badiou's general theory and Beckett's German letter of 1937. Such a
development dynamizes the dialectics of its own images and thus criticizes
the foundation of our belief in humanity's progress. Like a black hole, the
text thinks its own form and makes it become almost radiant, furthering
new concepts and chains of reasoning. Badiou makes us understand how
Beckett's texts always "think," even when they combine the bow and fiddle
of metaphysical *ritournelles* (to use Deleuze and Guattari's term). As long as
these texts assert the force of desire, as long as they let beauty surge in

language, they make us understand that, with words that go counter to the
demands of thought, a negation can be an affirmation, and vice versa.

As discussed in chapter 3, Beckett's self-canceling statements keep affirming the domination of teeming undecidables in *The Unnamable*. The narrator
hesitates so symptomatically and so systematically that it is hesitation itself
that turns into an ontological assertion: "There is at least a first affirmation,
I mean negation, on which to build."[66] The reversibility or indifference
between "yes" and "no" is a recurrent theme in the novel. In another passage, the narrator imagines a dialogue between a master and workers who
had the task of plugging holes somewhere:

> But commanded to say whether yes or no they filled up the holes, have
> you filled up the holes yes or no, they will say yes and no, or some yes,
> others no, at the same time, not knowing what answer the master
> wants, to his question. But both are defendable, both yes and no, for
> they filled up the holes, if you like, and if you don't like they didn't, for
> they didn't know what to do, on departing, whether to fill up the holes
> or, on the contrary, leave them gaping wide.[67]

Can these workers fill the holes in knowledge that Truth will produce
according to Badiou? Or will we never know? Will there be an event, or
none, or just our endless waiting for the Event? Is there any hope? On this
vexed point, Beckett's answer rings very much like Kafka's famous quip:
Kafka had told his friend Max Brod that there was "plenty of hope, an
infinite amount of hope—but not for us."[68] Similarly, the narrator of *The
Unnamable* reassures us: "Is there then no hope? Good gracious, what an
idea! Just a faint one perhaps, but which will never serve."[69] Once more,
Adorno formulated the proximity between his two favorite writers in his
last note taken on *The Unnamable*: "Is nothingness the same as nothing?
Everything in B[eckett] revolves around that. Absolute discardment,
because there is hope only when nothing is retained."[70] Badiou may have
been tempted to rewrite the "nothing" as a philosophical or poetic "nothingness" too quickly, which led him to compare Mallarmé and Beckett.
Suggestive as it is, such abolished nothingness ultimately leads to a misreading, or to the invention of a final "event."

In all these cases, a dose of humorous skepticism helps. However, there
is one point upon which one cannot tergiversate. Given the baffling proliferation of reversible actions and events, given the pervasive undecid-
ability affecting all statements, what stands out is the need, the duty even,
to state and, hopefully, speak as well as possible. This is indeed the only law
of "saying." Whether the injunction to "know happiness" at the end of *Ill*

Seen Ill Said is a way of heralding an event, of being this event, or a denial
of this same event marked by future happiness, the promise of happiness it
contains is linked with the beauty of language. There cannot be a "happy
ending" if there is no ending, but happiness survives as long as language
does. Thus, if the main events of the past can be summed up by images like
the family photographs of *Film*, such pictures will have to be torn one by
one by the protagonist in order to be free. What trauma is Buster Keaton
running away from in *Film*? We will never know. However, in spite of all,
the images soon return. Even if the imagination is "dead," it revives itself
and keeps imagining. As Kant, Coleridge, and Badiou state with different
vocabularies, the Imagination of the event must first die as fancy in order
to be reborn as ethical power. Its serial rebirth posits the imagination as a
force (*Einbildungskraft*) capable of carrying out an imperative to speak as
well as possible; here is the first condition, a formal condition to be sure,[71]
for any assertion about the domain of freedom. In Beckett's later texts, if
the imagination is a force, freedom is its form.

CHAPTER II

Lessons in Pigsty Latin:
The Duty to Speak

Form, Beckett felt, would never be divorced from ethical value, but could not for all that be evacuated as such. This is why he staunchly rejected Adorno's imputation that Kafka had influenced him. What distinguished them was Kafka's use of form, a form that he did not like, as he told Israel Shenker in 1956: "You notice how Kafka's form is classic, it goes on like a steamroller—almost serene. *It seems* to be threatened the whole time—but the consternation is in the form. In my work there is consternation behind the form, not in the form."[1] Consternation is an excellent term to describe the effect of a laughter that laughs at itself or that laughs halfway, as in the "xanthic laughter" of *Texts for Nothing*, while contemplating the radical absence of any ending even in a catastrophe.

For Beckett, as for Proust, a central concern for style will give rise to an ethics that is also a "bathetics," a worship of the low under all its shapes, while adhering to a law of formal expressivity. Form dominates when style replaces the belief in the substantial unity of the soul. Beckett's ethical position has been defined by Jacques Lacan in his critique of the soul as the seat of affects. For Lacan as for Beckett, there is no soul burning in hell, only the hellish torture that language can inflict to one. The same language is a medium with which one will keep playing with, thus perpetuating the torture, but the torture has to be accomplished according to some rules. These rules give one a certain duty. This duty is that of "saying well," that is a *bien dire* that also means saying the "good." One ought to express one-self as best as one can, whether facing the most horrible or the most trivial incidents of one's life.

Echoing Dante's condemnation of the Sullen in Canto 7, Lacan dis-cusses their sin, which is called "sadness." For Lacan, such sadness should not be construed as "a state of the soul" because it is quite simply a "moral failing." Lacan then develops the analysis: "it is simply a moral failing, as Dante, and even Spinoza, said: a sin, which means a moral weakness, which is, ultimately located only in relation to thought, that is, in the duty to speak well, to find one's way in dealing with the unconscious, with the structure."[2] The sadness that Spinoza characterized as a diminution of our being in the *Ethics* is here equated with a despair facing language, or rather a lack of courage in applying language to what eludes us for being unconscious. Sadness is the sin of human speakers who fail to use lan-guage to battle with their unconscious. It is not simply a psychoanalytic cure, like Beckett's stint with Bion in London; the whole effort of litera-ture in its most irreducible straining toward expression would come under the heading of this double injunction: to have the courage to say, and to obey the duty to say well. The Roman rhetorician Quintilian, who appears in *Murphy* ("Scratch an old man and find a Quintilian"[3]), simi-larly extolled the ability to "speak well." Book 12 of his *Institutio Oratoria* gave specific instruction to develop and facilitate the idea launched by Cato that the good man was a *"vir bonus, dicendi peritus"* (a "good man speaking well)."

This duty to "speak well" explains why Beckett's writings are framed and kept together by rhetorical categories, so much so that the category of the "poetical" can apply to them all. Marjorie Perloff has demonstrated once and for all that a text like *Ill Seen Ill Said* ushers in a "new poetry,"[4] whereas *Watt* proves that Beckett was, consciously or unconsciously, a Wittgensteinian writer who obeyed the famous injunction: "Philosophie dürfte man eigentlich nur dichten."[5] Not only philosophy, but also novels and plays have to be written as well as poetry: they are all *Dichtung*. A similar rule was brandished by Schopenhauer when he wanted to debunk the obfuscating and opaque language of Hegel. One can tackle this injunc-tion from the angle of translation. If Beckett writes an idiosyncratic "poetry of thought," how can it be translated? Or as Heidegger would say, to use the example already taken, how can one translate *logos*?

Beckett's intuitive philosophy of language relies on a peculiar type of poetic diction, and therefore cannot avoid being caught up in formulations that are not universal, because they evince the presence of idioms that are not identical in all natural languages. Alain Badiou commenting Beckett has played a role in shaping these questions since he was quite daring when translating Beckett's texts into philosophical statements as we have just seen.[6] If one believes that Beckett's strategy was of the formalist kind, that he borrowed quotes and philosophemes from famous and obscure thinkers in order to compose his nonsystem of philosophy, we reach the problem of the untranslatable. As discussed in chapter 4, when we meet Belacqua's Italian teacher who doubted that it was possible to translate Dante's *qui vive la pietà quando è ben morta*, the question of translation dovetails with burning issues of ethics.

Beckett's stylistic evolution has often been construed as moving away from the erudite and reaching the gnomic, as slowly rejecting the Joycean polyglottic puns of *Dream of Fair to Middling Women* to attain the ethereal grace of the last poems or television plays, or of purely visual pieces like *Quad* in which words disappear altogether. An asymptotic curve toward wordlessness or verbal "strangury" would underpin the poetry itself. To stick to the theme of the curse of birth, one moves from the learned obscurities of the poem "Sanies I":

> müüüüüüüüüde now
> postwalloping now through the promenaders
> this trusty all-steel this super-real
> bound for home like a good boy
> where I was born with a pop with the green of the larches
> ah to be back in the caul with no trusts
> no fingers no spoilt love[7]

to dense and crisp verse translations of Chamfort's maxims of consternation and desolation:

> sleep till death
> healeth
> come ease
> this life disease[8]

via the bare statements of the last French poems adequately dubbed *mirlitonnades*, meaning doggerel or "kazoo music":

> chaque jour envie
> d'être un jour en vie

non certes sans regret
un jour d'être né.[9]

One of the *Mirlitonnades* offers a superbly minimalist rewrite of *"Rien n'aura eu lieu que le lieu"* of *Un Coup de Dés*, which is muted to an echolalic diminuendo whispering of negativity:

rien nul
n'aura été
pour rien
tant été
rien
nul[10]

However, we may note Beckett's preference for *nul* instead of *néant* (nothingness). *Nul* is more discrete, more grammatical or mathematical, and much less a philosophical concept. If these examples testify to an evolution toward minimalism, another tendency is observable in Beckett's writings—the wish to condense thought to the maximum by delivering maxims, proverbs, and *sententiae*. This condensation appears in "Whoroscope," a miracle of concision if we compare it with the volumes on the life of Descartes that Beckett had perused in Dublin and Paris. Even if this poem was Beckett's way of sending up *The Waste Land*, it makes the French philosopher ascend from the sordid farces of everyday life vaudevilles to a sublime elevation, as shown by the following passage:

so I'm not my son
(even if I were a concierge)
nor Joachim's my father's
but the chip of a perfect block that's neither old nor new,
the lonely petal of a great high bright rose.[11]

If it is not immediately clear why these lines should "prove God by exhaustion," as Beckett's note states, the note has been taken as announcing a literary program of diminution and impoverishment. However, *exhaustion* has other meanings, like using up completely, or trying out all the elements of a series; those meanings are deployed in *Watt*, with the difference that in that novel it is the very absence of God, a divine being hollowed out by serial and repetitive permutations, that is "proved by exhaustion."

Thus the distribution of logorrhea as opposed to concision in Beckett's works refuses to follow a simple arc or obey a clear-cut teleology. For instance, concision dominates in an early poem like "Gnome" (1934):

Spend the years of learning squandering
Courage for the years of wandering
Through a world politely turning
From the loutishness of learning[12]

The rhyme-scheme based on a recurrent *-ing* pattern is even more held together by the imperative verb "Spend." The imperative releases the wandering "gnome" from the thrall of the gnomic and pushes him into the open. Beckett's work is far from monolithic, even when its resources lie in proverbs, maxims, and witty sayings. Beckett's formalism is not that of other modernists like Eliot who tend to oppose form (or culture) and chaos (or contemporary history). In the 1960s Beckett could still describe his effort as an attempt "to find a form that accommodates the mess."[13] "Formalism" suggests that the force of certain word combinations—their rhythms, shapes, and patterns—override whatever thought is contained in them. Such formalism could be aligned with the experiments of the *Oulipo* group, whose members would endlessly rewrite proverbs and retranslate famous poems, systematizing a tendency already present in André Breton's or Paul Eluard's Surrealist poems.

As a translator of poems, Beckett realized that the most difficult thing is not to render complex verse but simple lines. How can one find an adequate equivalent for Guillaume Apollinaire's anaphoric ending in "Zone" with his celebrated "Soleil Cou Coupé"? Beckett came as close as possible to perfection, but here had to admit defeat. "Zone" ends with:

Adieu Adieu
Soleil cou coupé

Beckett changes the point of view from the neck to the head, which suggests a Bataillean vision of an acephalic man; the image is solid, but lacks the subtly stuttering strength of the original:

Adieu Adieu
Sun corseless head[14]

Beckett schooled himself as a translator in the prewar years, and soon was ready to face more demanding challenges—his own. His stint with creative translation began early. A good example of his skills can be found in *Beckett in Black and Red*. His diligent translations for the *Negro* anthology were his way of thanking Nancy Cunard for the publication of "Whoroscope" and the prize that crowned it. With this huge book, Cunard wanted to reconstruct a "black" history by going back to African cultures, and then studying the "negro" diaspora. For her, Beckett translated articles by Raymond Michelet, Georges Sadoul, or Benjamin Peret, but had to be creative when battling with Ernst Moerman's poem on Louis Armstrong, which starts with a trumpet flourish:

> Un jour qu'Armstrong jouait au loto avec ses soeurs
> Il s'écria: "C'est moi qui ai la viandre crue."
> Il s'en fit des lèvres et depuis ce jour,
> Sa trompette a la nostalgie de ce premier baiser.[15]

Beckett mixes up echoes of Anglo-Irish and African-American phrases like "li' ole fader Mississippi" in a perfectly jazzy overture:

> suddenly in the midst of a game of lotto with his sisters
> Armstrong let a roar out of him that he had the raw meat
> red wet flesh for Louis
> and he up and he sliced him two rumplips
> since when his trumpet bubbles
> their fust buss[16]

The lack of punctuation and capitalization reinforces the poetic "swing" with its string of easygoing American colloquialisms. More difficult was the translation of Crevel's impassioned attack on European sexual hypocrisy facing black women of which we caught a glimpse in chapter 2. Crevel took no prisoners and did not even spare Baudelaire who had a life-long entanglement with Jeanne Duval, his notoriously promiscuous mulatto mistress. "The Negress in the Brothel" was so litigious that the text had to be omitted from the table of contents; it was glued to the volume at the last minute to avoid censorship.

Crevel dazzles the reader with erotic jests and bawdy puns, jumping from dizzy associations of images to wild sexual and political rants. Here is a typical parallel:

> Ainsi, notre civilisation analytique a consacré parallèlement le double
>   règne du bordel où l'on baise
> du salon où l'on cause[17]

This is translated bravely:

> Thus our civilization splits up into the holy and divided kinesis of: In the
>   Brothel: Sexual intercourse.
> In the Drawing-Room: Social intercourse.[18]

Beckett finds witty equivalents for Crevel's devastating fury in the portrayal of the "Negress" of the metropolitan brothels:

Et qu'elle n'ait pas le mal du pays. Là-bas, dans son continent original, avec ses négrillons de frères, des administrateurs, des généraux et qui sait? peut-être ce maréchal qui a mérité réputation d'impérator romain, jouent à "je t'encule et tu me suces." Pourquoi la colère secouerait-elle une famille qui a si bien réussi.

Vraiment ce serait à vous ôter l'envie d'aller porter sa goutte militaire, sa goutte religieuse aux sauvages.[19]

However, Beckett somewhat tones down the sexual content while being as sarcastic as Crevel:

And Sarah need not be homesick. For what are they doing, governors, generals and even the Imperial Roman marshall himself? Playing with the picaninnies: which is only tit for tat. The heart of so prosperous a family shall not be troubled.

After that I propose to withdraw my subscription from the Society for the Diffusions of the White Man's Moral and Physical Complaints among Savage Peoples.[20]

We also hear in the prostitute's "black conch" the echo of a tidal wave threatening to "engulf every capitalistic fortress, from brothel to cathedral."[21] These felicities confirm the connection between the politics of translation and the stylistic provocations of the avant-garde in the 1930s.

Ludovic Janvier explained that, when translating *Watt* with Beckett, they aimed at rendering sounds and rhythms more than sense: "the absolute similarity of terms or the perfect adequation between words and expressed idea would at times count less than the rhythmic or aural situation of the word in a syntagm."[22] Janvier lists some failures while registering felicitous *trouvailles*, as when they found an equivalent for Goff's evocation of his wife's "wom":

When Larry leaped in my wom.
Your what? . . .
You know, said Goff, her woom[23]

This became in French "ma trice" then declined as "sa trice."[24]

In his last years, however, Beckett began to despair of translation as a possible practice. He had been striving so relentlessly for a literary idiom that would be "idiomatic" that in the end, his texts could not be translated. This happened with *Worstward Ho*. When Mel Gusow met Beckett in the summer of 1985, he found the writer in a state of depression, a symptom of which being that he failed to translate his own text: "He had been trying to translate *Worstward Ho* into French and was having extreme difficulty. 'I can't translate it,' he confessed. 'I can't translate the first word.' With an urgency, he said, 'I've gagged myself,' then added in a moment of Beckettian humour, 'Life's ambition.'"[25]

What is even more remarkable is that Beckett had managed to translate himself so regularly up to this point. Even if critics have pointed out minimal differences between the style of *L'innommable* and that of *The Unnamable*, both texts feel equally "original." *The Unnamable* loses some of the strength and subtlety of the French original, as we can see in a passage from the lyrical ending culminating with "I can't go on, I'll go on."[26] Close to the beginning of a sentence of three pages that calls up the image of a huge prison and ends with an endless flow of words, we find this:

> repartir, dans cette immensité, dans cette obscurité, faire les move-
> ments de repartir, alors qu'on ne peut pas bouger, alors qu'on n'est
> jamais parti, on le con, faire les mouvements, quells mouvements, on
> ne peut pas bouger, on lance la voix, elle se perd dans les voûtes, elle
> appelle ça les voûtes, c'est peut-être le firmament, c'est peut-être
> l'abîme, ce sont des mots, elle parle d'une prison[27]

Here is Beckett's condensed English version:

> start again, in this immensity, this obscurity, go through the motions
> of starting again, you who can't stir, you who never started, you the
> who, go through the motions, what motions, you can't stir, you launch
> your voice, it dies away in the vault, perhaps it's the abyss, those are
> words of a prison[28]

Beckett had to battle against French grammar, which makes an explicit feminine of "voice." The last segment is clearer in French; "elle parle" refers to the voice, whereas the English has to combine "those are words" with "prison." The incongruous pun "on le con" is rendered weakly by "you the who." Rhyming is the key to echo "Oh le con," a French insult implying that the subject has been stupid enough never to leave his home, while suggesting a general deficiency ascribed to the neutrality of language. Beckett preferred *you* to the neutral *one*, which creates an interesting inner dialogism while missing the weird echo of *on/con*.

This segment calls up an intractable problem of self-translation brought to by *Worstward Ho*; Beckett, when trying to translate "On. Say on. Be said on. Somehow on"[29] into French thought that there was no French equivalent for the reversal of "On" into "No."[30] Indeed, his own translation of *Waiting for Godot* systematically renders "En avant" as "On." Three syllables would be prohibited in the terse idioms of the text, but a solution would have been to use Beckett's "*on le con.*" A more radically Beckettian version might have begun thus: "C'on. Dis c'on. Qu'on dise c'on. Dis-continue. Dit pris, compris, non pas qu'on prie."[31] Would this have flown or crawled? Obviously, Beckett was not ready yet for Oulipian exercises that would have delighted Georges Perec, like rewriting *The Unnamable* by using only mono-syllabic words.

Nevertheless, Beckett has crafted a text halfway between prose and poetry that pushed the limits of the English language to new extremes of condensation. One may assert that the text reads better as philosophy; such is the contention of Alain Badiou who, as we have seen, placed *Worstward Ho* next to Heraclitus, Plato, and Mallarmé. If *Worstward Ho* is a "philo-sophical treatise, a treatment in shorthand of the question of being,"[32] Badiou's matrix has combined Beckett's concepts before incorporating them in his system; this proves that the untranslatable is not the unthink-able, provided philosophers are willing to extend their vocabulary. Even if, as I argued, one may object to the presence of an "event" in the last pages of *Worstward Ho*, Badiou allows Beckett's text to "think" beyond the "quaquaquaqua" of Lucky's rant in *Waiting for Godot*. Badiou's concepts and Beckett's idiosyncratic verses tend indeed to converge, as shown by a French poem from 1977 presenting the quandary of "eyes" and "hands" unable to hold whatever is deemed to be the "good":

> ce qu'ont les yeux
> mal vu de bien
> les doigts laissé
> de bien filer
> serre-les bien
> les doigts les yeux
> le bien revient
> en mieux[33]

A translation might be:

> What good eyes
> have ill seen
> what good fingers
> let slip
> hold them tight
> fingers eyes
> the good returns
> bettered

This uncharacteristic optimism is soon debunked, for the next stanza, which stages the heart and the heads, ends on a perfect reversal:

ce qu'a de pis
le coeur connu
la tête pu
de pis se dire
fais-les
ressusciter
le pis revient
en pire.[34]

Literally:

what worse has
the heart known
what worse has
the head told itself
make them resuscitate
then the worse returns
worsened.

The solution would be to provide a simple paraphrase capable of respecting the text's idiosyncrasies, a commentary struggling less against the text's willful ironies than against Beckett's tendency to pure reduction. Whenever an expressive form can be found, then the "worse" has been warded off, as one sees in the statement made by Beckett to Charles Juliet in 1973. Juliet had asserted that an artist cannot be original without disposing of a rigorous ethics. For once, Beckett disagreed and he replied rather testily: "What you say is right. But moral values are not accessible. They cannot be defined. To define them, one would have to make a value judgment, which is impossible. . . . Paradoxically, it is through form that artists can find a solution. By giving form to the non-form [*l'informe*]. Only at this level might there be an underlying affirmation."[35] In terms that, once more, call up both Badiou's and Bataille's concepts, Beckett displaces ethics toward a minimalist formalism: given the nonavailability of positive values, the courage to create forms by struggling against the informal defines the sole ethical program worth the effort.

It is most likely that Badiou's philosophical paraphrases would have been acceptable for Beckett. Whenever he explained his themes himself, which was rare enough, he would resort to a kind of philosophical poetry. For instance, in 1976, Beckett summed up for Morton Felman, who had

composed a score for *Film*, the dominant themes of his work. Before Felman could take any note, Beckett scribbled a few lines for him:

> To and fro in shadow
> from outer shadow to inner shadow
> from impenetrable self to impenetrable unself
> by way of neither.[36]

This gave birth to a short text entitled "Neither," which is, indeed, neither
poetry nor philosophy. It ends with:

> then gently light unfading on that unheeded neither
> unspeakable home.[37]

Of course, this looks very much like the later poems ("something there" or
"thither" come to mind[38]), while being not far from the later plays (*Foot-
falls*) or the later translations ("To and Fro" recurs in the translation of a
poem on Saint Theresa by Mexican poet Alfonso Reyes). This suggests
that by the late 1970s, Beckett could formulate his writing practice in a
poetic and philosophical way.

The effort to stick to gnomic concision took Beckett away from the
Latinate diction capable of condensing an argument in a neat but wordy
one-liner, of which Seneca and Augustine provided models that he relished. Even if Beckett loved the "shape" of such sentences, he longed to
reach a degree of condensation in which the abstract and the concrete,
the particular and the general, the personal and the universal would be
fused, without for all that completely identifying form and meaning—as
Joyce had.

Beckett's first novels, *Murphy* above all, betray the limitations of his
method. If striking sentences can be remembered as in the evocation of
Murphy's mind in chapter 6, the attempt to have all characters speak in a
gnomic mode ends up being disappointing or predictable. Neary's exhor-
tations in chapter 10 unleash a "battle of wits" during which the three
accomplices explain why they need Murphy. In the dense crossfire of verbal
pyrotechnics, all the characters end up speaking like the author, who himself speaks like a book. Here is Miss Counihan expressing her disdain facing Celia: "One of the innumerable small retail redeemers . . . lodging her
pennyworth of pique in the post-golgothan kitty."[39] Precisely, the sole
exception in this game of verbal one-upmanship is Celia who remains
simple when she states: "I was the last exile."[40] This fits her character, her
naïve but staunch resistance to her partner's gnomic style; Celia describes
accurately the effect of Murphy's series of witty *pointes*: "She felt, as she felt

so often with Murphy, spattered with words that went dead as soon as they sounded; each word obliterated, before it had time to make sense, by the word that came next. It was like difficult music heard for the first time."[41] In *Murphy*, Beckett refused to take his minor characters as more than puppets: they gesticulate for a while, they utter amazing sallies, but never really become credible. As he explained, the "comic exaggeration" of their speeches was to evoke "the Hermeticism of the spirit."[42] However, soon after he would need the *bathos* of low comedy in order to deflate the same hermeticism.

Beckett learned the true art of the low, which is also the art of the flow (even if this flow can turn into strangury, that slow urinal discharge drop by drop) during the war. We can compare the torrential but often shallow witticisms of *Murphy* with the fluid ease with which the first paragraph of *Watt* describes the complexity of the position of jealous desire. We are told that Mr. Hackett likes only one bench in the street: "The seat, the property very likely of the public, was of course not his, but he thought of it as his. This was Mr. Hackett's attitude toward things that pleased him. He knew they were not his, but he thought of them as his. He knew they were not his, because they pleased him."[43] Hackett desires what is not his, because were this his, he would not desire it. Therefore he has to claim as his what is not his. He will stop desiring as soon as the object appears as truly his. We find a similar analysis of desire in *Murphy* when we follow the tribulations of Neary the "yearning" philosopher, but they take several pages. Here, two lines suffice to sketch Hackett's paradox. However, *Watt* soon starts dilapidating its riches and exhausts itself in endless lists and serial permutations.

One-liners reappear in the Addenda as the excremental refuse excluded by the hermeticism of the spirit. One needs to know both French and German to understand the pun linking *Erde* with *merde* in the parody of Goethe presented by "die Merde hat mich wieder" that I discussed in chapter 8.[44] This verbal echo nevertheless appears as Beckett's cryptic note to himself: it will launch the entire narratological program of *How It Is*, a novel first written in French with a title presenting an untranslatable pun: *Comment c'est*, a phrase in which we can hear *Commencer* (How to begin). How could one find an equivalent? Facing this quandary, Beckett the self-translator remained silent. He knew that this is "*How It Is*" with his two languages, both full of treacherous black holes. The point was to leave room for suspension dots in an architecture of silences with "numerous repeats." This is what we hear about the older protagonist of "Enough": "He was not given to talk. An average of a hundred words per day and night. Spaced out. A bare million in all. Numerous repeats. Ejaculations. Too few for even a cursory survey. What do I know of man's destiny? I could tell you more about radishes. For them he had a fondness. If I saw one I would name it without hesitation."[45] The French original puns on *radis* so as to suggest *–dis* as in *redis* (say it again).[46] Let us see out of which soil these namable radishes grow.

CHAPTER 12

An Irish Paris Peasant

Beckett's silences were often triggered by the contemplation of catastrophes, disasters, and ruins. One of the most moving meditations about a city in Beckett's oeuvre is the evocation of the bombed city of Saint-Lô, a completely obliterated city that he called "The Capital of the Ruins."[1] The city had been flattened by a US air force raid in June 1944. For a few months, Beckett worked as a volunteer in the Irish hospital established there in 1945. In a sense, all the cities in which he lived could be called "capitals of the ruins" as well. The short text entitled "Lessness" begins with this statement in block capitals: "RUINS TRUE REFUGE" and then develops it,[2] rehearsing the same words all over again: "One step in the ruins in sand on his back in the endlessness he will make it."[3] The equation of "ruins" and "refuges" could apply to Dublin as well as to Paris, the two cities around which his imaginative life revolved. Born a Dubliner, but having been raised in the posh suburb of Foxrock, Beckett could be called a Parisian because he spent more than half a century of his life in that capital.[4] However, one finds very little of the "city of light" in his works. On the contrary, they teem with evocations of lush or melancholy Irish landscapes, or of Irish suburbs and small French villages. One could say that his imagination had remained caught up in evocations of the melancholy or lush (according to season) landscapes around Foxrock: the ruins concern first the remains of gentility in this suburb less of Dublin than of Dun Laoghaire, with its still beautiful golf course.

Whenever Beckett evokes these green and shiny landscapes, jarring images crop up, as when Arsene mentions "the crocuses and the larch turning green every year a week before the others and the pastures red with uneaten sheep's placentas."[5] The cycle of nature evoked here, as in many other texts, mixes the horror of birth with the specter of death. The result is always the same, a disabused contemplation of same old "muckball": "the endless April showers and the crocuses and then the whole bloody business starting all over again. A turd."[6] Nature means an eternal return of the same, spelling out cycles of pain or boredom facing the spectacle of digestive or reproductive excretion. Why this apparently cynical view of pastoralism? At times, Beckett's cynical pastoralism encroaches with visions of cities, all of which are threatened by disaster, as Lisbon had been for the philosophers in the eighteenth century. In a poem in French, Beckett writes: "Sur Lisbonne fumante Kant froidement penché."[7]

Voltaire had written a famous "Poem on Lisbon's disaster," while Kant published no fewer than three essays about the catastrophe in the year following the earthquake. There was no way one could make sense of such a cataclysm in the context of religious discourse then: the Lisbon catastrophe had taken place early on All Saints' Day of 1755, when most people were in churches that collapsed on them, while the red-light district of the Alfama, located higher, was spared this havoc. Kant, who was twenty-four then, argued that the catastrophe was due to natural causes, wrongly attributing them to fiery gases arising from the interior of the earth. Beckett mentions this rational attitude in the French poem quoted above, adding a list of past catastrophes like those that may have caused the extinction of the mammoths. But in a very Proustian vein, he ironically links a vanished species like the dinotherium with the lost memories of our first kisses:

> comme si c'était d'hier se rappeler le mammouth
> le dinothérium les premiers baisers . . .[8]
> [As if it was yesterday, remember the mammoths
> the dinotherium the first kisses . . .]

Indeed, given the suddenness and scope of the devastation in Lisbon, Kant's rationalism, any rationalism, would be forced to accept the truth of Voltaire's irrefutable remark: "Of destruction Nature is the empire." The new rationality would have to examine as "coldly" as possible the connection between Nature, Reason, and Destruction. And thus, because Beckett perceived the cycle of nature everywhere, even in those doomed cityscapes, he rarely used cities as a backdrop for local color and idiomatic characterization as one sees in the works of authors like Eliot, Joyce, Céline, or Proust.

For Beckett, Lisbon, London, Dublin, or Paris meant people, either alive or dead, more than sites one visits. Paris offers a good example; it provided first of all a cultural milieu, defined by social networks and a specific use of language. It was the place where a certain French was spoken, and this slangy idiom durably impacted Beckett's works. Parisian French bathes the texts in all its changing moods, from racy slang to abstract concepts and the murmurs of marital bickering. Besides its layered idioms, Paris offered a convenient site for productive work—up to a point. Fears of sterility would be assuaged by late night drinks and conversations, until the network of friendships and obligations became too heavy a burden. One can distinguish four moments in Beckett's progressive introduction to Paris, which correspond to different stages in his becoming Parisian.

As we have seen, the first period was an early and fruitful initiation, the two years spent at the École Normale Supérieure from November 1928 to September 1930. Beckett's fortunate meeting with Thomas McGreevy opened the doors to the Joyce family. This nuclear family soon included an "Odeonia" dominated by Adrienne Monnier and Sylvia Beach, with the group of experimental writers and artists gathered by Eugene Jolas around *transition*. Next to Dublin, so provincial and Puritan then, Paris offered everything at once. It was the Paris of the Quartier Latin that Beckett knew intimately, with inroads near the Invalides and the quays of the Seine explored during walks with Joyce. In two years, Beckett went out a lot, visited the Louvre and galleries, was a theatergoer and devoured the new magazines and little reviews. Often taken for Joyce's secretary, he was in the habit of ending up dead drunk at the end of the dinners launched by Joyce to mark birthdays, publications, and other rituals. It was in Paris that Beckett discovered Surrealism, a movement that left a deep imprint on him. It was in Paris that Beckett became a writer and started publishing poems and essays.

The second period was brief but intense and lasted from January 1932 to July 1932. It was marked by Beckett's decision to reject all values but literature: he would be an "artist" like Joyce. Such a momentous decision was made after the breakup with Joyce over the plight of his daughter Lucia and a parallel breakup with Peggy Sinclair. The decision led to the refusal of an academic career in Dublin. When Joyce later realized that

Lucia's dementia had not been caused by Beckett, he invited him back into his circle, and the collaboration with Jolas's *transition* turned into a regular partnership. This is the moment when Beckett completed the redaction of *Dream of Fair to Middling Women*, an unpublishable novel not only because it was hardly readable but also too close to the style of *Finnegans Wake*.

The third period was highly dramatic; it followed the stay in London that serves as the basis for *Murphy* and the aborted trip to Germany. It contains instances of near death, first when Beckett was stabbed by a pimp near the impasse of Villa Coeur-de-Vey in 1938, and then when he barely avoided being arrested by the Gestapo in 1942. It lasted from October 1937, when Beckett settled in Paris, to August 1942, when he rushed out of his apartment fleeing the police as they were catching the members of the Gloria resistance network. This moment defines Beckett's maturity: he leaves behind the immaturity of the "artist as a young man" and becomes a writer who shares his life with a woman. He is ready to make life-changing decisions. In autumn 1937, Beckett left Dublin for Paris, where, after a few attempts and delays he found a lasting refuge, the small apartment at 6 rue des Favorites (fifteenth arrondissement), not very far from the metro station Vaugirard. Visitors would say that the place looked more like a studio than an apartment, and they found it situated too far from the fashionable sixteenth arrondissement or the livelier areas of Montparnasse or the Latin Quarter. Such distance was needed by Beckett, by then engaged in liaisons with several women. After the near-fatal stabbing in January 1938, Suzanne Deschevaux-Dumesnil came to share the rue des Favorites apartment.

The French poems evoking this period treat themes that revolve around sterile lovemaking, solipsist isolation, the *taedium vitae*, and the fear of death. They are markedly different from the first poems in English; the style is less allusive and polyglot puns are rare. This paring down of the language corresponds to Beckett's immersion in spoken French. At times, we see a medievalist Paris called up, as in the poem "être là sans mâchoires sans dents," in which we meet Roscelin, the nominalist teacher of the notorious Abélard:

> être là sans mâchoires sans dents
> où s'en va le plaisir de perdre
> avec celui à peine inférieur
> de gagner
> et Roscelin et on attend
> adverbe oh petit cadeau[9]
> [to be there without jaws without teeth

where the pleasure of losing goes
barely inferior
to that of winning
and Roscelin and we are waiting
an adverb oh little gift]

The eleventh-century nominalist philosopher insisted that words refer to real objects. Abélard turned against Roscelin and denounced him as a heretic. He was punished for his misdeeds—Abélard's castration for his notorious dalliance with Héloïse is evoked in the first line, as being "without jaws without teeth." More surprising is the connection established between *on attend* (one is waiting) and an adverb; the verb could become adverbial in *en attendant*, as we find it in the French title of *Waiting for Godot*. Beckett implies here that *waiting* is less a present participle than an adverb that can be attached to any verb. This suggests an empty time, although really lost for the woman of Les Halles: paid by the hour, she is waiting for her *petit cadeau*, the usual euphemism for the payment of a prostitute's services. Thus time cannot be "killed" even in a mindless coition— for someone is always waiting. Therefore waiting defines the whole human condition, an idea that *Waiting for Godot* exploits in many ways. The same poem uses the slangy phrase *qu'elle mouille* (make her wet), a term that Beckett had found in the *Journal* of Jules Renard. Renard had written cynically: "Aussi navrant que le 'attendez que je mouille' d'une vierge' [As distressing as a virgin saying "Wait whilst I moisten"]."[10] The context shows that Beckett highlighted the delayed or impossible sexual enjoyment, but the lyrical finale of the poem conquers all the sexual and metaphysical hesitations by a diction full of submerged puns caught in an incremental and pulsating rhythm:

et vienne
à la bouche idiote
à la main formicante
au bloc cave à l'œil qui écoute
de lointains coups de ciseaux argentins[11]
[that she should come
to the idiot mouth
to the formicating hand
to the vena cave of the heart to the eye listening to
distant and silvery scissors strokes]

The pun on *fourmi* (ant) and *fornication* reappears in *Happy Days* where it triggers a moment of hilarity. In this wry Parisian vignette situated in a brothel of Les Halles, the tinkling of scissors wielded by the Parchae seems to announce a peaceful and ethereal death.

The dialectics of this Parisian period, whether nominalist or idealist, absorb the negative so as to convert it into a positive, as we see in "Rue de Vaugirard":

à mi-hauteur
je débraye et béant de candeur
expose la plaque aux lumières et aux ombres
puis repars fortifié
d'un négatif irrécusable[12]
[halfway
I declutch and gaping with candor
expose the plate to lights and shadows
then cycle off strengthened
by an irrefutable negative]

Images coming from different technologies are spliced: the bicycle—used by Beckett to go from rue des Favorites (a street merging with rue de Vaugirard) to Montparnasse—and photography. The subject becomes a camera recording a vision in black and white. The darkness of the negative is kept in reserve, as it were, after the poet stops to observe and then begins pedaling again. Darkness highlights a "white" candor thanks to a process of purification by evacuation or of transformation by inversion. The dialectical twist relies on a series of oppositions: shadows and light, love and indifference, isolated self and the vastness of the world. In the end, as Adorno would suggest, a good dose of negativity can bring health and happiness.

Such couplings lead to a de-doubling of the self, as one witnesses in "Arènes de Lutèce," one of the rare descriptive Paris poems.[13] The scene is the Gallo-Roman ruins of the amphitheater situated between rue Monge and rue des Arènes, two names quoted in the poem. A character is seen entering the space with a woman, but from higher up than the steps, and then he sees himself walking in. Is it a doppelganger or can he see himself entering the space? A green dog is running, little girls push a hoop; it is cold, rainy, and misty; then the narrator suddenly shudders and feels reunited with himself. Some details are specific: we are told that the basis of the neoclassical statue there is that of Gabriel de Mortillet. The urban space with "the empty steps, the high houses, the sky/ giving us its light too late" provides a backdrop for a metaphysical quest for identity.[14] Beckett was tickled by the fact that the statue of the Arènes de Lutèce dedicated to the staid and bearded scientist de Mortillet actually represents a young woman. This impressionist poem might contain the blueprint for *Film*. While Buster Keaton flees the camera's gaze along high walls straight out of the New York of the Great Depression, "Arènes de Lutèce" is a Parisian hymn to a no less depressed urban and antique arena in which the division continues, not only between self and other, but also between self and self.

In spite of the dispirited tone of those Paris poems, this period corresponded to a moment of peace and hard-won equanimity. Beckett was fully integrated in the group of *transition*; he was at ease among the second wave of the English-speaking "pilgrims" who spent their nights chatting and drinking in Montparnasse. Montparnasse was the hub for the American expatriates, whereas French misfits like Jean Genet preferred the pimps and transvestites of Clichy and Pigalle to those of Montparnasse. Beckett did not follow the Surrealists, then relayed by Walter Benjamin in exile, to the small cafés of the nineteenth-century *passages* around the *grands boulevards*. He largely ignored Paris *rive droite*, except for the poem about Les Halles. His friends lived between Odéon and Les Gobelins, like Geer van Velde whose studio was on boulevard Arago, while from 1934 to 1939, Joyce lived in the seventh arrondissement at 7 rue Edmond Valentin.

Soon Beckett called his neighborhood the "commune de Vaugirard," which implies a sense of shared community.[15] If he could deplore his relative distance from Montparnasse, he felt comfortable in spite of the noise made by the neighbors—or perhaps because of the noise.[16] The French poems "Ascension," "The Fly," and "Prayer" were written soon after his taking possession of the new premises, and evoked features of this new life. An inner silence was opposed to the noise from outside, and from this confrontation he unleashed new dreams and fantasies, finding a boon in the soothing contemplation of nothing. The neighbors may scream loudly about a soccer game on the radio, but this is not distracting enough: the voices do not prevent the return of ghastly visions, the image of his beloved dying, blood spurting from her mouth, covering bed sheets. In another poem, the fly on the windowpane reminded the poet of a material, although transparent divide between the world and his subjectivity. Once the fly was squashed by the poet's thumb, it made the sea and the sky tumble together in a cosmic shipwreck.[17]

The fourth period is by far the longest and the most stable. Beckett came back to Paris in 1946 and reoccupied his apartment of rue des Favorites. Starting in 1953, he spent more and more time in his country cottage at Ussy. Finally, in January 1971, he moved to 38 boulevard Saint Jacques, a more comfortable apartment from which he could see the prison of La Santé and where he stayed until his final illness forced him to go to a clinic. The Paris in which Beckett lived was mainly *rive gauche* Paris from the Latin Quarter to Saint-Germain and Montparnasse. It stretched far south into the fifteenth arrondissement. Place names mentioned in the texts are mostly found there, from rue de Vaugirard to the Arènes de Lutèce. Beckett spent a lot of time in the cafés of Montparnasse including le Dôme, le Select, and la Coupole. He would meet his friends in the restaurant Les Îles Marquise on rue de la Gaieté, famous for its fish dishes, and whose Beaujolais wine Beckett never stopped praising.

Beckett's Paris was to accrue memories as years went by. In 1965, in an untypical outburst of enthusiasm, he told Lawrence Harvey that "every building, every bench" in Paris held memories for him.[18] However, talking of his wish to go to Paris in April 1933 when he had to stay in Dublin, he mentions his refusal to take root anywhere: "I am sure you were right to go to Paris. . . . Of course your letter made me wish very much to be there. The sensation of taking root, like a polypus, in a place, is horrible, living on a kind of mucous [*sic*] of conformity."[19] More than thirty years elapsed between these letters, but Beckett never wanted to "take root" in Paris. This he reserved for Ussy, his true refuge.

In Beckett's texts, Paris is everywhere and a nowhere, and accompanies plots as a shifting referential tissue. The ending of the eighth "Text for nothing" is a good warning for those who want to identify local references. At the end of meditation on how language, alone, can break the silence, the narrator zooms in on a specific place. He daydreams of being a blind and deaf passerby. He would wander aimlessly in Paris, but then he gropes his way into a metro station where he starts begging for money. Where is he? He appears first on Place de la République, precisely "at pernod time," the sacred hour of the *apéritif*.[20] A little later, he passes along United Stores (Magasins Réunis), wondering whether he is not on Place de la Bastille instead. Or perhaps his infirmities led him to the cemetery of Père-Lachaise. This shows how warped, twisted, and unreliable Beckett's Parisian geographies are. They only rely on exact topographies in order to exploit objective puns; the street named Godot de Mauroy, which stretches from the Madeleine Church to Saint Lazare station, still has at number 21 an Irish pub called *Molly Malone*, in a remarkable superposition of Joycean and Beckettian characters. Near rue de Vaugirard (fifteenth arrondissement), there is an Impasse de l'Enfant Jésus whose original name was "cul-de-sac de l'Enfant-Jésus," which was its official name in 1760. When the appellation was felt demeaning, it was renamed "Impasse," not a much more positive association, except that the offending *cul* (arse) had been deleted. This genealogy was not lost for *Eleutheria* and the French *Murphy*. In *Eleutheria*, Victor is discovered "still living in Impasse de l'Enfant-Jésus."[21] Upon hearing the address, Victor's aunt concludes that Victor must be extricated from it. Victor's "grand refusal" consists in exerting his freedom by doing absolutely nothing. Here is the life program called by the Glazier a "negative anthropology."[22] Christ living in an impasse, a dead end, a cul-de-sac, or a "blind alley," isn't this as forceful an image as when T. S. Eliot meditates on the sacred infant called "the Word without a word" by Lancelot Andrews in a perfect oxymoron, *Verbum infans*?[23] Beckett did not have to invent the name; the street still exists and leads from hospital Necker, formerly hospital of l'Enfant-Jésus, to rue Vaugirard. That the Holy Manger should be located in a "blind alley" adds a theological paradox to a Surrealist aesthetics of found objects.

Parisian places, often named, even in *The Unnamable*, are never described. Beckett agreed with André Breton's anathema against descriptions. In *Nadja*, Breton's own prohibition led him to replace Paris streets, squares, hotels, or monuments with black-and-white photographs, which paradoxically reinforced the sense of a Parisian context. One could not imagine Beckett's texts decorated with photographs, except perhaps for the Paris poems already mentioned. Beckett's Paris is above all a literary space in which one catches glimpses of the ghosts of other writers, like Apollinaire, whose *Zone* that he translated, and Céline, whose dark *Voyage au bout de la nuit* he admired. Paris also functions as a synecdoche for Europe: like Joyce, Beckett felt that he was a European, albeit a strangely nihilistic one: "to my certain knowledge I'm dead and kicking above, somewhere in Europe probably, with every plunge and suck of the sky a little more over-ripe, as yesterday in the pump of the womb."[24]

Two French places offered deeper roots, Roussillon and Ussy. Knowlson's biography describes Roussillon during the war, when Beckett was hiding there. I have already mentioned the coincidence that the castle of Lacoste, where Sade had organized his last orgies before he was sent to jail for a very long time, was partly visible. In fact, Beckett may not have been aware of this. He was not interested in the rich history of the Vaucluse with the ferocious wars of religion that left scars in all villages. He may not have known that Roussillon was inscribed in troubadour legend, a legend memorialized in Ezra Pound's fourth Canto. The old castle of Roussillon was destroyed after a murder of mythical proportions. The troubadour Cabestan was murdered by the jealous lord of Roussillon—and then the lord served his cooked heart to his wife. Learning what the dish was, she declared that she would never taste any other meat, and threw herself out of the window. Her suicide led to the downfall of the lord: he was murdered and his castle destroyed, a fate that almost befell Sade's own castle nearby. There was enough destruction at the time for Beckett to search for mythical parallels.

Beckett may not have known that his neighbor, René Char, was the head of a Resistance unit of partisans nearby. Char invented a poetic language of packed images and taut action to jot down his impressions as a *maquis* leader in Vaucluse and Roussillon. Char vents his anger and frustration when one of his men is executed by German soldiers and he has to watch, hidden nearby, refusing to risk the lives of the others. One day the population of Céreste, just fifteen miles away from Roussillon, banded together against the SS so as not to divulge where Char was hidden. All this is in the wonderful *Feuillets d'Hypnos*. Beckett, who was to translate one of Char's poems for *Transition 49* after the war, found a release in similarly nervous, taut, and compressed language when he composed *Watt*. Whereas Char's crisp prose poems keep the smell, heat, and stony feel of the Lubéron landscapes, *Watt* revisits and explodes Irish landscapes. Nevertheless, his creative immersion and excavation, in line with the program outlined in *Proust*, ended up owing something to the peculiar geography of Roussillon, with its abandoned ochre quarries and steep caves offering welcome hiding places.

What Beckett experienced in Roussillon—a village that in 1942 lived in the nineteenth century, without running water or hot baths, and in which someone called Samuel had to be a Jew—was so different from the luxury of Foxrock or the sophistication of Paris that one is surprised to see that it had become the model for Beckett when he built a house of his own. When he had his country house built in Ussy-sur-Marne in 1953, he eschewed luxury but pursued the dream of a place where he could "disappear," that is become invisible, as he had in 1942. The idea of disappearing is sounded as early as 1948.[25] "All I want is to disappear in the country," is a leitmotiv that runs through the correspondence.[26] Whereas Paris looks more and more like a social hell peopled by old friends and new bores imposing schedules and obligations, Beckett associates Ussy with a refuge in which stillness, silence, solitude, teeming animals, and creativity blend together.

What is striking in the letters documenting Beckett's everyday life in Ussy is that he repeats the gestures learned when working for food in the Audes' farm near Roussillon: digging, weeding, cutting, planting, attacking roots, fighting against pests like moles, ants, or wild boars. "Ussy" has translated and rewritten Roussillon in its very sonorities. Digging became an obsession in Ussy because many of the trees planted in the garden would die year after year. This mindless activity became soothing after the death of his mother. Beckett did not need a psychoanalyst like Bion to point out to him the obvious link between digging and mourning; several letters show that he was aware of the association. Here is one from January 1951: "I long to be digging, digging over [*labourer*] as they say here. Went for a long walk yesterday, met no one,—yes, I did, a gravedigger coming out of a cemetery pushing a wheelbarrow."[27] This is interspersed with hilarious accounts of the conversations in local cafés. An old man barges in after his wife has had a bad fall, but wishes he could finish her off with his shotgun. The stories overheard from the locals are wickedly funny, as when Beckett in a sort of dead pan, just after mentioning the proofs for *Waiting for Godot*, adds: "It is snowing. The farm-workers are fucking the cows, perched on 3-legged milking stools. Bad for the cows, it seems. They are called 'juniors' and are driven away pitilessly."[28] No need to invent animalistic tramps like the poor man killed in the woods by Molloy—these animal lovers are now his neighbors.

However, digging, for Beckett, is not a metaphor for writing, as it is in a famous poem by Seamus Heaney. For Beckett, digging means really digging: digging the earth, making holes into a communal tomb that links us with nature.[29] His garden was no "paradise," as the etymology of the word would suggest. Was it a purgatory, then? The life of animals and plants was still caught up in the same pathos of "germination, maturation, putrefaction, the cyclic dynamism of the intermediate."[30] Was the meaning of this mediation revealed by the apparent lack of purpose of a purpose? Digging was not even beautiful as an activity; however, it remained an imperative following the form of duty. Indeed, "digging" led to the French verb of "labourer," which means more than digging. It implied for Beckett plowing and toiling with an earth that was a "terreau," a fertile humus whose decomposition included the mixture of human and inhuman matter. This activity also evoked a "labor" whose outcome might be the birth of something.

CHAPTER 13

The Morality of Form—A French Story

Contrary to what most critics have asserted, Beckett's decision to write in French so as to write "without style" was not a biographical accident, the consequence of his exile from Dublin to Paris. It was a matured decision that enacted a consistent literary program. Moreover, this program happened to be shared by other French writers of the period. The difference was that Beckett enacted it more consistently, more rigorously and over a longer period of time. Besides, the program was formulated early, just after his first stay in Paris. Quoting a startling phrase coined by Lucien, the character modeled after the philosopher Jean Beaufret, "Black diamond of pessimism,"[1] Belacqua recognized in the phrase a purity of diction that he had seen in Racine and Malherbe. This leads him to generalize about the French language: "But the writing of, say, Racine or Malherbe, perpendicular, diamanté, is pitted, is it not, and sprigged with sparkles; the flints and pebbles are there, no end of humble tags and commonplaces. They have no style, they write without style, do they not, they give you the phrase, the sparkle, the precious margaret. Perhaps only the French can do it. Perhaps only the French language can give you the thing you want."[2] This fragment of *Dream of Fair to Middling Women* was excerpted in *Disjecta*, which proves that Beckett found it important.[3] What remains to be teased out is the link established between those "diamonds" (one might be tempted to describe them as Baroque metaphors) and the alleged absence of a style. Not everyone would agree that Racine writes without style. Indeed, "black diamond of pessimism," a trope in which one discerns an echo of Nerval's famous "soleil noir de la Mélancolie," sounds more precious than homely. It would take Beckett twenty more years to iron out the tensions that this passage held in store for him.

Sparkling French, but without Style

Beckett had the advantage of having learned French young; the identification with the other idiom was made easier by his awareness that his name was of French extraction (*bequet*), a name that *Eleutheria* defines as betraying a "Greenland Jew mixed with an Auvergnat."[4] Then he was immersed in the experimental avant-garde of the *transition* group, in which at least three or four languages were always combined. He had witnessed the impact of Joyce's creation of a syncretic language fusing more than seventy separate languages. He had perceived that the grammar of *Finnegans Wake* remained fundamentally English. Joyce's invented idiolect would turn into a universal language only if one knew enough English. In this context, Beckett appeared as a belated Synge who did not have to go the Aran islands to forge a new idiom at Yeats's suggestion, because he found it in the exchanges between blue-collar workers drinking calvados in Parisian cafés or among the resilient peasants toiling in the Lubéron hills, when he and Suzanne were hiding from the Gestapo in Roussillon.

The idea of French that Beckett elaborated during his student's years took him in a different direction. When he taught French literature at Trinity (1930–1931), his chosen landmarks in the survey of French literature were Racine and the modern classicism represented by André Gide, later called "le style Nouvelle Revue Française." Beckett admired Racine's modernity less for its stylistic directness than for the complexities of psychological analysis it allowed: Racine was a forerunner of Freud.[5] The model that he followed when it came to write in French was Gide more than Proust.[6] Already in his spoof of French literary criticism, "Le Concentrisme," Becket compared the individualism of du Chas with Gide's position, for Gide, he claimed, would never be called an "individual"— high praise in the context.[7]

This 1930 essay was read by Beckett at the Modern Language Society of Trinity College. Inspired by Normalien "canulars" (the students' farcical, and often elaborate, practical jokes), or by the spoofs mounted by Surrealists like Duchamp who invented a Rrose Sélavy whom he shared with Robert Desnos at exactly the same time,[8] "Le Concentrisme" sends off the mannerisms of French literary criticism by inventing this writer, whose name calls up the Chas of *More Pricks Than Kicks*. In the fake biography, Beckett evinces a bawdy humor à la Duchamp when he puns on "les cons sont tristes" (cunts are sad) to present the new movement:[9] "Vous allez vous appeler les *Concentristes*."[10] We note in passing that du Chas rehabilitates the expression of "asinine sadness" typical of poor donkeys; in a good exemplification of animal bathos, du Chas apologizes to the modest animals that he wrongly insulted in the past.[11]

The verve with which Beckett sketches the career of Jean du Chas, a fictional nobody with a strong suicidal bent, is infectious. This spoof shows that Beckett's French was wiry, imaginative, and muscular. Its intensity is on par with the witty hyperboles and crazy conceits of *Murphy*. Sharing Beckett's date of birth, du Chas functions as a parodic alter ego in a satire calling up Gide's *soties*, the delightful pastiches of the decadents in *Paludes* or the farcical plot of *The Vatican's Cellars*. Beckett also mentions Paul Valéry, a writer who "decomposes in absolute propositions what he has not read,"[12] an insight confirmed by Pierre Bayard's witty book.[13] In fact, du Chas is everywhere and looks Beckett's equivalent of Pierre Ménard, a Borgesian double, an author whose posthumous work does not consist in copying *Don Quixote* but in gathering his *Journals* and *Cahiers* (shades of Valéry) before launching a movement tending toward its own disappearance. Du Chas's "Discourse of the Exit" is a *"reductio ad obscenum"* of academic discourse that does not spare Proust:[14] Proust would never blow his nose before 6 AM on Sundays! Jean du Chas's *con*centrism anaphorically echoes with *con*cierges, the janitors or doorkeepers who seem to obsess him as they fascinated Descartes in "Whoroscope." If du Chas has a family air with Descartes once renamed Seigneur du Perron, his name calls up "chas," the term for the feminine sexual organ in libertine literature. With extreme gusto Beckett's debunks the tired tropes of French biographical criticism while conveying his mounting doubts about literature.

Betraying that he is not a native speaker, Beckett adds a superfluous circumflex on *symbole* and mangles the plural of *démentir*. Such slips are rare. He mimes the logorrhea he had observed among the disciples of *transition*, a review in which the genre of the manifesto had been raised to the heights of self-parody. Ironically, Beckett participated in this genre when he cosigned the 1932 manifesto "Poetry is Vertical." It is as if the fictional "concentrism" had given birth to *transition* magazine's "verticalism." The du Chas spoof adds a touch of humor lacking among the apostles of the revolution of the word. Thus du Chas could only be born in Toulouse, because he was destined from birth "to lose." An inverse verticalism characterizes the author's biography; his life was horizontal:

> . . . une de ces vies horizontales, sans sommet, tout en longueur, un phénomène de mouvement, sans possibilité d'accélération ni de ralentissement, déclenché, sans être inauguré, par l'accident, d'une naissance, terminé sans être conclu, par l'accident d'une mort[15]

> [one of these horizontal lives, without a summit, all flat along the ground, the phenomenon of a movement that cannot accelerate or slow down, triggered without being inaugurated by the accident of a birth, terminated without being concluded by the accident of a death].

Du Chas sums up his wisdom as "*Va t'embêter ailleurs* [Go get bored elsewhere]."[16] This plebeian turn of phrase conveys that if *taedium vitae* cannot be eliminated, at least one should move it elsewhere, which rephrases Baudelaire's aspiration to go "Anywhere out of the world," but by anticipating its own exhaustion. A good cure of boredom brings you back to reality, which is more or less the lesson of *Waiting for Godot*.

In the 1930s, Beckett had not yet opted for the vernacular of the Paris "concierges" that he would make his after the war; he sounded stuck in academic verbiage. A similar stylistic hesitation between the high and the low reappears in "Les deux besoins," a 1938 manifesto written in French. It splices Racine, Proust, and Flaubert, and begins with an ironical epigraph from *The Sentimental Education*. Astutely distinguishing between the need to have and the need to need, that is need and desire (two important Lacanian categories), Beckett provides a diagram inspired by Pythagoras, in which the infinity of human desire leaves room for art.[17] Such diagrams will recur in the later work, from "All Strange Away" to *Quad*. There again, the style is epigrammatic: "Préférer l'un des testicules à l'autre, ce serait aller sur les plates-bandes de la métaphysique. A moins d'être le démon de Maxwell [To favor one of the testicles over the other would mean trespassing on the flower-beds of metaphysics. Unless you are Maxwell's demon]."[18] The choice of French is not yet the sign of an immersion in demotic speech. Beckett is as pedantic and allusive in French as in English, although more irreverent in French.

A new awareness of the lyrical potentialities of the French language came to Beckett when he began writing poetry in French after he settled in Paris. Then one observes a new and spontaneous fluency. Although, as we have seen, he had been stabbed near the heart by Prudent, the well-named pimp and almost died, as it were, by mistake, Beckett felt at home in Paris; he began drafting poems in French that developed earlier themes, the obsession with a dead fiancée, the sadness of physical love, the gnawing awareness of mortality. Their style is less allusive, less Joycean than the earlier poems in English. Puns are rare, litanies insistent. Beckett discovers a simpler lyrical voice that sings of loss, absence, and mourning.

In "Ascension," the loud radio of neighbors forces him to listen to a soccer match, the noise cut by memories of blood gushing from the mouth of the loved one. "The Fly" meditates on windowpanes that separate the poet from the outside world. The final mingling of sky and sea could come from a Rimbaud poem. In "Prayer," silence offers the only defense against fits of anxiety.[19] If anxiety accompanies sexuality, philosophy provides meager consolations. Beckett confirmed that his own French language derives from poetry when he explained to his German translator that he chose to write in French because of his need to be "ill equipped."[20] The French original reveals a pun. Beckett writes: "le besoin d'être mal armé,"[21] a phrase in which anyone, especially his addressee, will recognize a reference to Stéphane Mallarmé; it might be read as "the need to be Mallarmé." In fact, Mallarmé himself often played on the echoes of his name, highlighting the weakness of his body and his art that it revealed.

When Beckett wrote *Waiting for Godot* as a diversion from his relentless probing of the metatextual paradoxes of the novel in *Molloy* and *Malone Dies*, he created an instant French classic. This play is one of the most popular of the French repertoire. More details are recognizably local, in spite of the allegorical landscape, in the French version. The name Godot, which sounds so funny in French, may or may not refer to God. The word looks like an Italian name if we cut the final *t*—should we spell it "Godo"? We can think of *commedia dell' arte* characters praised by Beckett in his essay on Joyce.[22] Beckett had mentioned the Teatro dei Piccoli that brought to London and New York the ancient technique of commedia de l'arte in the 1920s.[23] Whoever has witnessed enthusiastic crowds of young spectators clap, cheer, and laugh at each joke in various theaters of the world, can conclude that *Godot* has become the modern equivalent of the Venetian comedies of the classical age. Since his essay on Joyce also foregrounded Dante, one cannot forget the eternal light surrounding the final appearance of God at the end of *Paradiso*; the very mention of its radiating form brings ineffable joy to the poet:

La forma universal di questo nodo
credo ch'i' vidi, perche più di largo,
dicendo questo, mi sento ch'i' godo.
[I think I saw the universal shape
which that knot takes; for speaking this, I feel
a joy that is more ample.][24]

Godo(t) would be a name promising an enjoyment to come, in the end-less deferral of divine parousia, the tantalizing evocation of a never-present apocalypse. However, to make sense of Godot's overtones as a French name, it is not sufficient to mention the mythical anecdote of Beckett wait-ing for a Paris bus on rue Godot de Mauroy, pursued by a prostitute who made fun of him by asking whether he was waiting for Godot.[25] Another detail is much more precious: the notebook of the first draft of *En Atten-dant Godot* at the Bibliothèque Nationale de France, shows that the first version dated October 9, 1948, pairs two old men named Lévy et Vladi-mir.[26] In the draft, it was only at the end of the first act that Beckett changed Lévy for Estragon or Gogo.[27] Didi derives from Vladimir, which evokes Lenin. We are told early that without Vladimir, Gogo-Lévy would only be a "little heap of bones."[28] Beckett hints at the death camps and their freeing by Russian troops, while obliquely paying homage to his old and dear friend Alfred Péron from the École Normale Supérieure. Péron, who was Jewish and had brought him to the Resistance, was not as lucky as Beckett when he was caught with other members of the Gloria network by the Gestapo. He died in Mauthausen in 1945. He survived in the camp longer than most because he had been protected by a pimp named Polo; Polo considered Péron as a poet. Estragon presents himself as a "poet," too:

VLADIMIR.—You should have been a poet.
ESTRAGON.—I was. (*Gesture towards his rags.*) Isn't that obvious?[29]

Angela Moorjani sees his name as a reference to the yellow color of tarragon, thus alluding to the yellow stars worn by Jews.[30] Through these emblematic characters, Beckett alludes to a recent history marked by the Shoah and Soviet communism. In this context, the fact of "waiting" as an adverb accompanying all actions becomes less an unbearable torture than a sign of survival. One enjoys the simple fact of being alive in lulls between terrifying and unpredictable outbursts of absurd violence:

VLADIMIR.—And they didn't beat you?
ESTRAGON.—Beat me? Certainly they beat me.

VLADIMIR.—The same lot as usual?
ESTRAGON.—The same? I don't know.[31]

In an unpublished talk, Felicia McCarren has shown that one of the
sources of the dialogic games played by Didi and Gogo, in which one
shifts from brotherly solicitude to bitter antagonism, is the superb ending
of Jean Renoir's film *La Grande Illusion*. In the 1937 film, two French soldiers escape from a German jail during World War I, Maréchal (Jean
Gabin) and Rosenthal (Marcel Dallo). One is a tough guy from the Paris
suburbs, the other comes from a rich Jewish family and cannot stand the
strain of trekking all night. They bicker, try to part their ways, get reconciled; solidarity allows them to survive. Beckett could not have missed the
resemblance between Rosenthal's name and that of his old Dublin friend
"Con" Rosenthal.

At a remove from the stage, one discovers a parallel lyrical modulation of
the poetic voice in the poems written at the time. A French poem from the
1940s evinces a musical mode of expression that recalls Verlaine or Eluard:

> je suis ce cours de sable qui glisse
> entre le galet et la dune
> la pluie d'été pleut sur ma vie
> sur moi ma vie qui me fuit me poursuit
> et finira le jour de son commencement[32]

This fluid evocation of Ireland's rainy summers presents a poet dog-
gedly walking along the beach in a soft fog. Here, Beckett translates himself perfectly, even if he cannot keep the double meaning of *je suis* ("I am"
and "I follow"). His elegant solution testifies to an equal command of lyrical poetry in both languages:

> my way is in the sand flowing
> between the shingle and the dune
> the summer rain rains on my life
> on me my life harrying fleeting
> to its beginning to its end[33]

We have left behind the Cartesian subject of the first poems: subjectivity has turned into a pure trace and become an Orphic path that one follows with the flow of time, as sand keeps dripping from the hourglass.
However, the versions soon diverge; here is the second stanza in French:

> cher instant je te vois
> dans ce rideau de brume qui recule

où je n'aurai plus à fouler ces longs seuils mouvants
et vivrai le temps d'une porte
qui s'ouvre et se referme[34]

A literal translation would be:

dear instant I see you
through a curtain of receding mist
where I won't have to tread long quicksand thresholds

Beckett's English is different—and much better:

my peace is there in the receding mist
when I may cease from treading these long shifting threshholds
and live the space of a door
that opens and shuts.[35]

Reaching this open and shut door, we may pause, fearing the risk of being swallowed in the quicksand of comparative translation studies. Not only is the file immense, but it yields no consistent protocol. Rules vary from text to text. At times Beckett translates himself faithfully, at times he takes huge liberties—the most obvious case being *Mercier and Camier* from 1974, which, as we have seen, is not at all identical with the French *Mercier et Camier* from 1946. In this case, Beckett produced a reduction more than a translation. He skipped entire pages, condensed dialogue, rendered the quest of the two old men less provocative and delirious, more subdued, more metaphysical. The first version abounded in grotesque details that were erased. The scenes of love-making were expunged; tantalizing hints about a sexual relationship between the two friends vanished. In many instances, Beckett did not bother to translate the profanities regularly uttered by Mercier; we have just: "Mercier used a nasty expression," or "He used another nasty expression."[36] In fact, paradoxically, the English version achieved what Beckett claimed the French language itself had done for him: writing without style, erasing stylistic markers of physicality, incongruity, and intertextuality. We still have witty exchanges between the characters whereas most of the verbal glitter has come off.

One has to be cautious when rehearsing the story of Beckett's descent into minimalism thanks to the use of French. If there is a clearly attested desire to write without style, it has to be inscribed in a broader tradition—not so much that of the "theater of the absurd" (a term one should reserve for Ionesco, another bilingual author) but of the new modernity ushered in by contemporary writers like Jean Genet or Georges Bataille. Or perhaps an author whom Beckett recognized quite early as an equal, an alter ego, and a close friend—Robert Pinget.

There was a remarkable literary complicity between Beckett and Pinget.[37] One glance at the opening paragraph of *Mahu, or the Material*, written before Pinget had met Beckett, presents evident parallels with Beckett's trilogy (*Molloy, Malone Dies*, and *The Unnamable*). Pinget uses unreliable narrators like Molloy and the Unnamable:

> This is the story I can't make head or tail of it, somebody said: 'You ought to write it down,' I can't remember who, perhaps it was me, I get everything mixed up, it's true sometimes when I'm being introduced to someone I concentrate so much that I take on the same face as the person and the friend who is introducing us doesn't know if it's me or the other one, he just leaves me to sort it out for myself.[38]

Pinget's novel was published by Éditions de Minuit in 1952, one year after *Molloy*, one year before *The Unnamable*.

I have mentioned important French predecessors like Bataille and Blanchot, but Louis-René des Forêts and Albert Camus were no doubt as crucial. In the 1940s, Beckett read Blanchot avidly, more as a gifted literary critic than as a novelist. The nocturnal eschatology composed by a series of dizzying dialectical reversals in *Thomas the Obscure*, whose version dates from 1941, calls up the deranged and serialist syntax of *Watt*. We also know that Beckett read with great interest the prophetic 1943 essay "From Dread to Language"—originally published in his first collection of essays called *Faux Pas*—in which Blanchot seems to sketch in advance Beckett's aesthetic program as he elaborated it with Duthuit, when he writes: "The writer finds himself in this more and more comical condition—of having nothing to write, of having no means of writing it, and of being forced by an extreme necessity to write it."[39] At the time Beckett was translating another essay by Blanchot for *Transition* in 1951, and he alludes to *Faux Pas* with admiration.[40] And as soon as Blanchot's essay *The Unnamable* was published in 1953, Beckett would recommend it to other critics and translators.[41] He was even hoping that Blanchot could write a survey of his works for Gallimard in 1960.[42] Unhappily, Blanchot, too busy, although very interested, had to renounce.

We do not know whether Beckett read des Forêts, whose experimental novel *Le Bavard* was published in 1946 to great acclaim. Like the narrator of *The Unnamable*, the narrator is a mere voice speaking endlessly and contradicting itself. This voice invents stories and then denies their authenticity while flaunting their lack of style: "One will remember that with an ostentation that might pass for excessive modesty, I did not avoid underlining the deliberate sparseness of my form, and I was the first to present hypocritical regrets that a certain monotony was the inevitable price to pay for its honesty."[43] Similar metatextual games with a fictional listener likewise dominate in Beckett's trilogy.

The *bavard* invented by des Forêts is an irrepressible chatterbox who keeps flaunting his endless garrulity in terms very similar to those used by Beckett in *The Unnamable*. The *bavard* thus says: "Now that I have chatted at some length with you, do you imagine that I have taken on some volume? Do you imagine me endowed with any other organ than my tongue? Can I be identified with the owner of the right hand that is now writing these letters? How can one know this? Don't wait until he denounces himself. Who, being in his place, wouldn't prefer to remain anonymous?"[44] Here, truly, the author has vanished; the flow of words entails that character, author, and readers only survive by trusting the medium of language, no matter how glib, desperate or absurd the statements that are produced may appear to be.

Writing Degree Zero

Rather than multiply converging examples taken from the French writers of the 1940s and 1950s, we can assume that these joint efforts correspond to a generational shift; this shift has been accounted for by Roland Barthes in very eloquent terms. In fact, one might say that Barthes's *Writing Degree Zero* (1953) offers the best gloss on Beckett's attempt to write without a style. The point of departure for *Writing Degree Zero* was the linguistic revolution brought about by the French Revolution.[45] Barthes highlights the profanities that marked the style of a revolutionary regicide like Hébert, who never began a number of *Le Père Duchêne* without using expletives such as "fuck!" and "bugger!" Hébert peppered the pages of his publication with obscenities in order to signal a revolutionary situation. By dramatizing two beginnings, the stylistic markers of popular anger flaunted by Le Père Duchêne and the departure embodied by the regicides of the French Revolution, Barthes spliced History and Text, both duly capitalized and united under the red banner of the absence of style. Thus *écriture*, according to Barthes, cannot be reduced to style. Barthes distinguishes *literature*, the field of the evolution of forms, *language*, a social medium granted to all speakers, and *style*, the writer's singularity, on par with biographical constraints, a "fate" handed down by the writer's body.[46] "Writing" deploys itself against style and language, it carves a space for freedom away from biographical determinations and social negotiations: "Placed at the center of the problematics of literature, which cannot exist prior to it, writing is thus essentially the morality of form, the choice of that social area within which the writer elects to situate the Nature of his language."[47]

Like Beckett, Barthes was engaged in a critical dialogue with Jean-Paul Sartre's dialectics of "commitment." *Writing Degree Zero* was published in 1947, months after the publication of Sartre's *What Is Literature?* Barthes's first chapter "What Is Writing?" quotes Sartre's first chapter, but its aim is to slyly invert Sartre's terms. Sartre had defined writing in terms of communication, as a collective response to a historical situation. Barthes wrenches the term from humanistic existentialism and neo-Marxist dialectics to endow it with a new dynamism. Sartre had two terms in a dialectic predicated upon the form and content division: language communicated ideas and style was the means of expression. By providing three terms, Barthes escaped from this conceptual deadlock. *Écriture* was emancipated from the dilemma in which one had to choose between a private discourse and the socially responsible position of the committed intellectual. *Writing* took upon itself features traditionally attributed to style while eschewing the formalism of stylistics.

It is crucial to understand that Beckett's point of departure was similar to that of Barthes. One key factor was Beckett's friendship with Georges Duthuit. As we saw, the first issue of the new *Transition* had translated into English a selection from Sartre's *What is literature?*, his brilliant but jaundiced critique of Surrealism. Those pages were introduced by the first section of Duthuit's long essay in several installments, "Sartre's Last Class."[48] There, Duthuit minimized the clash between Sartre and Breton and even invented an exchange of letters on anti-Semitism between Nietzsche and Céline. His point was that there was a broad agreement between all these authors' theses. Beckett, who had expressed his admiration for Sartre's *Nausea* before the war,[49] nevertheless seconded Duthuit in his rejection of Sartre's "engaged" literature along the lines defined by Barthes.

Barthes's essay introduced the idea of a "degree zero of *écriture*" by sketching a history of modernity stretching from the French Revolution to the *Nouveau Roman*, via Flaubert and Mallarmé. In 1953, Barthes's modernity was epitomized by the *Nouveau Roman*, which loosely included Beckett. The *Nouveau Roman's* catalogues, descriptive vertigo, games with pseudo-objectivity, and eccentric reduction of the human to the question of language were meant to destroy, Barthes claimed, a previous generation's grandiloquence. For Barthes, as for Beckett, writers like Alain Robbe-Grillet, Albert Camus, or Maurice Blanchot promoted a "neutral" style in which they saw a debunking of the belated political rectitude of many writers who were caught posturing in distasteful pseudo-heroics. Barthes pays homage to the work of Blanchot twice in *Writing Degree Zero*, and the second time he moves on from Blanchot's remarks on Mallarmé to what he coins as the "*neutral*."[50] The neutral, a concept on which Blanchot was to elaborate at length in subsequent essays, is neither one nor the other; it is a pseudo-transparent speech that "implies no refuge, no secret."[51]

Barthes mentions Camus and Céline as the main precursors of this new literature which uses a simple vernacular spoken in the streets, and which therefore rejects the high modernist idea of mastery over an array of ancient styles that will have to be recombined, parodied, ironized, and transcended. What is lost in the domain of modernist stylistics is a net gain for the ethics of the contemporary world. The blank and neutral writing is down-to-earth, it flows along with its endless store of popular idioms, which does not rule out countless self-reflexive games. This writing can truly embody the new "morality of form" that Barthes craves for. Above all, it has very little to do with a committed literature explicitly discussing political events of the times and transforming the poet or novelist into a public intellectual. In short, it breaks with Sartre's model.

Like Bataille, Barthes had fought his way out of Sartre's neo-Hegelian dialectics and found in Camus's *The Stranger* a present perfect tense that exemplified a "style-less style" and announced the "writing degree zero." With *The Stranger*, Camus launched a style of "indifference," according to Barthes who described the style of a new "absurd" as "flat and deep like a mirror."[52] Barthes's review of *The Stranger* dates from 1944. Camus's "flat" absurd was shared by Beckett's tramps, who decidedly have much in common with Meursault. In *The Stranger*, Barthes argues, "we see the beginning of a new style, a style of silence and silence of style, in which the voice of the artist—equally removed from sighs, blasphemy, and gospels—is a white voice, the only voice that can fit our unredeemable distress."[53] Barthes accepted the validity of Camus's ethical stance not because he endorsed Camus's moralism but because he saw in *The Stranger* the emergence of a new mode of writing. This flat writing alone could rise to the challenge of historical catastrophes.

This style-less writing finds its resources in the rhythms of a low and spoken French vernacular. The most visible predecessor had been Céline with the celebrated opening of *Voyage au bout de la nuit*: "Ça a débuté comme ça. Moi, j'avais jamais rien dit. Rien."[54] Then the famous first sentence of Camus's *The Stranger* introduced the recurrent trope of epistemic qualification and negation so typical of Beckett's French writing:[55]

"Aujourd'hui, maman est morte. Ou peut-être hier, je ne sais pas."[56] This style-less writing style was a pure "writing," a writing that, according to Barthes, was the only form of writerly response to the dramas of World War II, the Shoah, the sordid betrayals among Resistance members, the widespread use of torture in the Algerian war, the grim face of Soviet communism, and the dead end of a battered French colonialism.

Here was a site that Samuel Beckett had decided to inhabit, not as a militant but as a French writer—it was a new threshold, the space of a door that opens rather than shuts, and from which he could go on. It was a language to learn in and from and not just the language imposed by a capitalized Other, as the narrator of *The Unnamable* complains. We guess that much at the end of *Molloy*, when the eponymous hero comes home to find that some of his pets have died, like his bees and hens. Distraught, Molloy evokes the joys that his bees provided: they fascinated him, he studied their dances, interpreted their systems of signals, classified figures accompanying the hum and the height at which the dances were performed: "And I said, with rapture, Here is something I can study all my life, and never understand."[57] We are back to the critique of anthropomorphism that underpins all of Beckett's ethics and aesthetics.

In this case, if the bees have died, some of the birds have survived, which leads Moran, for the first time perhaps, to try and understand something new: "I tried to understand their language better. Without having recourse to mine."[58] Moran pottering about in his decayed garden parodies, as we have seen, Voltaire ending of *Candide* with "Il faut cultiver son jardin." This dilapidated garden allows Moran to be both at home and in exile; it is there as well that he hears a voice talking to him and coming from the outside: "I have spoken of a voice telling me things. I was getting to know it better now, to understand what it wanted. It did not use the words that Moran had been taught when he was little and that in his turn he had taught to his little one. So that at first I did not know what it wanted. But in the end I understood this language."[59] It would be reductive to identify this language with French.

What matters is that this new language reiterates the obligation to speak: the voice keeps asking for a report from Moran, which suggests that literature as such has been displaced by a radical exile before morphing into a writing of the outside. Its addressee is the same as its fictional origin: an unknown Other who can never be equated with God addresses a writing subject who survives, in spite of all, in the garden to which his world has shrunk. Here is the necessary quandary reached by Beckett. In the last decades of his life, he appeared caught up between a cul-de-sac—the dead end or a blind alley of a little street in a Paris arrondissement—and his solitary progression through literary work. Between a cul-de-sac and the injunction to *cultiver son jardin*, Beckett's solution was to invent his brand of pastoral cynicism. We know that cynical ethics militantly require a release from the demands of the polis. Diogenes was the first self-declared "cosmopolitan," which did not prevent him from questioning the dominant values of Athens and refusing to grant any dignity to the human.

Catastrophe, *or the Writing of the Disaster*

Beckett's "human"—caught in a garden that combines dying animals and barely surviving human diggers—presents us a broader humanity, a humanity at the limit, accepting the animal in itself, a humanity that has become stronger because of this acceptance of the stranger. It is therefore better fitted to resist oppression and humiliation. One sees this main concern in Beckett's later play *Catastrophe*. It begins when an irate, obnoxious, and arrogant director comes in, terrorizing his secretary. Huffing and puffing, he claims to be in a hurry, yet wants his cigar lit and relit. He lingers on details of color and gesture, yet checks his watch, eager to go to a political meeting after he is done with his theatrical business. He orders his assistant around while she instructs an old man who is silently standing on a podium. The director and the secretary try out hieratic poses for him: the old man has to move up his hands and join them as in prayer. He has to bare some flesh despite the cold, and his skin will be whitened for better effect, but he must not speak or lift his head. A single projector will highlight his head when he is exhibited as a living statue or *tableau vivant* in a forthcoming official gathering. If the old man is docile, if the eager assistant follows the orders dutifully jotted down in a notebook, the show will be a success, or at least will be greeted by loud applause from the audience. Beckett's 1982 dense allegory revolves around the meanings to give to its title, *Catastrophe*.

Why this title? We may remember Beckett's words to Alan Schneider, when he described *Endgame* as "the impossibility of catastrophe." In the later play, the impossibility remains, but it is precisely this impossibility that suggests hope. The word *catastrophe* is mentioned at the end, when the director finally looks satisfied with the awkward pose he has devised for the old man: "There's our catastrophe. In the bag. Once more and I'm off."[60] Much of the meaning of a play performed at the Avignon festival in 1982 at the request of a French association defending imprisoned artists is contained in its dedication to Václav Havel. The Czech dissident, later to become the first democratically elected president of Czechoslovakia, was

in jail at the time. Havel, who had been charged as a subversive, had been
targeted for his political work with Charter 77. The protagonist who stands
exposed and mute on a podium calls up the dire fate of an accomplished
playwright who had been prevented from writing in his cell. Beckett's
protagonist is made to strike a pose without any possibility of expressing
himself.

Beckett suggests some comedy but soon undercuts it. The assistant asks
tentatively: "What about a little . . . a little . . . gag?" The question makes
the director explode: "For God's sake! This craze for explicitation! Every i
dotted to death! Little gag! For God's sake!" However, she insists: "Sure he
won't utter?" He replies confidently: "Not a squeak."[61] The original French
is less ambiguous. "Un petit bâillon" means literally a "gag" in the mouth,
which loses the possibility of being understood as a quip or prank.[62] Nevertheless, a hermeneutic problem arises. If the director and the assistant
are afraid that the protagonist might speak out in public, how can the use
of a gag be an "explicitation"? The play's *i*'s are not so dotted and generate
other puns, as when the old man shivers, frozen in order to "freeze" at the
last minute in a perfect petrification.

This brings us back to the terrifying world of endless tortures, the
inquisitive quest for a final avowal from a helpless victim as depicted in
Rough for Radio II. There, we remember, a similar couple, the Animator and
the Stenographer, forced the poet Fox to confess an impossible guilt, alter-
nating coaxing and blows. In *Catastrophe*, the insinuation of torture is limited to the director's visible glee when told that the old man shivers in the
cold. When the assistant suggests that the protagonist might lift his head,
the director rejects this innovation vehemently: "Raise his head? Where do
you think we are? In Patagonia? Raise his head! For God's sake."[63] Beckett
slyly alludes to the then recent Falkland war, a military conflict opposing a
dictatorial Argentina sullied by a "dirty war" against "subversives" and a no
less muscular United Kingdom. In spite of the warning, the gesture to be
avoided at all cost takes place at the end: the old man raises his head and
stares at the audience, which is enough to silence the recorded applause.
The stage directions end with: "*The applause falters, dies. Long pause. Fade-
out of light on face.*"[64]

This short play does less to explicate than complicate the concept of
catastrophe. Or rather, the catastrophe is allegorized at several levels. The
first level is obvious: the exhibition intended by the director evokes the
idea of presenting an old man on a stage as a degraded victim or enemy.
This catastrophe is a scene of humiliation. The protagonist's hands are
twisted by disease perhaps contracted in jail. His bald head and his whit-

ened skin make him look weak, contemptible, and barely human. The political spectacle that the director organizes calls up the sinister Stalinist trials with their absurd accusations displaying broken and consenting victims. This leads to a first reversal: the entire system of totalitarian regimes can be called a "catastrophe" because it needs to make a spectacle of itself. Such "catastrophe" will be understood as a profane apotheosis, the visible reification of battered humanity. A second connotation of catastrophe sticks to its etymological meaning, which is that of a final reversal. Indeed, at the last second, the mute victim manifests his agency by his defiant stare. The catastrophe intervenes as the last act in the play. The condensed logic of mute gestures allows for a minimal resistance, strong enough to undo all the rest. One finds again the ethics of courage and resistance that Badiou and Adorno have described so powerfully.

There is another meaning implied by *Catastrophe*. The play was first performed on a stage in Avignon, written in French by an Irish writer about a Czech author and political prisoner. Its performance was successful, among other reasons, because news about it reached Havel in his jail, which boosted his morale, and finally, given the international outcry, led to his release.[65] However, at Avignon, the French audience was caught up in a bind. Should they clap at the end? Should they express their solidarity with the defiant protagonist by remaining silent? This was Beckett's innovative way of alerting spectators to what they had to construe as their ethical or political role, a role that comes closer to the sense of a dire consternation that he saw deriving from his own texts than any aesthetic elation.

Beckett's play mobilizes *catastrophe* in all these meanings, from a Greek word that keeps its entire poetological valence, the sudden reversal, the turning or literal strophe going against any historical situation that we perceive as theatrical. In the same way as there is a theater of war, there is a theater of catastrophe, in which the limits of the human are displayed. The hope is that such an overturning will entail change, a revolution that will not remain on a purely aesthetic level. It mobilizes the whole ethical or political perspective that one needs to bring to bear on any spectacle.

The poetological meaning needs to be explicated further. In *Malone Dies*, Malone evokes "catastrophe in the ancient sense" when he laments the sudden loss of his stick. Malone reflects that it is precisely because he has been deprived of the object that he can then understand the concept of the stick in itself. His negative Kantianism is a philosophy of deprivation. Malone comments: "So that I half discern, in the veritable catastrophe that has befallen me, a blessing in disguise. How comforting that is. Catastrophe too in the ancient sense no doubt. To be buried in lava and not turn a hair, it is then a man shows what stuff he is made of."[66] With this reference to the tortures of Dante's *Inferno*, Malone deplores the absence of a "catastrophe" in the sense it had for Greek rhetoricians: a turning, an overturning, the event precipitating the end of a play, whether a tragedy (usually the death of a hero) or a comedy (usually a marriage, or a sudden happy event). Aristotle's *Poetics* prefers the term *peripeteia*, or "reversal of fortune." It became the standard mode of ending a classical play. Stephen Dedalus remembers the term when he evokes the theme of banishment that he sees recurring in Shakespeare's plays: "it repeats itself, protasis, epitasis, catastasis, catastrophe."[67] Beckett had learned from Joyce the trick of not concluding his novels or plays. Thus the literal catastrophe is avoided. If most of Beckett's plays eschew a final *dénouement*—there is no final closure or disclosure, no conclusion, no last turn of the plot—*Catastrophe* is the exception.

Beckett's avoidance of a final dialectical reversal may have something to do with his frequentation of psychoanalysis in the thirties. The two years he spent on W. R. Bion's couch in London brought about a major trope: the sense that he had never been properly born, as Jung had explained in a famous lecture delivered in London.[68] The explanation, metaphorical as it was, provided a relief, a new "turning." If this was the case, then he would never really die either—such an insight allowed him to go on writing, finishing *Murphy* by killing off the main protagonist and then launch other projects. He had found his main theme, and Adorno understood it immediately as we have seen, that death itself is not a catastrophe: it is the impossibility of dying that is catastrophic. The forever dying Malone echoes this fantasy: "Yes, an old foetus, that's what I am now, hoar and impotent . . . has anything happened, anything changed? No, the answer is no, I shall never get born and therefore never get dead, and a good job too. And if I tell of me and of that other who is my little one, it is as always for want of love, well I'll be buggered. I wasn't expecting that, want of a homuncule, I can't stop."[69] And, in a distant echo of Descartes calculating the time it takes for his eggs to feel like perfect abortions, Malone adds that he wants to eat his creation: "I shall try and make a little creature, to hold in my arms, a little creature in my image, no matter what I say. And seeing what a poor thing I have made, or how like myself, I shall eat it."[70]

What Beckett's novels at the time of the novel trilogy and his later plays stage—even when they insist on bleakness, despair, and postapocalyptic situations as in *Endgame*—is that we have to survive the worst by the dark humor deriving from the notion that there has been even worse; we will live by facing an ancient catastrophe that has already happened, and this awareness keeps a certain panic active while muting what would have been pure horror or disabling terror. This is what the narrator of *The Unnamable* confesses: "I only think, if that is the name for this vertiginous panic as hornets smoked out of their nest, once a certain degree of terror has been exceeded."[71] He admits that this same terror makes him say that he is in a head, or is a head: he has been born into a text, which means in fact that his birth is an act of language. If Jung's revelation of the possibility that one can die because one has not been truly born had paved the way for a new insight into the essence of the catastrophe, it is because it announced a forceful idea later developed by Donald W. Winnicott in his last, posthumous paper, "Fear of Breakdown," published in 1974.[72] Barthes had read this paper and sums it up in his last book on photography in these terms: "I shudder, like Winnicott's psychotic patient, *over a catastrophe which has already happened.*"[73] The sudden elation that one can derive from such an insight is liberating, as Winnicott explains about certain suicidal patients. This elation may not generate a gushing enthusiasm; if it can bring a sense of triumph, it will have to be muted; because the catastrophe has already taken place, my triumph over the darkness of fate will always be somewhat belated—it is one that one will greet, but without applause.

However, Beckett's recurring catastrophe seems quite far from what Badiou had presented as a "constellation" if "Worstward Ho" had happened to merge with Mallarmé's "Un Coup de dés." Because the catastrophe engages language as well as past unconscious traumas, it seems much closer to what Blanchot has called the "writing of the disaster." In Blanchot's rather idiosyncratic evocation (it includes a personal account of several "primal scenes"[74]), disaster implies a bad arrangement of the stars in a catastrophic or "ill-starred" horoscope, while confirming that a fundamental "law" of fate remains and insists. Providing a fitting conclusion for this French chapter, Blanchot writes: "If disaster means being separated from the star . . . then it indicates a fall beneath disastrous necessity. Would law be the disaster? The supreme or extreme law, that is: the excessiveness of uncodifiable law—that to which we are destined without being party to it. The disaster is not our affair and has no regard for us; it is the heedless unlimited; it cannot be measured in terms of failure or as pure and simple loss."[75]

Coda: Minima Beckettiana

As Blanchot notes, disaster is not somber or terrifying. It should not evoke horror or desolation, even if it has to do with death and dying, for in its extreme exteriority it even generates a form of *gai savoir*.[1] Blanchot adds: "The disaster: stress upon minutiae, sovereignty of the accidental."[2] Indeed, the attention to minutiae of everyday life appears as a dominant theme in Beckett's later prose texts and letters, to the point that one can talk of a fascination for the minute "minima" of sensation—silence that is not fully silence, attention to distant echoes in the posture of one who is waiting all day for nothing, along with the simple pleasures taken in thinking, walking to and fro, and breathing: "Then little or nothing of note till the minima, these too unforgettable, on days of great recall, a sound of fall so muted by the distance, or for want of weight, or for lack of space between departure and arrival, that it was perhaps his fancy."[3] The term will allow me to move in conclusion toward Adorno's masterpiece of ethical writing, his *Minima Moralia*.

Beckett's nihilistic verve brought him close to the position of classical Cynicism, a school for which the main hero was Heracles because he could withstand anything, death included, as we see in Sophocles's *Women of*

Trachis. This position was stated in many of Beckett's letters, at least whenever he summed up what he thought of form and value. True values, then, are not just manmade, they must compete with the qualities of the earth, the hardness of the stone, and with the strength evinced by animals; indeed, for a Cynic like Diogenes, who had been quoted in "All Strange Away,"[4] any difference between animals and humans tends to vanish.

In Beckett's later texts, men, women, and animals appear as puppets buffeted by the winds of fate, blinded by instinct, led to death in a theater of futility, caught up in the swells of the unconscious before drifting toward final extinction. However, such a stark vision is not purely nihilistic since it aims at finding the true bedrock of values. This dark pathos recurs even in tender pastoral vignettes:

> In the fields, on the roads, I give myself over to deductions on nature, based on observation! No wonder I am irritable. It produces grim results. . . . One evening as we were on our way back to Ussy, at sunset, we suddenly found ourselves being escorted by ephemerids of a strange kind, "may-flies," I think. They were all heading in the same direction, literally following the road. . . . In the end I worked out that they were all going towards the Marne to be eaten by the fish, after making love on the water.[5]

At least, one might interject, those insects will have known love. Like Cousse's sublimely pathetic pig rushing headlong to slaughter, they too could exclaim: "I shall have lived."[6]

Beckett's humor appears when he compares beetles with humans, or humans with beetles. His garden at Ussy had been invaded by Colorado beetles, in French *doryphores*, a common pest in those regions, and he comments dryly: "I keep an eye on the love-life of the Colorado beetle and work against it, successfully but humanely, that is to say by throwing the parents into my neighbour's garden and burning the eggs. If only someone had done that for me!"[7] The ancient fantasy of "not being born" is reenacted here with a vengeance; at least, he will pass on to his neighbors the cycle of infestation and destruction. Such minimal incidents often led to the writing of short texts, like a superb "Fizzle" dated from the 1960s: "Three years in the earth, those the moles don't get, then guzzle guzzle, ten days long, a fortnight, and always the flight at nightfall. To the river perhaps, they head to the river."[8] At the end, the speaker sees his old loves and his previous lives carried along, all caught up in the same relentless death-drive.

A similar mood appears in 1960 when Beckett watches animals during walks at night along the Marne River. Describing to Barbara Bray a group of baby woodpeckers, with the mother in surveillance not far, he adds in French: "L'histoire que j'avais la naturelle."[9] The phrase "the history I knew, natural history" comes directly from *Comment C'est*. In *How It Is*, the text changes slightly and states: "or failing kindred meat a llama emergency dream an alpaca llama the history I knew my God the natural."[10] Nature and God have to be invoked together: universal history and the stories people tell themselves boil down to a "natural history," that is a cycle of birth, survival, and death in which humans and animals are undistinguishable.

We are caught up in the same affective cycles in which need and disgust alternate, as the narrator of *How It Is* writes: "when the great needs fail the need to move on the need to shit and vomit and the other great needs all my great categories of being."[11] I discussed previously how Beckett superimposed ethical cycles of pain and retribution on similarly cynical recapitulations. All those years Beckett observed local animals and people with the same fascinated interest, soon to get back to his literary toils, the only activity that mattered in the end.

To the strict imposition of limits, Beckett preferred to maintain a dynamic tension between all his spaces, and he achieved this mostly by keeping a double pole: there was first a Dublin-Paris axis, it was relayed by a Paris-Kassel axis or a Dublin-London axis; finally, in the end, we find a last binary alternation with the Paris-Ussy axis. Ussy was a point of rest after Paris and all the trips brought about by a successful literary career. Even when his career was filled with honors, life and death kept marking the extreme points of a swinging pendulum. These were not empty symbols: they were legible in the soil, in the trees, and in animals. The imperative to write entailed a measure of destruction, what with the burning of eggs, seeds, weeds, pests, and the remainders of painful memories. If Beckett's landscapes tended to be *paysages moralisés*, their allegories were never static. Like those of the English metaphysical poets, Beckett's dialectical images dance and think. Even the village elected for his creative solitude, the country house at Ussy, so far away from any romantic myth, conjured in its very signifier a collective pronoun (*Us*) allied with a deictic *Ici!* Here, you can be alone and with us.

Such a theater of consternation leaves room for communal reconciliation. Ussy offered a desk for the patient creation of verbal beauty. It was a site where the resilient force of hope could be invoked. As the narrator of "Enough" says: "Now that I am entering night I have kinds of gleams in my skull. Stony ground but not entirely. Given three or four lives I might have accomplished something."[12] The key is in the qualification:

"but not entirely." The original of the sentence that Badiou often quotes is more evocative: "Terre ingrate mais pas totalement [Barren soil but not totally]."[13] The Earth itself, because it is ungrateful in so many aspects but not in all, resists being equated with the dull totality of today's "globalized sphere."

Thanks to the earth, because it is thankless, but not devoid of gratitude in the end, the skull learns to resist. One of Beckett's ethical rules is that one has to resist one's resistance as well. In the tricky semantics of the qualification, in the lack of punctuation of a sentence that glides along in a continuous breath even when it sets a limit, the resistance of value is reasserted. Human value resists itself by putting a limit to its own fluidity. Two hard crusty spheres are superimposed when the gleaming skull acquires the earth's virtue of stoniness. Like Molly Bloom spinning on herself as the Earth, the ventriloquizing narrator lets his skull replay all the stories and even invent new ones. In this exchange between the dry, rocky substance of the world and the softer tissue of verbal creation, the sturdy ground of ontology allows the fictional flow—or, more modestly, its "ooze," as *Worstward Ho* has it[14]—to keep on running. Indeed, as long as Beckett's superb later texts, his fizzles and short texts "for nothing," are read and reread, they can "accomplish" years of extra life. In spite of all, ethical hope returns even as it flaunts its weakness and limitations.

As if to provide a last commentary on Beckett, one essay in Adorno's *Minima Moralia* captures the appeal of weakness when discussing the radiance of beauty. It is a beauty that is enjoyed simply in gold and precious stones. In a section entitled "Magic Flute," Adorno describes the process by which jewels have lost their magical features. Over time, they have forfeited their power to seduce or kill, and today, what they have retained is only beauty and value; the price to pay was the disappearance of any magic:

> In the magic of what reveals itself in absolute powerlessness, of beauty, at once perfection and nothingness, the illusion of omnipotence is mirrored negatively as hope. It has escaped every trial of strength. Total purposelessness gives the lie to the totality of purposefulness in the world of domination, and only by virtue of this domination, which consummates the established order by drawing the conclusion from its own principle of reason, has existing society up to now become aware of another that is possible. The bliss of contemplation consists in disenchanted charm. Radiance is the appeasement of myth.[15]

The last phrase could also be rendered as "Myth reconciled." The disenchanted charm of reconciled myth would define the moment when theory,

upholding the Kantian concept of aesthetics as disinterested contemplation, and ethics, those pithy maxims that help us to live on this earth, meet
in a historical logic of entropy, often called late capitalism, which is marked
by exhaustion and diminishment. However, the verbal magic of expressive
form is there to activate the "black diamond of pessimism" and make it
sparkle. Even if it only sparkles now and then, its intermittent rays prove
that beauty can flare again on the earth. The effulgence of value it manifests brings back those small things that quicken the heart.

ACKNOWLEDGMENTS

All my thanks to Jennifer Mondal who read the first draft of a different book and made useful suggestions, and to the two readers who read the typescript for the press, their astute comments were most helpful.

Parts of this book revise, distort, rephrase, and condense essays published in the last ten years, all of which have been "expurgated, accelerated, and reduced," to paraphrase *Murphy*:

"Unbreakable B's: From Beckett and Badiou to the Bitter End of Affirmative Ethics," in *Alain Badiou: Philosophy and Its Conditions*, ed. Gabriel Riera (Albany: State University of New York Press, 2005), 87–108.

"Formal Brilliance and Indeterminate Purport: The Poetry of Beckett's Philosophemes," *Fulcrum* 6 (2007): 530–550.

"Dangerous Identifications, or Beckett's Italian Hoagie," in *Joyce's Disciples Disciplined*, ed. Tim Conley (Dublin: University College Dublin Press, 2010), 1–14.

"Philosophizing with Beckett: Adorno and Badiou," in *A Companion to Samuel Beckett*, ed. S. E. Gontarski (Oxford: Wiley-Blackwell, 2010), 97–117.

"Beckett's Three Critiques: Kant's Bathos and the Irish Chandos," *Modernism/Modernity* 18, no. 4 (2011): 699–719, repr. in *Samuel Beckett and the Encounter of Philosophy and Literature*," ed. Arka Chattopadhyay and James Martell (London: Roman, 2013), 41–70.

"Bataille, Beckett, Blanchot: From the Impossible to the Unknowing," *Journal of Beckett Studies* 21, no. 1 (2012): 56–64.

"'Think, Pig!' Beckett's Animal Philosophies," in *Beckett and Animals*, ed. Mary Bryden (Cambridge: Cambridge University Press, 2013), 109–125.

"Paris, Roussillon, Ussy," in *Samuel Beckett in Context*, ed. Anthony Uhlmann (Cambridge: Cambridge University Press, 2013), 53–62.

"Beckett's Masson: From Abstraction to Non-Relation," in *The Edinburgh Companion to Samuel Beckett and the Arts*, ed. S. E. Gontarski (Edinburgh: Edinburgh University Press, 2014), 131–145.

"Love and Lobsters: Beckett's Meta-Ethics," in *The Cambridge Companion to Beckett*, 2nd ed., ed. Dirk Van Hulle (Cambridge: Cambridge University Press, 2015), 158–169.

"Beckett's French Contexts," in *History of Modern French Literature*, ed. Christopher Prendergast (Princeton, NJ: Princeton University Press, 2016).

Extracts from Samuel Beckett's unpublished "Philosophy Notes" reproduced by kind permission of the Estate of Samuel Beckett c/o Rosica Colin Limited, London.

NOTES

INTRODUCTION

1. Jean-Michel Rabaté, ed., *Beckett avant Beckett* (Paris: Presses de l'École Normale Supérieure, 1984). Beckett's abbreviation of the title as "B.A.B.*a*." hinted ironically that the collection could be taken as a basic primer.

2. See Anthony Cronin, *Samuel Beckett: The Last Modernist* (New York: HarperCollins, 1997).

3. On the topic of nothingness, see Daniela Caselli, ed., *Beckett and Nothing: Trying to Understand Beckett*, (Manchester: Manchester University Press, 2010).

4. One can think of Bruce Nauman's "Beckett Walk" videos (1968), or of Stan Douglas's "Monodramas" (1991) or "Video" (2007) based on Beckett's *Film*. This contemporary visual aspect was documented by the Paris exhibition *Samuel Beckett* shown at the Centre Pompidou in March–June 2007 and Judith Wilkinson's *Samuel Beckett: A Curated Life* (Bloomsbury, 2016) intelligently explores the numerous connections between Beckett and contemporary art.

5. Simon Critchley, Nicholas Strobbe, John Dalton, Peter Banki, "'Beckett is my hero (it's alright).' An Interview with Simon Critchley," *Contretemps*, no. 1 (September 2000): 2–20, http://sydney.edu.au/contretemps/1september2000/critchley.pdf.

6. Stephen John Dilks, *Samuel Beckett in the Literary Marketplace* (Syracuse, NY: Syracuse University Press, 2011).

7. Harold Pinter, "Samuel Beckett," in *Various Voices: Prose, Poetry, Politics* (New York: Grove Press, 1998), 55.

8. Samuel Beckett, *Disjecta: Miscellanous Writings and a Fragment* (London: John Calder, 1983), 95.

9. Walther von der Vogelweide quoted in Dirk van Hulle and Mark Nixon, *Samuel Beckett's Library* (Cambridge: Cambridge University Press, 2013), 84. The line "How on this earth one ought to live" is in the original "Wie man zer Werlte solte leben." The poet uses *zer* not *in*, thus a phrase closer to *zu der Welt* than *in der Welt*. Von der Vogelweide points to the responsibility we have *to* the world.

10. Blaise Pascal, *Pensées*, ed. Michel Le Guern, 2 vols. (Paris: Gallimard, 1977), 2:92, translated by A. J. Krailsheimer in *Pensées* (New York: Penguin, 1966), 212. Krailsheimer's translation tones down the original.

11. Laura Salisbury, in *Samuel Beckett: Laughing Matters, Comic Timing* (Edinburgh: Edinburgh University Press, 2012), quotes Beckett who had written to Desmond Eagan: "Democritus laughed at Heraclitus weeping + Heraclitus wept at Democritus laughing. Pick yr. Fancy" (230).

12. Erik Grayson, "An Interview with J. M. Coetzee," *Stirrings Still* 3, no. 1 (Summer 2006): 6.

13. J. M. Coetzee, "Samuel Beckett," in *Inner Workings, Literary Essays 2000–2005* (New York: Viking, 2007), 172.

14. Samuel Beckett, *Mercier and Camier* (New York: Grove Press, 1975), 56.

15. Ibid., 118.

16. Ibid., 117.

17. Ibid., 66.

18. Ibid., 67.

19. "Il faut cultiver notre jardin" is the last sentence of Voltaire's *Candide* (see www.ebooksgratuits.com/blackmask/voltaire_candide.pdf). We know that in 1937, Beckett read *Candide* with great pleasure; see *Samuel Beckett's Library*, 65.

20. Beckett's cynicism follows the classical type, not contemporary disabused pessimism. It aims at telling the truth, as Sloterdijk and Foucault have shown. See Peter Sloterdijk, *Critique of Cynical Reason* (Minneapolis: University of Minnesota Press, 1988), and Michel Foucault, *The Courage of Truth*, trans. Graham Burchell (London: Palgrave MacMillan, 2011).

21. For a discussion of the impact of this dream on Beckett, see chapter 5. Descartes's three dreams are translated by John Cottingham, *Descartes* (Oxford: Blackwell, 1986), 161–164. The passage of the third dream is quoted on page 163.

1. HOW TO THINK LIKE A PIG

1. Samuel Beckett, *En attendant Godot/Waiting for Godot*, bilingual ed. (New York: Grove Press, 2010), 140. The French has two terms for pig, *porc* and *cochon*; both have negative moral connotations, but *porc* is more biblical, closer to swine. When Estragon shrieks "Oh the swine!" after Lucky has kicked him, the French text has "La vache!" (102–103, also 107). "Hog" is used by Pozzo to refer to Lucky as well (see 75, 95, and 131). He is a "pig" (99, 121, 141, 147, 157, and 329) whereas in the French original, he is always called "porc," although not as often as he is called "pig" in English. Note that Estragon calls Vladimir a "punctilious pig" (267) and "pig-headed" (299).

2. Ibid., 141–142.

3. Georges Bataille, "La Pratique de la Joie devant la Mort," *Acéphale*, 1936–1939, facsimile reprint Jean-Michel Place, Paris, 1995, 11–23.
4. Georges Bataille, *Visions of Excess*, trans. Allan Stoekl (Minneapolis: University of Minnesota Press, 1985), 239.
5. Ibid., 235.
6. Ibid., 28.
7. Georges Bataille, "The Ultimate Instant," trans. Thomas Walton, *Transition 48*, no. 1 (January 1948): 60–69.
8. Ibid., 67.
9. Maurice Nadeau, "Georges Bataille and the Hatred of Poetry," *Transition 48*, no. 4 (n.d.): 112.
10. Ibid., 111.
11. Georges Bataille, *Choix de Lettres 1917–1962*, ed. Michel Surya (Paris: Gallimard, 1997).
12. Samuel Beckett, *Three Novels: Molloy, Malone Dies, The Unnamable* (New York: Grove Press, 1991), 39.
13. See Sylvie Patron, *Critique (1946–1996), Une encyclopédie de l'esprit* (Paris: Éditions de l'IMEC, 1999).
14. Georges Bataille, "Le silence de Molloy," *Critique*, no. 48 (May 15, 1951): 390; translation mine. Translated into English by Jean M. Sommermeyer in *Samuel Beckett: The Critical Heritage*, ed. L. Graver and R. Federman (London: Routledge and Kegan Paul, 1979), 55–64.
15. Bataille, "Le silence de Molloy," 395; translation mine.
16. Beckett, *Three Novels*, 25.
17. Bataille, "Le silence de Molloy," 395; translation mine.
18. Lawrence Graver and Raymond Federman, eds., *Samuel Beckett: The Critical Heritage* (London: Routledge and Keagan Paul, 1979), 56.
19. Bataille, "Le silence de Molloy," 390; translation mine.
20. See Van Hulle and Nixon, *Samuel Beckett's Library*, 80 and 234–235. I quote some of these underlined passages in chapter 9.
21. Georges Bataille had written an introduction for Marquis de Sade's *Justine ou les Malheurs de la Vertu* (Paris: Soleil Noir, 1950). See *Samuel Beckett's Library*, 80.
22. Peter Fifield, "'Accursed Progenitor!' *Fin de Partie* and Georges Bataille," in *Samuel Beckett: Debts and Legacies*, ed. Eric Tonning et al. (Leiden, NL: Brill, 2010), 107–121, shows that Bataille's testimony about his father—who died blind, syphilitic, and abandoned by all during World War I—did inspire the predicament of Hamm in *Endgame*.
23. Maurice Blanchot, "Sade's Reason," in *The Maurice Blanchot Reader*, ed. Michael Holland (Oxford: Blackwell, 1995), 75–76. The essay was published in *Les Temps Modernes* in October 1947 as "A la rencontre de Sade." In 1950,

Beckett translated a few pages from this essay for *Transition*; see *The Letters of Samuel Beckett*, vol. 2, *1941–1956*, ed. George Craig, Martha Dow Fehsenfeld, Dan Gunn, and Lois More Overbeck (Cambridge: Cambridge University Press, 2011), 211.

24. Blanchot, "Sade's Reason," 76–77.

25. Bataille, "Le silence de Molloy," 396.

26. Beckett, *Three Novels*, 21.

27. Ibid., 21.

28. Beckett, *Molloy*, 29.

29. See Thomas Trezise, *Into the Breach* (Princeton, NJ: Princeton University Press, 1990).

30. Beckett, *Disjecta*, 118–137.

31. Ibid., 120.

32. It is a similar question that led the philosopher and mathematician Gilles Châtelet to write a sweeping and accurate political diatribe entitled *To Live and Think Like Pigs: The Incitement of Envy and Boredom in Market Democracies*, trans. Robin Mackay (Falmouth, UK: Urbanomic/Sequence Press, 2014).

33. See Arthur Rimbaud, "L'impossible" (*A Season in Hell*), in *Collected Poems*, trans. Oliver Bernard (London: Penguin, 1986), 337–340. French poet Bonnefoy takes this concept to be Rimbaud's central concern; see Yves Bonnefoy, *Arthur Rimbaud*, trans. Paul Schmidt (New York: Harper and Row, 1973), 45.

34. Beckett, *Disjecta*, 121.

35. Ibid., 123.

36. Ibid., 126.

37. Ibid., 128.

38. Ibid., 131; translation mine.

39. Ibid., 132.

40. Samuel Beckett, *Mercier et Camier*, 186.

41. Ibid., 106.

42. Beckett, *Three Novels*, 165.

43. Giorgio Agamben, *Homo Sacer*, trans. Daniel Heller-Roazen (Stanford, CA: Stanford University Press, 1998), 1.

44. Giorgio Agamben, *The Open*, trans. Kevin Attell (Stanford, CA: Stanford University Press, 2004), 29, 33–38.

45. Jacques Derrida, *Séminaire La Bête et le Souverain* (Paris: Galilée, 2008), 1:407, 434. The discussion of *Homo Sacer* took place on March 10, 2002 (419–422 and 431–442).

46. Samuel Beckett, *Eleutheria* (Paris: Éditions de Minuit, 1995), 146.

47. Raymond Cousse, *Death Sty: A Pig's Tale*, trans. Richard Miller (New York: Grove Press, 1979). The original title is *Stratégie pour deux jambons* (Paris: Le Serpent à Plumes, 1979). Excerpts from the correspondence between Beckett and Cousse, as well as passages related to Beckett in Cousse's journal, have been published in *Les Episodes*, no. 18 (2003): 49–97.

48. Letter to Cousse from December 1, 1969, quoted in *Les Episodes*, no. 18 (2003): 86.

49. Cousse, *Death Sty*, 89–90. The original is funnier: "La durée de l'intermède est fonction de l'humeur plus ou moins massacrante de l'équarrisseur" (*Stratégie pour deux jambons*, 118). However, the translation adds a nice pun on "boudin" and "burden."

2. THE WORTH AND GIRTH OF AN ITALIAN HOAGIE

1. Beckett, *Disjecta*, 6. Hereafter cited in text as *D*.

2. *Our Exagmination Round His Factification for Incamination of Work in Progress*. The collection was published in May 1929 by Shakespeare and Company.

3. Lawrence Rainey annotated Beckett's essay in *Modernism: An Anthology*, ed. Lawrence Rainey (Oxford: Blackwell, 2005), 1061–1072.

4. Samuel Beckett, *Beckett in Black and Red: The Translations for Nancy Cunard's Negro (1934)*, ed. Alan Warren Friedman (Lexington: University Press of Kentucky, 2000), 73.

5. Rebecca West, "The Strange Necessity," in *The Strange Necessity* (London: Jonathan Cape, 1928), 3.

6. Rainey, *Modernism*, 1067n4.

7. James Knowlson, *Damned to Fame: The Life of Samuel Beckett* (New York: Simon and Schuster, 1996), 107.

8. Benedetto Croce, *What Is Living and What Is Dead of the Philosophy of Hegel*, trans. Douglas Ainslie (London: Macmillan, 1915).

9. Martin Heidegger, "Logos (Heraclitus, Fragment B 50)," in *Early Greek Thinking*, trans. D. F. Krell and F. A. Capuzzi (San Francisco: Harper and Row, 1984), 59–78.

10. Ibid., 77.

11. See Giacomo Leopardi, *Zibaldone*, ed. Michael Caesar and Franco D'Intino, trans. Kathleen Baldwin et al. (New York: Farrar, Straus and Giroux, 2013). *Zibaldone*, an extraordinary notebook full of philological insights, was apparently unknown to Beckett.

12. Samuel Beckett et al., *Our Exagmination Round His Factification for Incamination of Work in Progress* (London: Faber, 1972), 143.

13. James Joyce, *Finnegans Wake* (London: Faber, 1939), 497, lines 1–3.

14. Samuel Beckett, *The Complete Dramatic Works* (London: Faber, 1986), 116.

15. Samuel Beckett, *More Pricks Than Kicks* (London: Calder and Boyars, 1970), 9.

16. Dante Alighieri, *The Divine Comedy of Dante Alighieri: Purgatorio*, trans. Allen Mandelbaum (New York: Bantam, 1984), Canto 4:98–99 (35). All references to Dante come from this translation.

17. Samuel Beckett, *Nohow On: Company, Ill Seen Ill Said, Worstward Ho* (New York: Grove Press, 1996), 44.

18. Samuel Beckett, *The Complete Short Prose, 1929–1989*, ed. S. E. Gontarski (New York: Grove Press, 1955), 205.

19. Samuel Beckett, *Dream of Fair to Middling Women* (Dublin: Black Cat Press, 1992), 66.

20. Samuel Beckett, *The Letters of Samuel Beckett*, vol. 1, *1929–1940*, ed. George Craig, Martha Dow Fehsenfeld, Dan Gunn, and Lois More Overbeck (Cambridge: Cambridge University Press, 2009), 81.

21. Samuel Beckett, *Murphy* (New York: Grove Press, 1957), 65.

22. See Jacques Le Goff, *The Birth of Purgatory*, trans. Arthur Goldhammer (Chicago: University of Chicago Press, 1984), and Michel Vovelle, *Les âmes du Purgatoire, ou le travail du deuil* (Paris: Gallimard, 1996).

23. Beckett, *Complete Short Prose*, 159.

24. James Joyce, *Letters*, ed. Stuart Gilbert (New York: Viking, 1957), 1:241.

25. Beckett, *Three Novels*, 291.

26. Beckett, *Letters*, 1:519.

27. Samuel Beckett, *Proust and Three Dialogues with Georges Duthuit* (London: John Calder, 1976) 36–38.

28. Beckett, *Nohow On*, 97.

3. THE POSTHUMAN, OR THE HUMILITY OF THE EARTH

1. Joyce, *Finnegans Wake*, 36, line 6.

2. Knowlson, *Damned to Fame*, 105.

3. Quoted by Dougald McMillan, *Transition: The History of a Literary Era, 1927–1938* (New York: George Braziller, 1976), 179. See also Céline Mansanti, *La Revue transition (1927–1938): Le modernisme historique en devenir* (Rennes: Presses Universitaires de Rennes, 2009), 88–92 and 186–189.

4. See Roland McHugh, *The Sigla of Finnegans Wake* (London: Edward Arnold, 1976), for an excellent presentation of Joyce's visual abbreviations.

5. Joyce, *Letters*, 1:180.

6. I have discussed Molly's allegorical status and the function played by the sigla representing characters of *Finnegans Wake* in *Joyce Upon the Void: The Genesis of Doubt* (Houndmills, UK: Macmillan, 1991), 43–101.

7. Beckett, *Letters*, 1:545.

8. Ibid., 1:535.

9. Ibid., 1:546.

10. Ibid., 1:537.

11. Ibid., 1:536.

12. Ibid., 1:222.

13. Ibid.

14. Ibid.

15. Ibid., 1:227.

16. Ibid., 1:540.

17. Beckett, *Three Novels*, 305.

18. Ibid., 305, 306.

19. Samuel Beckett, *L'innommable* (Paris: Éditions de Minuit, 1953), 31.

20. Beckett, *Three Novels*, 300.

21. Beckett, *L'Innommable*, 22.

22. Ibid.

23. Beckett, *En attendant Godot*, 71.

24. Beckett, *Three Novels*, 338.

25. See the conversation between Derek Attridge and Jacques Derrida, "This Strange Institution Called Literature: An Interview with Jacques Derrida," in Jacques Derrida, *Acts of Literature*, ed. Derek Attridge (London: Routledge, 1992), 60–62. See also Daniel Katz, *Saying I No More: Subjectivity and Consciousness in the Prose of Samuel Beckett* (Evanston, IL: Northwestern University Press, 1999), and Asja Szafraniec, *Beckett, Derrida, and the Event of Literature* (Stanford, CA: Stanford University Press, 2007).

26. Joyce, *Finnegans Wake*, 18, lines 3–5.

27. Beckett, *Complete Short Prose*, 160.

28. Samuel Beckett, *Echo's Bones*, ed. Mark Nixon (New York: Grove Press, 2014), 3. "Casse-poitrine" is a slang term denoting an active partner in homosexual fellatio. Beckett found it in Pierre Garnier's 1883 book *Onanisme seul et à deux*.

29. Beckett, *Three Novels*, 383.

30. Ibid., 338.

31. See *Beckett's Dream Notebook*, ed. John Pilling (Reading, UK: Beckett International Foundation, 1999), 165.

32. Ibid. This was also drawn from Jules de Gaultier's book, one of the first books to launch Nietzschean ideas in France.

33. Beckett, *Three Novels*, 322.

34. Ibid., 324.

35. Ibid.

36. Ibid., 337.

37. Ibid., 372.

38. Ibid. Given its main theme—which can be said to be human language speaking of itself without a person, face, or voice—it is surprising to observe that the pages of *The Unnamable* are teeming with animals, cattle, dogs, rats,

termites, horses, pigs, ants, tapeworms, toads, hyenas, herrings (red), horn-owl, hornets, bluebottles, not counting Worm or the celebrated litany of "caged beasts born of caged beasts" (ibid., 386–387).

4. BURNED TOASTS AND BOILED LOBSTERS

1. Beckett, *More Pricks Than Kicks*, 21.
2. Ibid., 12.
3. Ibid., 21.
4. Ruby Cohn, *A Beckett Canon* (Ann Arbor: University of Michigan Press, 2001), 391n11.
5. See Mariko Tanaka, Yoshiki Tajiri, and Michiko Tsushima, eds., *Samuel Beckett and Pain* (Amsterdam and New York: Rodopi, 2012).
6. Beckett, *Collected Poems*, 38.
7. Marcel Proust, *Swann's Way*, trans. Lydia Davis (New York: Viking, 2002), 127.
8. Ibid., 125.
9. Ibid., 124.
10. Ibid., 125. See also, Marcel Proust, *À la recherche du temps perdu*, ed. Jean-Yves Tadié (Paris: Gallimard, Pléiade, 1987), 1:120.
11. Beckett, *More Pricks Than Kicks*, 21.
12. Ibid.
13. Proust, *Swann's Way*, 83.
14. Beckett, *How It Is* (New York: Grove Press, 1964), 132.
15. Jonathan Boulter, "'We have our being in justice': Samuel Beckett's *How It Is*," in Tanaka et al., *Samuel Beckett and Pain*, 173–200. See also, David Cunningham, "'We have our being in justice': Formalism, Abstraction and Beckett's 'Ethics,'" in *Beckett and Ethics*, ed. by Russell Smith (London: Continuum, 2008), 21–37, and Leo Bersani and Ulysse Dutoit, *Arts of Impoverishment: Beckett, Rothko, Resnais* (Cambridge, MA: Harvard University Press, 1993), 62–65.
16. Daniela Caselli, "Staging the Inferno in *How It Is*," in *Beckett's Dantes: Intertextuality in the Fiction and Criticism* (Manchester: Manchester University Press, 2005), 148–183.
17. Beckett, *Comment C'est* (Paris: Éditions de Minuit, 1961), 159.
18. Ibid., 150.
19. Beckett, *How It Is*, 124.
20. D. A. F. de Sade, "Lettre à Mademoiselle de Rousset," *Etudes Philosophiques*, 26 January 1782, quoted in Annie Le Brun, *Attaquer le Soleil*, (Paris: Musée d'Orsay / Gallimard, 2014), 17.
21. Ibid., 37.
22. Beckett, *Disjecta*, 81.

23. Dante Alighieri, *The Divine Comedy of Dante Alighieri: Inferno*, trans. Allen Mandelbaum (New York: Bantam, 1981), 65.

24. Ibid., 64. See also Dante Alighieri, *Opere*, ed. Fredi Chiapelli (Milan: Murcia, 1967), 474.

25. In "A Se Stesso," Giacomo Leopardi wrote: "Amaro e noia / La vita, altro mai nulla; e fango è il mondo [Life is merely bitterness and boredom, and the world is filth]." Leopardi, *Canti*, trans. Jonathan Galassi (New York: Farrar, Straus and Giroux, 2011), 234–235.

26. Beckett, *Dream of Fair to Middling Women*, 36.

27. Joyce, *Finnegans Wake*, 185, lines 17–26.

28. Beckett, *How It Is*, 62.

29. Ibid., 63.

30. Beckett, *Collected Poems*, 39.

31. Ibid., 39.

32. Beckett, *More Pricks Than Kicks*, 18.

33. Ibid., 20.

34. Ibid.

35. Ibid., 19.

36. Beckett, *Three Novels*, 372, and *The Unnamable*, 142. "Langoustes" are "spiny lobsters," slightly smaller than lobsters and devoid of any claw.

37. Beckett, *Three Novels*, 51.

38. Beckett, *Letters*, 2:458.

39. Beckett, *More Pricks Than Kicks*, 12.

40. Ibid., 11–12.

41. Joyce, *Finnegans Wake*, 121, line 11.

42. Beckett, *Collected Poems*, 18–19.

43. I am referring to Dalí's drawing from 1929 entitled "Parfois je crache par plaisir sur le portrait de ma mère." Dalí's mother had died when he was sixteen. When he saw the drawing, Dalí's father was enraged and threw his son out of the house, which provided a model for Beckett's numerous "expelled" sons of the French short stories.

5. "PORCA MADONNA!": MOVING DESCARTES TOWARD
GEULINCX AND PROUST

1. Samuel Beckett, *Collected Poems*, 40.

2. For Descartes's dreams, see Cottingham, *Descartes*, 160–164.

3. John Pentland Mahaffy, *Descartes* (Edinburgh and London: Blackwood, 1880), 138.

4. Edward Bizub, *Beckett et Descartes dans l'œuf. Aux sources de l'œuvre beckettienne: de Whoroscope à Godot* (Paris: Garnier, 2012).

5. L. Debricon, *Descartes: Choix de textes avec étude du système philosophique et notice biographique* (Paris: L. Michaud, 1909).

6. Beckett, *Collected Poems*, 14.

7. Maxime Leroy, *Descartes, le philosophe au masque* (Paris: Editions Rieder, 1929), 1:89–90. Freud's original letter has been lost and we only have Leroy's French translation.

8. I am quoting the excellent book by Kyoo Lee, *Reading Descartes Otherwise: Blind, Mad, Dreamy, and Bad* (New York: Fordham University Press, 2013).

9. Richard Watson, *Cogito Ergo Sum: The Life of René Descartes* (Boston: Godine, 2002; rev. 2007), 177.

10. Beckett, *Collected Poems*, 40.

11. Ibid., 42–43.

12. See Ann Lecercle, "*Echo's Bones:* La redoutable symétrie de l'oeuf pourri ou Une poétique de la suture," in *Beckett avant Beckett*, 47–78. The poems "Enueg 1" and "Sanies 2" are published in Beckett, *Collected Poems*, 6–8 and 14–15, respectively.

13. René Descartes, *L'Homme de Descartes et un Traité de la formation du fœtus du mesme auteur avec les remarques de Louys de La Forge* (Paris: Angot, 1664).

14. Beckett, *Collected Poems*, 244. The editors have added the final text of the poem and its annotations in an Appendix.

15. Beckett, *Collected Poems*, 242.

16. Leroy, *Descartes, le philosophe au masque*, 2:27.

17. Beckett, *Collected Poems*, 243.

18. Ibid., 244.

19. See James Joyce, *Ulysses*, ed. Jeri Johnson (Oxford: Oxford University Press, 1993), 38 and 198–199.

20. Beckett, *Murphy* (New York: Grove Press, 1957), 140.

21. See the discussion in Kyoo Lee, *Reading Descartes Otherwise*, 84–109.

22. Beckett, *Collected Poems*, 42, 243.

23. Ibid., 40.

24. Ibid., 43.

25. Ibid., 44.

26. Han van Ruler, Anthony Uhlmann, and Martin Wilson, eds., *Arnold Geulincx's Ethics with Samuel Beckett's Notes*, trans. Martin Wilson (Leiden: Brill, 2006); David Tucker, *Samuel Beckett and Arnold Geulincx* (London: Bloomsbury, 2012), 42–70.

27. Van Ruler et al., *Arnold Geulincx's Ethics*, 247 (for the text) and 337 (for Beckett's notes). Beckett quoted the Latin original of *Ethica*.

28. Thomas Dommange, "Geulincx ou la mécanique de l'ineffable," in *Notes de Beckett sur Geulincx*, ed. Nicolas Doutey (Besançon: Les Solitaires Intempestifs, 2012), 229–259.

29. Heinrich von Kleist wrote his essay "On the Marionette Theatre" in 1810. In this text, he argues that marionettes are superior to living dancers because they have no "affectation," no weight, and no cumbersome mind preventing a release of the full grace of their movements. A year later Kleist shot himself to death in suicide pact with his lover Henriette Vogel.

30. Friedrich Nietzsche, *On the Genealogy of Morality*, trans. Keith Ansell-Pearson (Cambridge: Cambridge University Press, 1994), 106.

31. See ibid., 107–110, and Friedrich Nietzsche, *Zur Genealogie der Moral* (Munich: Goldmann, 1966), 117.

32. Van Ruler et al., *Arnold Geulincx's Ethics*, 31–32.

33. Beckett, *Murphy*, 178.

34. Ibid., 62.

35. Ibid., 251–252.

36. Shane Weller, *A Taste for the Negative: Beckett and Nihilism* (Oxford: Legenda, 2005).

37. Jacques Lacan, *The Four Fundamental Concepts of Psychoanalysis*, trans. Alan Sheridan (New York: Norton, 1978), 103–104, 167–68, and 180.

38. Simon Critchley, *Very Little . . . Almost Nothing* (London: Routledge, 1997); Shane Weller, *Beckett, Literature, and the Ethics of Alterity* (Houndmills, UK: Palgrave Macmillan, 2006); Peter Fifield, *Late Modernist Style in Samuel Beckett and Emmanuel Levinas* (New York: Palgrave Macmillan, 2013).

39. Emmanuel Levinas, "The Other in Proust," in *The Levinas Reader*, ed. Sean Hand (Oxford: Blackwell, 1989), 160–165. On Levinas's analysis of Proust in his war notebooks see my *Crimes of the Future* (New York: Bloomsbury, 2014), 57–69.

40. Levinas, "The Other in Proust," 162.

41. Beckett, *Proust and Three Dialogues* (London: John Calder, 1970), 66.

42. Ibid., 89.

43. Ibid., 47.

44. Ibid.

45. Levinas, "The Other in Proust," 165.

6. FROM AN AESTHETICS OF NONRELATION TO AN ETHICS OF NEGATION

1. Beckett, *Letters*, 1:167.

2. See the excellent chapter "Talking Pictures: Beckett and the Visual Arts" in Mark Nixon, *Samuel Beckett's German Diaries 1936–1937* (London: Continuum, 2011), 132–161.

3. Beckett, *Letters*, 1:518.

4. See the account in Knowlson, *Damned to Fame*, 318–320.

5. Beckett, "Three Dialogues with Georges Duthuit," in *Disjecta*, 139 and 140.

6. Jane Bishop, Cécile Debray, and Rebecca Rabinow, eds., *The Steins Collect: Matisse, Picasso, and the Parisian Avant-Garde* (New Haven, CT: Yale University Press, 2011), 230, 232. Gertrude Stein owned Masson's *The Meal* (1922) and *Man in a Tower* (1924) (reproduced in *The Steins Collect: Matisse, Picasso, and the Parisian Avant-Garde*, 296–297) because in 1923, she had traded one Picasso for three Massons, thus becoming the first collector of Masson's work.

7. Clark V. Poling, *André Masson and the Surrealist Self* (New Haven, CT: Yale University Press, 2008), 158–159.

8. In the journal *Acéphale*, quoted in chapter 1, all illustrations were by Masson.

9. Beckett, *Disjecta*, 140.

10. See the essays by Steve Barfield, David Cunningham, Andrew Gibson, David A. Hatch, Lois Oppenheim, Jeremy Parrott, and Philip Tew in *"Three Dialogues" Revisited*, vol. 13 of *Samuel Beckett Today/Aujourd'hui*, ed. Marius Buning, Matthijs Engelberts, Sjet Houppermans, and Daniele de Ruyter-Tognotti (Amsterdam: Rodopi, 2003), 15–133. In *The Painted Word: Samuel Beckett's Dialogue with Art* (Ann Arbor: University of Michigan Press, 2000), Lois Oppenheim approaches Beckett's "decreative program" via Merleau-Ponty. See also David Lloyd, "Beckett's Things: Bram van Velde and the Gaze," *Modernist Cultures* 6, no. 2 (October 2011): 269–295.

11. Pascale Casanova, *Samuel Beckett: Anatomy of a Literary Revolution*, trans. Gregory Elliott (London: Verso, 2007).

12. Clement Greenberg, "Symposium: Is the French Avant-Garde Over-rated?," in *The Collected Essays and Criticism*, vol. 3, *Affirmations and Refusals, 1950–1956* (Chicago: University of Chicago Press, 1993), 155.

13. Daniel Albright, "Beckett and Surrealism," in *Beckett and Aesthetics* (Cambridge: Cambridge University Press, 2003), 1–24.

14. Poling, *André Masson and the Surrealist Self*, 153.

15. Beckett, *Letters*, 2:204.

16. Ibid., 2:161.

17. Georges Duthuit, ed., *Transition 48*, no. 1 (January 1948): 104–120. See also Eugene Jolas, *Critical Writings, 1924–1951*, ed. Klaus H. Kiefer and Rainer Rumold (Evanston, IL: Northern University Press, 2009), 184–199.

18. Beckett read "Peinture Tragique" in *Temps Modernes*, no. 4, January 1, 1946, 725–729; also in André Masson, *Le Rebelle du Surréalisme, Ecrits*, ed. Françoise Will-Levaillant (Paris: Hermann, 1976), 119–124. *Les Temps Modernes* published the first part of "Suite" in July 1946 before rejecting the second part.

19. Henri Maldiney, *Regard, Parole, Espace* (Lausanne: L'Age d'Homme, 1965). Maldiney denounces the "false dilemma of painting: abstraction or reality" in *Regard*, 8.

20. Beckett, *Letters*, 2:133.

21. Masson, "Une peinture de l'essentiel" (1956), in *Le Rebelle du Surréalisme*, 174.

22. Beckett, *Disjecta*, 139.

23. Duthuit, "Matisse and Byzantine Space," *Transition 49*, no. 5, 1949, 29.

24. André Masson quoted in Aron Kibedi-Varga, *Autour d'André Du Bouchet*, ed. Michel Collot (Paris: Presses de l'École Normale Supérieure, 1986), 117.

25. André Du Bouchet, "Three Exhibitions: Masson—Tal Coat—Miró," *Transition 49*, no. 5 (1949): 89.

26. Clement Greenberg, "Review of Exhibitions of Joan Miró and André Masson," *Collected Essays and Criticism*, vol. 1: *Perceptions and Judgments, 1939–1944*, ed. John O'Brian (Chicago: University of Chicago Press, 1986), 208.

27. Ibid., 209.

28. Ibid.

29. Clement Greenberg, "Modernist Painting" (1960), in *Collected Essays and Criticism*, vol. 4, *Modernism with a Vengeance, 1957–1969* (Chicago: Chicago University Press, 1993), 85.

30. Beckett, *Letters*, 2:86.

31. Ibid., 2:83.

32. Ibid., 2:86.

33. Ibid.

34. Ibid.

35. Duthuit, "Sartre's Last Class," *Transition 48*, no. 2 (1948): 109.

36. Duthuit, "Sartre's Last Class," *Transition 48*, no. 3 (1948): 60.

37. Ibid., 61.

38. Beckett, *Letters*, 2:94.

39. Ibid., 2:131.

40. Ibid., 2:139.

41. Ibid., 2:140.

42. Ibid.

43. Sigmund Freud, *New Introductory Lectures on Psycho-analysis*, trans. James Strachey (New York: Norton, 1989), 77 and 202.

44. Trinity College Library MS 10971/7, "Psychology," in *Notes Diverse Holo: Catalogues of Beckett's Reading Notes and Other Manuscripts at Trinity College, Dublin, with Supporting Essays*, ed. Matthijs Engleberts, Everett Frost, and Jane Maxwell (New York: Rodopi, 2006), 160.

45. Immanuel Kant, *Critique of Practical Reason and Other Writings in Moral Philosophy*, trans. Lewis White Beck (Chicago: University of Chicago Press, 1949), 258.

46. Ibid., 259.

47. Wilhelm Windelband, *A History of Philosophy, With especial reference to the formation and development of its problems and conceptions*, trans. James H. Tufts (1901; repr. Westport, CT: Greenwood Press, 1979), 568.

48. Windelband, *History of Philosophy*, 563–564.

49. Freud, *New Introductory Lectures*, 77.

50. *Notes Diverse Holo*, 160.

51. Beckett, *Disjecta*, 118.

52. Freud, *New Introductory Lectures*, 77.

53. Ibid., 202.

54. Beckett, *Disjecta*, 141.

55. Beckett, *Proust*, 31.

56. Adam Winstanley shows that Beckett read Leonardo's Notebooks because of a recent review by Maurice Blanchot. See Adam Winstanley, "A 'whispered *disfazione*': Maurice Blanchot, Leonardo da Vinci, and 'Three Dialogues with Georges Duthuit,'" *Journal of Beckett Studies* 22, no. 2 (2013): 135–160.

57. Leonardo da Vinci, "Of the deluge and the representation of it in painting" and "Description of the deluge," in *The Notebooks of Leonardo da Vinci* (New York: George Braziller, 1955), 914–920.

58. Da Vinci, "Philosophy," in *Notebooks of Leonardo da Vinci*, 75.

59. Beckett, *Disjecta*, 141.

60. Beckett, *Letters*, 2:187.

61. Sigmund Freud, *Leonardo da Vinci and a Memory of His Childhood*, trans. Alan Tyson (New York: Norton, 1989), 16; translation modified.

62. Beckett, *Letters*, 2:149–150.

63. Peter Fifield's study of the links between Beckett and Levinas explains very well the relation of nonrelation; see Fifield, *Late Modernist Style in Samuel Beckett and Emmanuel Levinas* (London: Palgrave Macmillan, 2013).

64. Bram van Velde, "Some Sayings," *Transition 49*, no. 5 (1949): 104.

65. Beckett, *Disjecta*, 141.

66. Paul Celan, *Atemwende*, in *Gesammelte Werke* (Frankfurt: Suhrkamp, 1986), 2:97.

7. BECKETT'S KANTIAN CRITIQUES

1. Martha Nussbaum, "Narrative Emotions: Beckett's Genealogy of Love," *Ethics*, no. 98 (1988): 225–254; repr. in Martha Nussbaum, *Love's Knowledge: Essays on Philosophy and Literature* (Oxford: Oxford University Press, 1990), 286–313.

2. Ibid., 289.

3. Ibid., 297. See also Beckett, *Three Novels*, 25.

4. Nussbaum, "Narrative Emotions," 298.
5. Ibid., 309.
6. Ibid.
7. Beckett, *Murphy*, 164.
8. Nussbaum, "Narrative Emotions," 302.
9. Ibid., 304.
10. Ibid., 299.
11. Ibid., 76 and 78.
12. Martha Nussbaum, "Cultivating Humanity: A Classical Defense of Reform in Liberal Education," in *Norton Anthology of Theory and Criticism* (New York: Norton, 2010), 2330.
13. Simon Critchley, *Very Little . . . Almost Nothing* (London: Routledge, 1997), 262.
14. Ibid., 178.
15. Ibid., 259.
16. Ibid., 265.
17. Ibid., 262.
18. Bjørn K. Myskja, *The Sublime in Kant and Beckett: Aesthetic Judgement, Ethics and Literature* (Berlin: Walter de Gruyter, 2002), 1–2.
19. Myskja, *Sublime in Kant and Beckett*, 52.
20. Ibid., 50.
21. See Van Hulle and Nixon, *Samuel Beckett's Library*, 163–168.
22. Beckett, *Letters*, 1:32–33.
23. Myskja, *Sublime in Kant and Beckett*, 280.
24. Ibid.
25. Beckett, *TCD MSS 10967, Philosophy notes*, Manuscript Department, Trinity College Library Dublin, 229 verso, and Windelband, *History of Philosophy*, trans. James H. Tufts (1893; repr. Westport, CT: Greenwood, 1979) para. 39, 551. See also Beckett's notes on "History of Western Philosophy," in *Notes Diverse Holo*, 87.
26. Beckett, *TCD MSS 10967*, 230 verso, and Windelband, *History of Philosophy*, 553.
27. Windelband, *History of Philosophy*, 553.
28. Beckett, *TCD MSS 10967*, 230 verso, and Windelband, *History of Philosophy*, 554.
29. Beckett, *TCD MSS 10967*, 231 verso, and Windelband, *History of Philosophy*, 556.
30. Beckett, *TCD MSS 10967*, 231 verso, and Windelband, *History of Philosophy*, 556.
31. Windelband, *History of Philosophy*, 556.
32. Beckett, *Letters*, 1:581.

33. Ibid., 1:622.

34. Immanuel Kant, *Critique of Pure Reason*, trans. Guyer and Wood (Cambridge: Cambridge University Press, 1998), 91.

35. Beckett, *Three Novels*, 329.

36. Beckett, *Letters*, 1:643.

37. Beckett, "Whoroscope" Notebook, Beckett International Foundation of the University of Reading, UoR MS 3000, 84.

38. Samuel Beckett, *Watt* (New York: Grove Press, 1953), 354.

39. See Sara Crangle and Peter Nicholls, eds., *On Bathos: Literature, Art, Music* (London: Continuum, 2010).

40. Beckett, *More Pricks Than Kicks*, 11.

41. Ibid.

42. Kant, *Prolegomena to Any Future Metaphysics*, trans. Gary Hatfield (Cambridge: Cambridge University Press, 2004), 125.

43. Ibid., 127.

44. Beckett, "Whoroscope," 80.

45. Ibid.

46. Richard Ellmann, *James Joyce*, 2nd ed. (Oxford: Oxford University Press, 1982), 648.

47. See Linda Ben-Zvi, "Samuel Beckett, Fritz Mauthner and the Limits of language," *PMLA* 95, no. 2 (March 1980): 183–200, and Matthew Feldman, "Beckett and Philosophy, 1928–1938," in *Samuel Beckett: Debts and Legacies*, ed. Erik Tonning, Matthew Feldman, Matthijs Engelberts, and Dirk Van Hulle (New York: Rodopi, 2010), 163–180. See also Feldman's groundbreaking *Beckett's Books: A Cultural History of Samuel Beckett's "Interwar Notes"* (London: Continuum, 2006), 116–146.

48. Fritz Mauthner, *Beiträge zu einer Kritik der Sprache*, 2 vols. (Frankfurt: Ullstein, 1982), 2:477; translation mine. Feldman provides a different translation in "Beckett and Philosophy,"174.

49. Mauthner, *Beiträge*, 2:477.

50. Ibid., 2:478.

51. Ibid., 2:532; copied by Beckett in "Whoroscope," 81.

52. Immanuel Kant, *Practical Philosophy*, trans. Mary J. Gregor (Cambridge: Cambridge University Press, 1996), 125–131.

53. "Kraus's Review of Ulrich's *Eleutheriologie*," trans. Mary J. Gregor in Kant, *Practical Philosophy*, 125–131. C. J. Kraus wrote the review of Ulrich's book at Kant's request.

54. Beckett, *Murphy*, 131.

55. Beckett first wanted to call his play *L'éleuthéromane*; see Knowlson, *Damned to Fame*, 331.

56. Samuel Beckett, *Eleutheria*, trans. Michael Brodsky (New York: Foxrock, 1995), 3.

57. Ibid., 166.
58. Beckett, *Eleutheria* (Paris: Éditions de Minuit, 1995), 167.
59. Beckett, *Letters*, 1:245.

8. DIALECTICS OF ENLITTLEMENT

1. Samuel Beckett, *Eleutheria*, trans. Barbara Wright (London: Faber, 1996), 44–45.
2. Ibid., 45.
3. Jorge Luis Borges, "Tlön, Uqbar, Orbis Tertius," in *Collected Fictions*, trans. Andrew Hurley (New York: Penguin, 1998), 69.
4. Quoted in Dougald McMillan and Martha Fehsenfeld, *Beckett in the Theatre* (New York: Riverrun Press, 1988), 231.
5. Jonathan Little, *The Kindly Ones*, trans. Charlotte Mandell (New York: HarperCollins, 2009).
6. Beckett, *Letters*, 1:607.
7. Beckett, *Watt*, 155–56; hereafter cited in text as *W*.
8. Knowlson, *Damned to Fame*, 307.
9. See Max Horkheimer and Theodor W. Adorno, *Dialectic of Enlightenment*, trans. Edmund Jephcott (Stanford, CA: Stanford University Press, 2002), 63–93.
10. Roland Barthes, *Sade, Fourier, Loyola*, trans. Richard Miller (Berkeley: University of California Press, 1989), 152–153.
11. Kant, *Practical Philosophy*, 428.
12. Walter Benjamin, "Goethe's Elective Affinities," in *Selected Writings*, vol. 1, *1913–1926*, ed. Marcus Bullock and Michael W. Jennings (Cambridge, MA: Harvard University Press, 1996), 299.
13. Kant, *Practical Philosophy*, 426–427.
14. Jacques Lacan, *The Ethics of Psychoanalysis*, trans. by Dennis Porter (New York: Norton, 1992), 202.
15. See Beckett, *Letters*, 2:210.
16. Pierre Klossowski, *Sade My Neighbor* (Evanston, IL: Northwestern University Press, 1991), 41.
17. Marquis de Sade, *The 120 Days of Sodom and Other Writings*, trans. Austryn Wainhouse and Richard Seaver (New York: Grove Press, 1966), 673. Hereafter cited in text as *120 Days*.
18. Beckett, *Three Novels*, 111.
19. Ibid.
20. Beckett, *Three Novels*, 111.
21. Beckett, *Complete Dramatic Works*, 182–185.
22. Ibid., 275–284.
23. Ibid., 276.
24. Mauthner, *Beiträge*, 1:364–372.

25. Ibid., 1:24.
26. Ibid., 1:25.
27. Slavoj Žižek, "Language, Violence and Non-violence," *International Žižek Studies* 2, no. 3 (2010): 26–36.
28. J. M. Coetzee, "Postscript: Letter of Elisabeth, Lady Chandos, to Francis Bacon," in *Elizabeth Costello* (London: Penguin, 2003), 227–230.
29. Beckett, *Three Novels*, 46.
30. Beckett, *Molloy*, 68.
31. Beckett, *Three Novels*, 46; Beckett, *Molloy*, 68.

9. BATHETIC JOKES, ANIMAL SLAPSTICK, AND ETHICAL LAUGHTER

1. Beckett, *Complete Dramatic Works*, 371.
2. Christopher Ricks, *Beckett's Dying Words* (Oxford: Oxford University Press, 1993).
3. Beckett, *En attendant Godot*, 333.
4. Beckett, *Complete Dramatic Works*, 216–217.
5. Ibid., 327.
6. Sándor Ferenczi, "Laughter," in *Final Contributions to the Problems and Methods of Psycho-Analysis*, vol. 3, trans. by Eric Mosbacher (New York: Basic Books, 1959), 177.
7. Ibid., 178.
8. My translation of a passage from the preface to *Madame Edwarda* quoted in Van Hulle and Nixon, *Samuel Beckett's Library*, 235.
9. Ibid.
10. Georges Bataille, preface to *Madame Edwarda*, trans. Austryn Wainhouse, in *The Bataille Reader*, ed. Fred Botting and Scott Wilson (Oxford: Blackwell, 1997), 225.
11. See Anca Parvulescu, *Laughter: Notes on a Passion* (Cambridge, MA: MIT Press, 2010), and Laura Salisbury, *Samuel Beckett: Laughing Matters, Comic Timing* op. cit.
12. Beckett, *Disjecta*, 157.
13. Sigmund Freud, *The Joke and Its Relation to the Unconscious*, trans. by Joyce Crick (London: Penguin, 2003), 46; emphasis in original.
14. Sándor Ferenczi, "The Elasticity of Psycho-analysis Technique," in *Final Contributions*, 3:93.
15. See *New Yorker*, September 22, 2014, 93.
16. Sándor Ferenczi, "Laughter," in *Final Contributions*, 3:180.
17. Ibid., 180.
18. Ibid., 179.
19. Beckett, *Three Novels*, 101.
20. Beckett, *Watt*, 48.

21. Arsene tells Watt: "And though in purposelessness I may now seem to go, yet I do not, any more than in purposelessness then I came, for I go now with my purpose as with it when I came, the only difference being this, that then it was living and now it is dead" (Beckett, *Watt*, 58).

22. Windelband, *History of Philosophy*, 154.

23. Beckett, *Complete Dramatic Works*, 101.

24. Simon Critchley, *On Humor* (London: Routledge, 2002).

25. Beckett, *Watt*, 25.

26. Ibid., 14–15.

27. Beckett, *Complete Dramatic Works*, 106.

28. Ibid., 116.

29. Theodor Adorno, "Trying to Understand *Endgame*," in *Notes on Literature*, 1:257.

30. Ibid., 264.

31. Ibid., 259.

32. See Adorno, "Notes on Kafka," in *Can One Live after Auschwitz? A Philosophical Reader*, ed. Rolf Tiedemann (Stanford, CA: Stanford University Press, 2003), 227. Kafka's "The Hunter Gracchus" is reprinted in Kafka, *The Complete Stories* (New York: Schocken, 1983), 226–230.

33. Beckett, *Complete Dramatic Works*, 133.

34. Adorno, "Trying to Understand *Endgame*," 269–270.

35. Letter of November 21, 1957, in *No Author Better Served: The Correspondence between Samuel Beckett and Alan Schneider*, ed. Maurice Harmon (Cambridge, MA: Harvard University Press, 1998), 23.

36. Ibid.; emphasis in original.

37. Beckett, *Letters*, 1:529.

38. Quoted in *Beckett's Dream Notebook*, ed. by John Pilling (Reading, UK: Beckett International Foundation, 1999), 31.

39. Beckett, *Complete Short Prose*, 107.

10. STRENGTH TO DENY: BECKETT BETWEEN ADORNO AND BADIOU

1. Franz Kafka, "He," in *The Great Wall of China and Other Short Works*, ed. and trans. Malcolm Pasley (London: Penguin, 1973), 112.

2. For a good analysis of the role of laughter and the writing for the stage in Badiou's works, see Joseph Livak's introduction to Alain Badiou, "Badiou the Comedian" in *Ahmed the Philosopher, 34 Short Plays for Children and Everyone Else*, trans. Joseph Livak (New York: Columbia University Press, 2014), 1–21.

3. Adorno's most systematic confrontation with Beckett was to remain posthumous—it appeared in *Aesthetic Theory*, ed. Gretel Adorno and Rolf Tiedemann (Frankfurt am Main: Suhrkamp, 1970), translated by Robert

Hullot-Kentor as *Aesthetic Theory* (Minneapolis: University of Minnesota Press, 1997).

4. Adorno's aesthetics has been presented by Marc Jimenez as a "negative aesthetics" in *Vers une esthétique négative. Adorno et la Modernité* (Paris: Le Sycomore, 1983). Beckett often appears in this book, as when Jimenez quotes P. V. Zima, *Pour une sociologie du texte littéraire* (Paris: 10/18, 1978), who paralleled Adorno's and Lucien Goldmann's diverging theories about the "positivity" or "negativity" of Beckett's *oeuvre*. See *Vers une esthétique négative*, 250–251.

5. Badiou's first lecture on Beckett was given in June 1989 and published as "Samuel Beckett: L'Écriture du Générique et l'Amour" (Paris: Les Conférences du Perroquet, 1989). It contains must of the theses on Beckett elaborated in later works.

6. Adorno, "Trying to understand *Endgame*," 241.

7. Alain Badiou, "Tireless Desire," in *On Beckett*, ed. and trans. Alberto Toscano and Nina Power (Manchester: Clinamen Press, 2003), 37–38. Hereafter cited in text as *OB*.

8. Rolf Tiedemann, "'Gegen den Trug der Frage nach dem Sinn': Eine Dokumentation zu Adornos Beckett-Lektüre," in *Frankfurter Adorno Blätter 3* (Munich: Text+Kritik, 1994), 25; translation mine. For a good translation and excellent commentaries by Dirk Van Hulle and Shane Weller, see Adorno's "Notes on Beckett," *Journal of Beckett Studies* 19, no. 2 (2010): 157–178.

9. Adorno, "Trying to understand *Endgame*," 246.

10. See the condensed essay from 1963 in Theodor W. Adorno, *Can One Live after Auschwitz? A Philosophical Reader*, ed. Rolf Tiedemann (Stanford, CA: Stanford University Press, 2003), 162–181.

11. Adorno, "Trying to understand *Endgame*," 247–248.

12. Ibid., 243.

13. Tiedeman, *Frankfurter Adorno Blätter 3*, 24; translation mine.

14. Ibid., xx; translation mine.

15. See Siegfried Unseld's account, as reported by Knowlson, *Damned to Fame*, 428.

16. In a muted manner; see Adorno, "Trying to understand *Endgame*," 267.

17. "*Endspiel* wird blosses Spiel sein. Nichts weniger. Von Rätseln and Lösungen also kein Gedanke. Es gibt für solches ernstes Zeug Universitäten, Kirchen, Cafés du Commerce usw" (Beckett, *Disjecta*, 114; translation mine).

18. Tiedeman, *Frankfurter Adorno Blätter 3*, 25.

19. Adorno, *Aesthetic Theory*, 134.

20. Tiedeman, *Frankfurter Adorno Blätter 3*, 26.

21. "Die Bahn des Romans: Reduktion des Reduzierten," in Tiedemann, "Eine Dokumentation zu Adornos Beckett-Lektüre," 38.

22. Ibid., 61.

23. Ibid.

24. Ibid., 67.

25. Ibid., 44.

26. Ibid., 73.

27. Adorno, *Aesthetic Theory*, 153–154.

28. Ibid., 250.

29. Ibid., 347–348.

30. Beckett, *Complete Dramatic Works*, 60.

31. Adorno, *Aesthetic Theory*, 234.

32. Theodor W. Adorno, *Negative Dialektik* (Frankfurt am Main: Suhrkamp, 1970), 371–372, translated by E. B. Ashton as *Negative Dialectics* (New York: Continuum, 1983), 380–381; translation modified.

33. Adorno, *Negative Dialektik*, 371–372.

34. Alain Badiou, *Beckett, L'increvable désir* (Paris: Hachette, 1995).

35. Stanley Cavell, "Ending the Waiting Game," in *Must We Mean What We Say?* (Cambridge: Cambridge University Press, 1976), 117.

36. Andrew Gibson, *Beckett and Badiou: The Pathos of Intermittency* (Oxford: Oxford University Press, 2006). This is a fascinating book with a misleading title; it should have been called *Badiou and Beckett*.

37. "Agamben, Rancière, and Proust all shed an important light on a dimension of Beckett's work that Badiou conspicuously neglects" (Gibson, *Beckett and Badiou*, 284).

38. Ibid., 285.

39. I discuss this shift in *Jacques Lacan: Psychoanalysis and the Subject of Literature* (Houndmills, UK: Palgrave, 2001), 69–84.

40. Beckett, *Disjecta*, 172.

41. See *Pourquoi Ecrivez-vous? 400 écrivains répondent*, *Cahier Spécial Libération*, 1er décembre 1988, ed. Daniel Rondeau and Jean-François Fogel, p. 3.

42. Beckett, *Complete Short Prose*, 187.

43. See Bruno Clément, *L'Oeuvre sans qualités. Rhétorique de Samuel Beckett* (Paris: Seuil, 1994), 179–195.

44. Samuel Beckett, *Ill Seen Ill Said*, in *Nohow On*, 80.

45. Franz Kafka, "Aphorism 69," in *Great Wall of China*, 91.

46. Beckett, *Watt*, 71.

47. Ibid., 71.

48. Beckett, *Complete Short Prose*, 175.

49. Here, Badiou is commenting on the finale of *Ill Seen Ill Said*: "First last moment. Grant only enough remain to devour all. Moment by glutton moment. Sky earth the whole kit and boodle. Not another crumb of carrion left. Lick chops and basta. No. One moment more. One last. Grace to breathe that void. Know happiness" (Beckett, *Nohow On*, 97).

50. Beckett, *Nohow On*, 128.

51. Ibid., 107.

52. Gibson, *Beckett and Badiou*, 257.

53. Ibid., 287.

54. Ibid., 289, 288.

55. Ibid., 197.

56. Samuel Beckett, *Le Dépeupleur* (Paris: Éditions de Minuit, 1970), 55.

57. Antoinette Weber-Caflisch, *Chacun son dépeupleur: sur Samuel Beckett* (Paris: Éditions de Minuit, 1994).

58. Primo Levi, *Si c'est un homme*, trans. Martine Schruoffeneger (Paris: Julliard, 1990). See *Chacun son dépeupleur*, 41–43.

59. Adorno, "Trying to Understand *Endgame*," 245–246.

60. Ibid., 266.

61. Adorno's "Notes on Beckett," *Journal of Beckett Studies* 19, no. 2 (2010), 173.

62. Ibid., 246.

63. Adorno, *Aesthetic Theory*, 30.

64. Ibid., 320–321.

65. Ibid., 30.

66. Beckett, *Three Novels*, 339.

67. Ibid., 365.

68. I quote Werner Hamacher's version from "The Gesture in the Name: On Benjamin and Kafka," in *Premises*, trans. Peter Fenves (Stanford, CA: Stanford University Press, 1999), 303.

69. Beckett, *Three Novels*, 366.

70. Adorno's "Notes on Beckett," *Journal of Beckett Studies* 19, no. 2 (2010): 178.

71. For all this, I am indebted to Rodolphe Gasché's superb meditation on Kant's *Critique of Judgment*, entitled *The Idea of Form: Rethinking Kant's Aesthetics* (Stanford, CA: Stanford University Press, 2003).

11. LESSONS IN PIGSTY LATIN: THE DUTY TO SPEAK

1. Beckett, *Critical Heritage*, 148.

2. Jacques Lacan, *Television*, trans. Denis Hollier, Rosalind Krauss, and Annette Michelson (New York: Norton, 1990), 22; translation modified. "Devoir de bien dire" was translated as "the duty to be well-spoken," which tones down the "imperative of saying" crucial for Beckett.

3. Beckett, *Murphy*, 17.

4. Marjorie Perloff, "Between Verse and Prose: Beckett and the New Poetry," in *On Beckett: Essays and Criticism*, ed. S. E. Gontarski (New York: Grove Press, 1986), 191–206.

5. "Philosophy ought really to be written only as a poetic composition," Ludwig Wittgenstein, *Culture and Value*, trans. by Peter Winch (Chicago: University of Chicago Press, 1980), 24.

6. See Gibson, *Beckett and Badiou*.

7. Beckett, *Collected Poems*, 12.

8. Ibid., 200.

9. Ibid., 213.

10. Ibid., 214.

11. Ibid., 243.

12. Ibid., 55.

13. Quoted by Tom Driver, "Beckett by the Madeleine," *Columbia University Forum* 4, no. 3 (Summer 1961): 25, and Beckett, *Critical Heritage*, 219.

14. *Collected Poems*, 149.

15. Beckett, *Beckett in Black and Red*, 186.

16. Ibid., 11.

17. Ibid., 174; literally: "Thus our analytic culture has consecrated in parallel the double realm of the brothel in which one fucks and the salon in which one chats."

18. Ibid., 70.

19. Ibid., 176.

20. Ibid., 72–73.

21. Ibid., 73.

22. Ludovic Janvier, "Au travail avec Beckett," in *Cahier de l'Herne Samuel Beckett* (Paris: Editions de l'Herne, 1976), 105.

23. Beckett, *Watt*, 11.

24. Janvier, "Au travail avec Beckett," 108.

25. Mel Gusow, *Conversations with and about Beckett* (New York: Grove Press, 1996), 50.

26. Beckett, *Three Novels*, 414.

27. Beckett, *L'innomable*, 204.

28. Beckett, *Three Novels*, 409.

29. Beckett, *Nohow On*, 101.

30. Knowlson, *Damned to Fame*, 601.

31. Edith Fournier translated this beginning as: "Encore. Dire encore. Soit dit encore. Tant mal que pis encore"; see Beckett, *Cap au Pire* (Paris: Éditions de Minuit, 1991), 7.

32. Badiou, *On Beckett*, 80.

33. Beckett, *Complete Poems*, 214.

34. Ibid., 215.

35. Charles Juliet, *Rencontre avec Samuel Beckett* (Montpellier: Fata Morgana, 1986), 27–28; translation mine.

36. Knowlson, *Damned to Fame*, 557.
37. Beckett, *Complete Short Prose*, 258.
38. Beckett, *Complete Poems*, 202 and 206.
39. Beckett, *Murphy*, 232.
40. Ibid., 234.
41. Ibid., 40.
42. Beckett, *Disjecta*, 103.
43. Beckett, *Watt*, 5.
44. Ibid., 251.
45. Beckett, *Complete Short Prose*, 192.
46. Samuel Beckett, "Assez," in *Têtes-Mortes* (Paris: Éditions de Minuit, 1972), 47.

12. AN IRISH PARIS PEASANT

1. Beckett, *Complete Short Prose*, 275–278.
2. Ibid., 197.
3. Ibid., 200.
4. See Pascale Casanova, *The World Republic of Letters*, trans. M. B. DeBevoise (Cambridge, MA: Harvard University Press, 2007).
5. Beckett, *Watt*, 45.
6. Ibid., 46.
7. Beckett, *Collected Poems*, 98. A translation might be: "Over Lisbon still smoldering, Kant coldly bent, meditating."
8. Ibid., 98.
9. Ibid., 93.
10. Beckett jotted this down in preparation for *Dream of Fair to Middling Women*, but did not pursue it. See John Pilling's annotation in *Beckett's Dream Notebook*, 30.
11. Beckett, *Collected Poems*, 93.
12. Ibid., 100.
13. Ibid., 101.
14. Ibid.
15. Beckett, *Letters*, 1:643.
16. Ibid., 1:626.
17. The poems accompany a letter to Thomas McGreevy mentioning the new apartment; see *Letters*, 1:630–632.
18. Knowlson, *Damned to Fame*, 473.
19. Beckett, *Letters*, 1:153.
20. Beckett, *Complete Short Prose*, 134.
21. Beckett, *Eleutheria*, 28.
22. Ibid., 146.
23. See T. S. Eliot, "Gerontion," in *Poems* (New York: Knopf, 1920), 5.

24. Beckett, *Complete Short Prose*, 133.
25. Beckett, *Letters*, 2:95, 97.
26. Ibid., 2:555.
27. Ibid., 2:217.
28. Ibid., 2:332.
29. For a wonderful discussion of "digging" and "digging in" in Beckett's letters, see Daniel Gunn's introduction to Beckett, *Letters*, 2:lxxi–lxxv.
30. Beckett, *Disjecta*, 29.

13. THE MORALITY OF FORM—A FRENCH STORY

1. See Beckett, *Dream of Fair to Middling Women*, 47. Beckett added "black" to an expression found in a letter from Beaufret in 1931. See John Pilling, "A Companion to *Dream of Fair to Middling Women*," special issue, *Journal of Beckett Studies Books* 12, nos. 1–2 (2004): 92.
2. Beckett, *Dream of Fair to Middling Women*, 48.
3. See Beckett, *Disjecta*, 47.
4. Beckett, *Eleutheria*, 136.
5. Brigitte Le Juez, *Beckett avant la lettre* (Paris: Grasset, 2007), 115.
6. John Bolin, *Beckett and the Modern Novel* (Cambridge: Cambridge University Press, 2013), 17–42, provides an excellent analysis of the links between Beckett and Gide.
7. Beckett, *Disjecta*, 40.
8. Robert Desnos excelled in the obscene spoonerisms called *contrepêteries* attributed to Rrose Sélavy: "Rrose Sélavy demande si les *Fleurs du Mal* ont modifié les moeurs du phalle [Rrose Sélavy wonders whether *Flowers of Evil* have modified phallic habits]" (Desnos, *Corps et biens* [Paris: Gallimard, 1968], 46).
9. See the terrible puns attributed by Duchamp to Rrose Sélavy, like "ovaire toute la nuit" (open all night/all ovary at night) and the famous L.H.O.O.Q. in Marcel Duchamp, *Notes* (Paris: Flammarion, 1999), 133–155.
10. Beckett, *Disjecta*, 40.
11. Ibid., 40.
12. Ibid., 39.
13. Pierre Bayard, *How to Talk about Books You Haven't Read*, trans. Jeffrey Mehlman (New York: Bloomsbury, 2007). Valéry gave a posthumous tribute to Proust without having read much of his work. The glibness of the tribute must have struck Beckett as he was working on *Proust* then.
14. Beckett, *Disjecta*, 41.
15. Ibid., 38.
16. Ibid.
17. For more details on this diagram, see my *The Ghosts of Modernity* (Gainesville: University Press of Florida, 1996), 153–154.

18. Beckett, *Disjecta*, 55–56.

19. See Beckett, *Letters*, 1:630–633, for the original version.

20. Beckett, *Letters*, 2:464.

21. Ibid., 2:462.

22. "Dicendo questo, mi sento ch'i' godo [Saying this, I feel a great joy],"
Paradiso, Canto 33, line 93.

23. Beckett, *Disjecta*, 19.

24. Dante Alighieri, *The Divine Comedy, Paradiso*, trans. Allen Mandelbaum (New York: Bantam, 1986), 300–301.

25. Deirdre Bair, *Samuel Beckett: A Biography* (New York: Simon and
Schuster, 1978), 382.

26. See Knowlson, *Damned to Fame*, 344, and Jackie Blackman, "Beckett
Judaizing Beckett," *Samuel Beckett Today/Aujourd'hui*, no. 18 (2007): 325–340.

27. Angela Moorjani, "Whence Estragon?," *Beckett Circle* 32, no. 2 (Fall
2009): 7.

28. See Beckett, *En attendant Godot*, 13.

29. Ibid., 21.

30. Moorjani, "Whence Estragon?," 7.

31. Beckett, *En attendant Godot*, 11–13.

32. Beckett, *Complete Poems*, 118.

33. Ibid.

34. Ibid.

35. Ibid.

36. Samuel Beckett, *Mercier and Camier*, 26. See also Steven Connor,
"'Traduttore, traditore,'—Samuel Beckett's Translation of Mercier et
Camier," www.english.fsu.edu/jobs/num1112/027_CONNOR.PDF.

37. See Martin Mégevand, "Pinget Seen by Beckett, Beckett According
to Pinget: The Unpublishable," *Journal of Beckett Studies* 19, no. 1 (2010):
3–14.

38. Robert Pinget, *Mahu or the Material*, trans. Alan Sheridan-Smith
(London: Dalkey Archive, 2005), 7.

39. Maurice Blanchot, "From Dread to Language," trans. Lydia Davis, in
The Station Hill Blanchot Reader (Barrytown, NY: Station Hill, 1999), 345.

40. See Beckett, *Letters*, 2:216–219.

41. Ibid., 441–443.

42. Beckett, *The Letters of Samuel Beckett*, vol. 3, *1957–1965*, ed. George
Craig, Martha Dow Fehsenfeld, Dan Gunn, and Lois More Overbeck (Cambridge: Cambridge University Press, 2014), 331–332.

43. Louis-René Des Forêts, *Le Bavard* (Paris: Gallimard, 1973), 151.

44. Ibid., 152.

45. Roland Barthes, *Le Degré Zéro de l'écriture*, in *Oeuvres Complètes*, vol. 1, *1942–1965*, ed. Eric Marty (Paris: Seuil, 1993), 139.

46. Roland Barthes, *Writing Degree Zero*, trans. A. Lavers and C. Smith (New York: Noonday Press, 1968), 10–11.

47. Barthes, *Writing Degree Zero*, 14–15.

48. Georges Duthuit, "Sartre's Last Class," *Transition 48*, no. 1 (1948): 7–20.

49. See Beckett, *Letters*, 1:626.

50. Barthes, *Writing Degree Zero*, 37 and 76–77.

51. Ibid., 77.

52. Roland Barthes, "Réflexion sur le style de *L'Étranger*," in *Oeuvres Complètes*, 1:63.

53. Ibid.

54. Louis-Ferdinand Céline, *Voyage au bout de la nuit* (Paris: Gallimard, 1952), 7.

55. For a detailed analysis of Beckett's rhetoric, see Bruno Clément, *L'Oeuvre sans qualités*.

56. Albert Camus, *L'Étranger* (Paris: Gallimard, Folio, 2012), 9. In a letter of August 1959 to Barbara Bray, Beckett says that he has been amused by Sigmund Freud's rejection of Céline's *Voyage au Bout de la Nuit*, a novel that Freud had been forced to read by Marie Bonaparte; just after, he praises Blanchot's *Livre à venir*, but decides not to read it because it would "get in his way." See *Letters*, 3:237.

57. Beckett, *Three Novels*, 169.

58. Ibid., 175.

59. Ibid., 175–176.

60. Samuel Beckett, *Catastrophe*, in *Complete Dramatic Works*, 460.

61. Ibid., 459.

62. Samuel Beckett, *Catastrophe et autres dramaticules* (Paris: Éditions de Minuit, 1986), 77.

63. Beckett, *Catastrophe*, in *Complete Dramatic Works*, 460.

64. Ibid., 461.

65. Knowlson, *Damned to Fame*, 598.

66. Beckett, *Three Novels*, 254.

67. Joyce, *Ulysses*, 174.

68. I have discussed this moment and its aftermath in *The Cambridge Introduction to Literature and Psychoanalysis* (Cambridge: Cambridge University Press, 2014), 60–70.

69. Beckett, *Three Novels*, 225.

70. Ibid., 226.

71. Ibid., 350.

72. Donald W. Winnicott, "Fear of Breakdown," *International Review of Psychoanalysis*, no. 1 (1974): 103–107.

73. Roland Barthes, *Camera Lucida*, trans. Richard Howard (New York: Noonday Press, 1981), 96.

74. Maurice Blanchot, *The Writing of the Disaster*, trans. Ann Smock, 72, 114–116, 125.

75. Ibid., 2.

CODA: MINIMA BECKETTIANA

1. Maurice Blanchot, *The Writing of the Disaster*, trans. Ann Smock (Lincoln: University of Nebraska Press, 1986), 5.

2. Ibid, 3.

3. Beckett, *Complete Short Prose*, 228.

4. Ibid., 175.

5. Beckett, *Letters*, 2:162.

6. Cousse, *Death Sty*, 96.

7. Beckett, *Letters*, 2:232.

8. Beckett, *Complete Short Prose*, 238.

9. Beckett, *Letters*, 3:348.

10. Beckett, *How It Is*, 14.

11. Ibid.

12. Beckett, *Complete Short Prose*, 187.

13. Samuel Beckett, "Assez," in *Têtes-Mortes* (Paris: Éditions de Minuit, 1972), 35.

14. See *Nohow On*, 119, 120, 122, 124.

15. Theodor W. Adorno, *Minima Moralia*, trans. E. F. N. Jephcott (London: Verso, 2002), 224–225. Dennis Redmond translates slightly differently: "In the magic of what reveals itself in absolute powerlessness, of what is beautiful, complete and void in one, the appearance of omnipotence is negatively reflected back as hope. It has escaped every test of strength. Total purposelessness denies the totality of what is purposeful in the world of domination, and only by virtue of such repudiation, which the existent fulfills in its own principle of reason out of the latter's consequentiality, has the existing society, to this day, become conscious of a possible one. The bliss of contemplation consists of disenchanted magic. What radiates, is the reconciliation of mythos" (http://members.efn.org/~dredmond/MinimaMoralia.html, part 3, Aphorism 144).

INDEX

Abélard, Pierre 174–175
abortion 66, 83–85, 137, 198
Adorno, Theodor W. 2–4, 9–10, 43, 46,
  92, 95, 109, 114–115, 131–132, 133–45,
  147, 152–156, 158, 176, 197–198, 200,
  203–204, 234n15
aesthetics 75–85, 99, 118–120, 135, 139
Agamben, Giorgio 20–21, 41, 153, 155
Albright, Daniel 218n13
Alexander, Archibald 98
Althusser, Louis 142
animals 13–15, 18, 21–22, 36, 49–52, 56,
  103, 116, 129, 184, 194–195, 201–202,
  213n38
anthropomorphism 9, 18, 20–21, 39, 40,
  46–47, 67, 102
apathy 15, 17, 115, 117. See ataraxy
Apollinaire, Guillaume 162, 179
Aristotle 62, 64, 68, 92, 95, 97, 130, 136,
  140, 198
Armstrong, Louis 163
Artaud, Antonin 80
ataraxy 114–118
Attridge, Derek 213n25
Aude family 114, 180
Augustine (Saint) 32, 65, 93, 168
Ausonius 59
Austin, John Langshaw 2, 142

Bacon, Francis 100, 113
Badiou, Alain 3–4, 10, 46, 92, 134–136,
  139, 142–157, 160, 166–167, 197, 199,
  203, 225n2
Bair, Deirdre 232n25
Balzac, Honoré de 6, 42, 106
Barrès, Maurice 97
Barfield, Steve 218n10
Barthes, Roland 10, 44, 115, 191–194, 199

Bataille, Georges 8, 10, 12, 13–18, 36, 56,
  58, 78–80, 85, 89–90, 94, 96, 126–127,
  162, 167, 189–190, 209nn21,22
bathos 55, 98, 100–104, 106, 118, 125, 132,
  158, 169, 184
Baudelaire, Charles 88, 153, 163, 185
Bayard, Pierre 231n13
Beach, Sylvia 173
Beaufret, Jean 61, 97, 182
beauty 73, 90, 94–96, 99, 118–119, 144,
  146, 156–157, 202–204
Beckett's works discussed: Catastrophe 195–199;
  Concentrisme (Le) 183–185; *Dante . . .*
  Bruno . Vico . . Joyce 23–30; *Dante and the*
  lobster 49–51, 58; *Eleutheria* 105–109;
  Endgame 30, 131–133, 140; *Film* 47, 157,
  168; *From an Abandoned Work* 45; *How It*
  Is 52–55, 145, 202; *Human Wishes* 127–
  128, 133; *Ill Seen Ill Said* 146; *Krapp's Last*
  Tape 125; *Mercier and Camier* 7–8, 20;
  Molloy 14–15, 17, 57, 93, 119–122, 125,
  129; *Murphy* 71–72, 91; *Proust* 74, 88–89;
  Rough for Radio II 120; *Text 3* 51–52, 55,
  56; *Three dialogues with Georges Duthuit*
  77–85; *Unnamable (The)* 15, 41–48, 156,
  165; *Watt* 109–114, 117–118, 129–132,
  147–148; *Waiting for Godot* 11–12, 141;
  Whoroscope 59–68; *Worstward Ho* 149–151
Belacqua 30–32, 34–36, 45, 49–50, 52,
  56–58, 71–72, 101, 160, 182
Benjamin, Walter 115–116, 134, 139,
  153–155, 177
Benn, Gottfried 139
Ben-Zvi, Linda 102, 222n47
Bergson, Henri 125–126
Berkeley, George 69, 102
Bernhard, Thomas 121
Bersani, Leo 214n15

235

Bion, Wilfred Ruprecht 57, 100, 159, 181,
    198
birth trauma 66, 128–129, 131
Bishop, Jane 218n6
Bizub, Edward 60–61
Blackman, Jackie 232n26
Blanchot, Maurice 9, 10, 15–16, 44, 97,
    110, 115–116, 135, 144, 190, 192–193,
    199–200, 220n56, 233n56
Bloch, Ernst 139
body (the) 12, 14, 16, 21, 35–36, 43–45, 52,
    55, 60, 64, 66–67, 72, 83, 93–94, 106, 128
Bolin, John 231n6
Bonaparte, Marie 233n56
Bonnefoy, Yves 210n32
Borges, Jorge Luis 109, 184
Boulter, Jonathan 53, 214n15
Bray, Barbara 201, 233n56
Brecht, Bertolt 72, 139
Breton, André 18, 79–80, 83–84, 162, 179,
    192
Brion, Marcel 38
Brod, Max 156
Browning, Robert 60
Bruno, Giordano 5, 23, 26–28, 34, 36
Bürger, Peter 154
Burnett, John 98

Cabestan, Guillem de 179
Cain 50, 58, 101
Camus, Albert 9, 43–44, 190, 192–193
Cantor, Georg 142
Carducci, Giosuè 97
Carnap, Rudolf 97
Casanova, Pascale 78, 218n11, 230n4
Caselli, Daniela 207n3, 214n16
Cassirer, Ernst 100–103
catastrophe 89–90, 132, 141, 158, 195–196
Caterina da Siena 13
Cato 159
Cavell, Stanley 3, 92, 142
Celan, Paul 91, 142–143, 153
Céline, Louis-Ferdinand (Destouches) 173,
    179, 192–193, 233n56
Cervantes, Miguel de 184
Cézanne, Paul 40–41, 80
Chamfort, Nicolas 160
Char, René 80, 180
Châtelet, Gilles 210n32
Christ (Jesus) 56–58, 64, 127, 129, 179
Christina, Queen of Sweden 60, 67, 68
Clément, Bruno 146
Clerselier, Claude 63
Coetzee, John M. 6, 95, 121

Cohen, Hermann 100
Cohn, Ruby 50
Coleridge, Samuel Taylor 157
Connor, Steven 232n36
Cottingham, John 208n21, 215n2
Cousse, Raymond 8, 21–22, 100, 201,
    211nn47,49
Crangle, Sara 222n39
Crevel, René 24, 163–164
Critchley, Simon 2, 3, 95, 97, 130, 217n38
Croce, Benedetto 27–30
Cronin, Anthony 207n2
Cunard, Nancy 24, 162
Cunningham, David 214n15, 218n10
cynicism 39, 92, 138, 144, 148, 175, 195,
    200–201, 208n20

Dalí, Salvador 12, 18, 58, 215n43
Da Messina, Antonello 83
Dante (Alighieri) 4, 8, 9, 23, 28–33, 36–37,
    49–57, 64–65, 71–72, 76, 110, 132,
    159–160, 186, 198
Da Vinci, Leonardo 88–90, 220n56
Debray, Cécile 218n6
Dedekind, Richard 142
De Gaulle, Charles (General) 80
De Gaultier, Jules 47, 213n32
Deleuze, Gilles 3, 41, 92, 142, 155
De L'isle-Adam, Villiers 33
De Mauroy, Godot 178, 187
Democritus 5, 18, 208n11
De Mortillet, Gabriel 176–177
Derain, André 84
Derrida, Jacques 3, 20–21, 44, 53, 66, 152,
    213n25
De Rousset, Mademoiselle 54
Descartes, Joachim 65
Descartes, René 5, 9, 11, 41, 44, 57–58, 59–
    68, 71, 76, 84, 97, 100–101, 104–105,
    116–117, 121, 125, 137, 139, 143, 145,
    147–149, 161, 184, 188, 198, 208n21
Deschevaux-Dumesnil, Suzanne 174
Des Forêts, Louis-René 190–191
Desnos, Robert 184, 231n8
Dilks, John 3
Diogenes 148, 201
Dommange, Thomas 69, 216n28
Douglas, Stan 207n4
Doutey, Nicolas 216n28
Driver, Tom 229n13
Dublin 27–28, 38–39, 45, 50, 61, 84, 161,
    171–174, 178, 182, 188, 202
Du Bouchet, André 80–82
Duchamp, Marcel 18, 71, 85, 184, 231n9

Duthuit, Georges 12, 41, 77–85, 190
Dutoit, Ulysse 214n15
duty 46, 156, 158–159, 181
Duval, Jeanne 163

Eagan, Desmond 208n11
Earth (the) 39, 45, 181, 203
Ecole Normale Supérieure 1, 18, 26, 37, 61,
    97, 173, 183
Eliot, Thomas Stearns 2, 28, 39, 60, 179
Eluard, Paul 162, 188
Epictetus 94
Esslin, Martin 96, 139
eternal return 26, 53, 89–90, 201–202
ethics 46–47, 49–58, 90–91, 93–94, 96, 99,
    104, 110, 123, 145, 147–148, 150–152,
    154, 158–162, 167, 173
existentialism 4, 43–44, 80, 84, 137, 144, 192

Fehsenfeld, Martha 223n4
Feldman, Matthew 102, 222n47
Felman, Morton 167–168
Fénéon, Félix 84
Ferenczi, Sándor 126–128, 131
Fifield, Peter 209n22, 217n38, 220n63
film 2, 47, 125, 154, 157, 168, 177
Flaubert, Gustave 8, 42, 66–67, 185, 192
Fogel, Jean-François 227n41
formalism 87, 122, 114–116, 162
Foucault, Michel 66, 208n20
Fournier, Edith 149, 229n31
Freud, Sigmund 5, 10, 48, 61–62, 70,
    85–89, 119, 125–126, 128, 183, 216n7,
    233n56

Galassi, Jonathan 215n25
Galileo Galilei 67, 109
Garnier, Pierre 213n28
Garve, Christian 101
Gasché, Rodolphe 228n71
Genet, Jean 80, 177, 189
Geulinx, Arnold 4–5, 10, 18, 34, 45, 57–58,
    67–73, 75–76, 91, 97, 101, 137
Gibson, Andrew 142–143, 151–152,
    218n10, 227n36
Gide, André 80, 183–184, 231n6
Gilbert, Stuart 80
Gillet, Louis 80
Giotto di Bondone 52
Goethe, Johann Wolfgang 118, 169
Goldmann, Lucien 226n4
Grayson, Erik 6, 208n12
Greenberg, Clement 79, 82–83, 218n12
Guattari, Félix 41, 155

Gunn, Daniel 231n29
Gusow, Mel 164, 229n25

Haerdter, Michael 109
Hamacher, Werner 228n68
Haneke, Michael 121
Harvey, Lawrence 61, 178
Hatch, David 218n10
Havel, Václav 195–197
Hayden, Josette 114
Heaney, Seamus 181
Hébert, Jacques 191
Hegel, Georg Wilhelm Friedrich 18, 27,
    29–30, 43–44, 57, 70, 96–98, 139, 141,
    144, 159
Heidegger, Martin 28, 43–44, 61, 97,
    137–138, 159
Heine, Heinrich 50
Héloïse d'Argenteuil 175
Hemingway, Ernest 91
Heracles 200
Heraclitus 5, 28, 87, 143, 149, 166, 208n11
Hofmannsthal, Hugo von 113, 121
Homer 26, 38–39, 45
Horkheimer, Max 109
Hosea 56
humanism 9, 14–15, 18, 20, 39, 46–47,
    83–84, 91, 96, 114, 117, 138, 144, 192
Hume, David 102
humility 2, 5, 9, 18, 37, 45, 68–70, 91
Husserl, Edmund 44, 97, 137, 143, 145, 147
Hussen, Andreas 154

identification 7, 22, 23–24, 29, 31–32
impossibility 2, 17–18, 82, 85, 132, 149, 198
impotence 41, 43, 69, 73, 91, 121, 133,
    144–145
informal 26, 167
Ionesco, Eugène 140, 189
Irrationality 60, 63, 65, 68, 109–110
Ireland 7, 40, 172
Ishiguro, Kazuo 21

Janvier, Ludovic 164, 229n22
Jarry, Alfred 73
Jelinek, Elfriede 121
Jimenez, Marc 226n4
Johnson, Samuel 100, 128, 133
Jolas, Eugene 25, 28, 79–80, 102, 173–174,
    218n17
Joyce, James 2, 4, 6, 8, 9, 21, 23–45, 51, 55,
    57–58, 60–61, 63–64, 76–77, 80, 93,
    110, 116, 121, 154, 160, 168, 173, 177,
    179, 183, 186, 198, 203

Joyce, Lucia 37, 173–174
Juliet, Charles 167, 229n35
Jung, Carl Gustav 102, 198–199

Kafka, Franz 6, 9, 36, 132, 134, 137–138,
    143, 147, 153–154, 156, 158, 225n32
Kahane, Jack 109
Kant, Immanuel 9–10, 47, 73, 82, 85–88,
    91–107, 109, 114–122, 130, 132, 143,
    146, 148, 152, 157, 172, 197, 204,
    228n71, 230n7
Katz, Daniel 213n25
Kaun, Axel 34, 77
Keaton, Buster 125, 157, 177
Keats, John 20, 94–95
Kibedi-Varga, Aron 219n24
Kleist, Heinrich von 69, 217n29
Klossowski, Pierre 110, 116–117
Knowlson, James 3, 232n26
Krailsheimer, Alban J. 208n10
Kraus, Christian Jakob 104

Lacan, Jacques 9, 28, 61, 73, 116, 142, 144,
    145, 149, 158–159, 185, 228n2
laughter 9, 12, 17, 46–47, 95, 121–134,
    137, 158
Lautréamont (Isidore Ducasse) 16
Lawrence, David Herbert 40
Lecercle, Ann 216n12
Le Goff, Jacques 32, 212n22
Lee, Kyoo 63, 216n8 and 21
Leibnitz, Gottfried Wilhelm 104
Le Juez, Brigitte 231n5
Lenin, Vladimir 187
Léon, Paul 80
Leopardi, Giacomo 28, 55, 97, 211n11,
    215n25
Leroy, Maxime 61–65
Leventhal, A. J, "Con" 188
Levi, Primo 152
Levinas, Emmanuel 10, 73–75, 91, 217n39,
    220n63
Lisbon earthquake 20, 172–173, 230n7
Littel, Jonathan 109
Livak, Joseph 225n2
Lloyd, David 218n10
Locke, John 102
Lorrain, Claude (Gellée) 40
Lo-Ruhama 56
Lowell, Robert 91
Lucretius 93
Lukacs, Georg 137–138
Luther, Martin 33

MacGreevy (also McGreevy), Thomas 4,
    38, 40, 100, 109, 133, 230n17
Mahaffy, John Pentland 60–61, 65–66
Mailer, Norman 91
Maklès, Rosa and Sylvia 80
Maldiney, Henri 81, 218n19
Malebranche, Nicolas 69
Malherbe, François de 182
Mallarmé, Stéphane 134, 143, 149–150,
    156, 161, 166, 186, 192, 199
Malraux, André 80
Malthus, Thomas Robert 109
Manet, Edouard 84
Mansanti, Céline 212n3
Mantegna, Andrea 83
Marcuse, Herbert 139
Marxism 134, 137–138
Masson, André 77–83, 88–90, 218n6
Matisse, Henri 80–81, 84
Mauss, Marcel 18
Mauthner, Fritz 97, 102–103, 106, 120–121
Maxwell, James Clerk 185
McCabe, Henry 50
McCarren, Felicia 188
McHugh, Roland 212n4
McMillan, Dougald 212n3, 223n4
Mégevand, Martin 232n37
Melville, Herman 32
Michelet, Raymond 163
Mirabeau, Honoré Gabriel 103
modernism 2, 77, 82–83, 85, 143, 154, 162,
    193, 212n3
Moerman, Ernst 163
Monnier, Adrienne 173
Moore, George 70
Moorjani, Angela 187, 232n27
Moses 103
Myskja, Bjørn 95–98

Nadeau, Maurice 13, 80
Napoléon (Bonaparte) 55
Nauman, Bruce 207n4
Nerval, Gérard de 185
Nicholls, Peter 222n39
Nicolas of Cues 102
Nietzsche, Friedrich 5, 12–13, 18, 47, 53,
    69–70, 74, 81, 87, 90, 93, 95–98, 120,
    192
Nixon, Mark 217n2
non-relation 40–41, 91, 119
nothingness 2, 13, 15, 68–73, 90–91, 96,
    112, 137, 140–142, 156, 200, 203, 207n3
Nussbaum, Martha 4, 92–95, 97